G000080353

Meeting
The Masters

A Spiritual Apprenticeship

Meeting
The Masters

A Spiritual Apprenticeship

William Wildblood

AXIS MUNDI
BOOKS

Winchester, UK
Washington, USA

First published by Axis Mundi Books, 2012
Axis Mundi Books is an imprint of John Hunt Publishing Ltd., Laurel House, Station Approach,
Alresford, Hants, SO24 9JH, UK
office1@o-books.net
www.o-books.com

For distributor details and how to order please visit the 'Ordering' section on our website.

Text copyright: William Wildblood 2011

ISBN: 978 1 78099 168 9

All rights reserved. Except for brief quotations in critical articles or reviews, no part of this
book may be reproduced in any manner without prior written permission from the publishers.

The rights of William Wildblood as author have been asserted in accordance with the Copyright,
Designs and Patents Act 1988.

A CIP catalogue record for this book is available from the British Library.

Design: Stuart Davies

Printed and bound by CPI Group (UK) Ltd, Croydon, CR0 4YY
Printed in the USA by Offset Paperback Mfrs, Inc

We operate a distinctive and ethical publishing philosophy in all
areas of our business, from our global network of authors to
production and worldwide distribution.

CONTENTS

Introduction

Although this book is written in the form of an autobiography, it is not actually about the writer at all. It is about the spiritual path and the experiences of an individual on it. It could be any individual. It is often said that there are many ways to God. That is not quite correct. There is really only one way though it may take many different forms, especially in the earlier stages. But, as it progresses, the outer differences are increasingly shed and the path of one soul becomes the path of each and every soul. This book is about the path of one soul but that soul is not fundamentally different to any other so its lessons are the lessons that come to us all on the journey home.

I should make one further remark in this brief introduction. This is not a work of fiction. Everything that is written here is true. There is nothing made up, nothing added, nothing even embellished a little to make it prettier for publication. All happened as is written. I know that many people will be unwilling or unable to accept that but few of such would be drawn to read a book of this kind anyway. Of those who are so drawn I am optimistic that there will be some who, without giving it uncritical acceptance (I hope nobody does that), have an inner response of intuitive assent. Others might allow that it has at least the possibility of truth. The book is addressed to them in the hope that it may inspire them to continue with their own journey.

Chapter I

Exile

Throughout my childhood I was conscious of a feeling of exile. From as early as I can remember I felt a stranger in a world in which I did not fully belong. It also seemed clear to me that there was more to the world than I was led to believe by my parents, teachers and the commonly accepted wisdom of the day but I lacked the language and conceptual framework in which to express that awareness. Not having the means to give shape or form to my instinctive recognition of the transcendent dimension to life led to profound dissatisfaction with the world around me; indeed, at times, to near despair when I felt myself besieged on all sides by the soulless products of modernity. Certain aspects of the Christianity I grew up with I found sympathetic, particularly the figure of Christ himself, but the religion itself seemed formalistic and empty, the burnt out ashes of a once mighty fire which was preached by priests who might be good and kind men but who had no understanding of the inner reality behind their religion. As I grew older I found some solace in books, particularly works of mythology which seemed to come from a time before recorded history when humanity lived more closely in tune with the natural and spiritual worlds, but really anything that stimulated my imagination and made the world seem more than a dull mechanical realm with nothing behind external appearances. To some this might seem a typical case of adolescent escapism. Others, to my mind wiser, will recognise that the attempted escape was one from prison, an escape not away from but into reality.

The natural world was also a source of comfort to my juvenile self. Growing up in post war London in the early 1960s, one of the few things I recall with much affection are the parks and gardens. The living, growing qualities of nature, its freedom from mechanical predictability, helped alleviate a sadness caused by my feelings of separation from something though I knew not what, and I was often taken out of myself by its beauty. I say beauty and it's easy to say and then pass on but what do we really mean by that word? What causes us to appreciate and value beauty? Surely it is not just prettiness of form. I think it is a sense that something is right, is as it ought to be. It is recognition of a truth and harmony that confirms our innermost feelings and tells us that there is a world beyond that of everyday experience despite what we may have been educated to believe. True beauty of form points to a reality that transcends form and that is precisely what defines genuine beauty as opposed to the many imitations and counterfeits of it.

I remember a holiday in Cornwall and encountering the sea for the first time. As we approached our destination by the coast there was a competition to see who would be the first to see the sea. You could smell it before you could see it which added to our increasing excitement. Suddenly there appeared a thin strip of silver which grew bigger and bigger. Then all at once as we cleared the brow of a hill there it was, the huge ocean which to a four year old seemed as boundless as anything could be. The first sight of it was almost overwhelming and left me feeling both small and large at the same time. Small because of the littleness of the 'me' confronted by that vast expanse of water, large because somehow I, or something in me, was one with its vastness. I knew then in a vague, undefined but unarguable way that what I felt within had some substance to it.

When, on another trip to Cornwall with my family, we visited the rocky promontory of Tintagel, I had my first exposure to one of the sacred sites of the Western Mysteries. Naturally I knew nothing of that tradition then nor was I aware that some places truly are places of power but my lack of knowledge did not stop me being deeply affected by the castle and, more especially, its setting. The sea, the stones, the wind and mist all combined to thrust me back into an archaic past when the veil between the spiritual and material worlds dissolved much more readily than it does now. The ruined castle and the stories around it may be of medieval origin but the site surely resonates to something much older. As I walked round it with the seagulls calling out their harsh, primeval cries, I felt the presence of a living past when the world was much closer to its spiritual source. As always with such experiences there was a painful sense of something precious that is now lost.

Another holiday, this time in Scotland, introduced me to mountains and lochs. The sense of wildness and remoteness one encounters in the Highlands I found similarly ego-stripping though it's highly unlikely I would have thought of it in those terms at the time. When I swam in Loch Ness with a cousin who lived nearby, and who probably derived much amusement from impressing his younger relative with scary stories, its great depth translated in my mind into psychological terms. The possible presence of a monster lurking beneath no doubt helped as well. At the other end of the vertical scale, I still remember as one of the most exhilarating moments of my life lying on my back in the heather with my grand-father watching a golden eagle glide majestically through the sky. It was a concentration of fiery beauty set against the clear, blue empyrean and, as it rose upwards, a startlingly apt symbol of the individual soul mounting up into pure spirit.

Isolated experiences like these of being taken out of myself and made aware of something much bigger might have come now and then but they did not fundamentally alter the monotony of the world I perceived around me or the artificial life that I felt I was expected to lead. Living in a world based on a materialistic conception of life is like living below permanent cloud cover with no understanding that there is sunlight behind it. I often felt a kind of spiritual claustrophobia and wondered why no-one around me seemed to feel the same. But they didn't or, if they did, there was no apparent sign of it. Yet there was a route to partial freedom and it was provided by the imagination. That was key for the child I was. Imagination was real in the way that normal external life was not. It had an intensity absent from the mundane everyday world. It could peel back the surface of the world and look at the many layers within.

Please remember these are the experiences of a child, come down, like all children, from the spiritual plane, but recollecting (possibly) rather more of its origins than most. At the same time, these experiences are doubtless not as rare as I might have thought back then. Almost certainly we all have them to a degree. The question is what is that degree and how quickly are they eroded by life on the material plane? I should also make clear that, while I do claim they indicate some kind of spiritual sensitivity, I have no illusions that they are any indication of an advanced spiritual state since to one in such a state the veils of the material world would not have seemed so opaque. In Buddhist terms, *Samsara*, the impermanent world of becoming, and *Nirvana*, the changeless world of being, appear as two separate states to the unenlightened but to the enlightened are seen as one, the former being perceived as the activity of the latter, not real in its own terms but real when seen in the light of spirit as its phenomenal expression. Thus a greater soul than I would not have felt so trapped by the world of matter but would have realised it to be a projection of spirit. So I was certainly not free but I did at least recognise that I was bound and how many of us can say even that?

At school I did quite well until about the age of ten when I jumped a year to a higher class and, as a consequence, floundered. My mother thought it was because when I could excel without trying I would do so but, if I had to work for success, I would give up, partly through laziness and partly through a fear of failure. I cannot deny there was some truth in that but it was not the whole story. In my new class, among older children, I felt frightened and exposed. Already ill at ease in the world, this produced a further sense of alienation. Was it a coincidence that my grandmother, to whom I had been quite close, died at around this time? Perhaps it was but the two events did take place very close together, and the loss of the one person who I felt understood something of my sensitivities, and did not just regard them as self-indulgence or an

5

annoying affectation, must have had some effect.

For the benefit of any astrologers who may be reading these lines let me say that I haven't looked at the transits and progressions going on at that time but that's because I've never found astrology particularly illuminating from a predictive point of view. Sometimes links can be found between chart and event (though usually, it must be said, only detectable afterwards in the light of what has happened) but often it requires a rather flexible interpretation to align the two. On the other hand, I do believe that the horoscope can be very revealing about a person's character, and I believe it because I have seen evidence for it on numerous occasions. For example, I am in many respects a typical Virgo with the virtues and faults of that sign even though, as any astrologer will tell you, the sun sign is only the tip of the astrological iceberg. Looking below the waterline, my ruling planet is the Moon (Cancer ascendant) which is conjunct Saturn in Scorpio and square Pluto. Most of what that would imply to an astrologer applies to me. I have been called both emotionally distant (Saturn) and emotionally intense (Scorpio/Pluto) at the same time. I was also very shy as a child. Mercury is conjunct Neptune in Libra in my birth chart and I have already spoken of how important the imagination was for me in my youth. So I have no doubt that even if our understanding of the correlation between an individual's character and the position of the planets in the heavens at the time of his birth is still fairly rudimentary, there is one. We should not forget, however, that the horoscope only applies to the outer self. I don't suppose that everyone born at the same time as the Buddha, and there presumably were such, attained enlightenment.

At boarding school in the late sixties and early seventies, like many of my contemporaries, I discovered drugs, specifically psychedelic ones. The changes in perception I experienced on taking LSD were another confirmation of much I had felt earlier. However I also recognised the artificiality of the experience, and the fact that it would not lead anywhere except possibly downwards. I have read that there is a saying in Islam to the effect that one should enter houses by their doors from which pithy comment you could make the analogy that the attempt to storm the kingdom of heaven by means of psychedelic drugs is like forcing an entry through the rear window. What is more, you never get much beyond the downstairs of the building before you are ejected. Nevertheless I must be honest and say that even though the limitations and "cheating" aspect of LSD were very apparent to me, experiencing the effects of psychedelic drugs did give some kind of validation to the strong but uncorroborated intuitions I had always had. It opened up the possibility of a spiritual path. However the sixteen year old me was completely ignorant of any spiritual or mystical traditions and had no guidance whatsoever. I did occasionally go to church but the stained glass and architecture meant more to me than the services and who can really blame me for that? As for religions other than Christianity, and Church of England Christianity at that, I knew next to nothing.

I did poorly at school, seeing absolutely no point to any future that was laid out for me. I did however have a creative phase that lasted for about a year during which I wrote poetry of an almost visionary nature. I am referring to the style not the quality, though some of it seemed reasonable enough to me then without, it must be conceded, giving Coleridge or Blake anything to worry about. Nevertheless my imagination was stimulated to near fever pitch and words poured out of me much to the detriment of my schoolwork, which I thoroughly neglected. At the time I saw the inspired poet as the only truly awake human being and, while I may have modified that view somewhat since, I still see the poet as one whose inner eye is beginning to open since the creative imagination is surely the first stirrings of what eventually becomes full spiritual vision. The upshot of all this, though, was that when I left school I had but a single 'A' level to my name, a very poor return for my parents' investment in my education.

One out of the ordinary experience I had during my teenage years I should mention here. It occurred when I was staying at a friend's house in the country. He had gone off somewhere for a couple of hours so I decided to go for a walk over a nearby golf course. It was summer and there was still plenty of light at around 6 o'clock when I set out. I had no particular interest in golf but the combination of the smooth, undulating fairways with the green woods that bordered the course made it a pleasant place in which to take a stroll. I was in a peaceful mood, aided by the fine weather and attractive surroundings. There were a few puffy white clouds but they did not disturb the clear blue sky or obscure the brightness of the sunshine in any way. It was a perfect summer's evening. As I walked round the practically empty course, my feeling of content gradually increased to the point where I began to have the impression I had stumbled into a little corner of paradise that had somehow miraculously survived the Fall. A feeling of benevolence hung heavy in the air and made me glad that my evening stroll was turning out even better than expected. Then I looked up at the sky. It was like Botticelli's Venus come to life. Afterwards, so inspired was I by this event, I wrote a poem about it and that did seem to me to capture something of its nature but it is long since lost and the muse has not visited me for many years so I must do the best I can to describe it in more prosaic fashion.

I saw a goddess. She was standing somewhat like Venus in the painting but far up in the sky. To my vision she seemed as though formed out of the clouds but do not take that to mean this was just a shape made by the clouds that vaguely resembled a woman to my over-heated imagination. It was nothing like that at all. There was a presence and a shining intensity that made any such interpretation quite absurd. Besides, when I say that she seemed as though formed out of the clouds, I do not mean that the clouds had moved into a position that gave a rough suggestion of her shape. There were no longer any clouds as such. There was just her. Her form and figure was absolutely clear, distinct and real. You couldn't say she was beautiful as that would have trivialised the splendour of her appearance. She was far beyond mere earthly beauty. She was refulgent with glory. Her hair seemed to stream in a powerful wind

8

or it may be that the power was coming from her because she radiated tremendous majesty and command. She was standing in front of a throne, and in two lines to either side of this throne were rows of beasts of the mythical sort one might see in heraldry or alchemical works. When, some years later, I saw 17th century Hermetic illustrations, they reminded me a little of what I saw that day. The beasts, who were all standing upright, seemed to be shuffling their feet or hooves a little nervously, their heads bowed in respect and adoration. They were paying homage to their deity, a homage that she received and accepted not as though she was some kind of authority figure who demanded obedience from her feudal underlings but as a natural part of the hierarchical order of things. There was no indication that they were aware of me. They were far off in the heavens, figuratively and perhaps even literally in another world to which I had somehow gained access. I felt as if I were a privileged witness to a sacred ceremony.

Even now I cannot say what any of this means or if it means anything at all. Nor can I say if it was objectively real. I have no doubt that in some sense it was real but what that sense might be doesn't really matter. Its relevance to me at the time was that it was a breakthrough into a higher dimension, and whether I witnessed something true or was tapping into an ancient archetype from the archaic past or even tuned into some psychic imprint or thought-form on the astral plane is immaterial. It was an experience of something beyond the physical world, not a spiritual experience more a psychic one but still a loosening of the bonds of the materialistic straitjacket I was struggling with. I have never encountered anything of the kind again except in literary form when I read of the vision of Isis as related in Apuleius's *The Golden Ass*, a book, I should say, I had never heard of at the time though it is true that I had loved the stories of the ancient Greek gods and goddesses from the age of 8 or 9.

As with my psychedelic experiences, though, I had no way to build on this vision or take it forwards in any practical sense, and so it remained an illuminating but isolated event in the spiritual gloom of my adolescence. I never spoke of it because there was nothing to be said about it and nor did I even think of it much after a few weeks. As it couldn't be interpreted within the framework of the knowledge of the world I had at the time, after a while I just set it aside.

Chapter 2

The Call Home

When I left school I did a couple of jobs because I had to do something and, because I knew no better and saw no point to ordinary existence, I drank too much alcohol and smoked too much marijuana. However by the age of 21 I had definitely had enough of that futile existence. I read many of the great novels of the past during this time, Balzac, Dostoyevsky, Herman Hesse and so on, and learnt a good deal from them, but I had begun to tire of fiction. These great works of art may contain many truths but they remain fiction. None of this was getting me anywhere. I frequented a metaphysical bookshop in the Old Brompton Road, looking for something that might take me further. I had some familiarity with the popular gurus of the day but regarded those that I knew of as fakes and frauds who only attracted the gullible and naïve. If that was spirituality, I wasn't interested.

The feeling that drives most human beings onto a serious spiritual path is that there must be more to life than this. When that feeling becomes almost unbearable, something will usually happen. The powers that be must have taken pity on me or perhaps it was that the time was now right for pre-ordained events to manifest themselves, since it would be my contention that you are a disciple of spiritual teachers on inner levels long before this transmits itself to the physical plane. Whatever it was, the fact is that I was knocking rather desperately and the door opened.

In June of 1978 I was approached in the Old Brompton Road bookshop by a man in his late fifties. He introduced himself as Michael Lord and began talking to me, recommending a couple of books which I bought. We had lunch together and discussed topics such as vegetarianism and reincarnation which were not quite as familiar subjects for discussion then as now. Prior to this I, in common with most of my contemporaries, had regarded vegetarians as rather silly eccentrics but I became one practically straightaway. There were two aspects to this decision. Reluctance to inflict unnecessary suffering on fellow creatures makes sense to anyone not ruled by their stomach, whether spiritually inclined or not, but, for those who are so inclined, purity, that is to say, rendering the body less coarse and more susceptible to impression from the higher worlds, is an additional factor to take into account. Meat is a food that dulls sensitivity. A vegetarian diet will not make you a more spiritual person but it will make you more finely attuned if you follow a spiritual practice.

I also became a believer in reincarnation from that day. I had come across it before, of course, but only in its more sensational aspects with people claiming to be this or that famous historical character. There used to be quite a few Cleopatras and Napoleons in former times. Now, together with its associate, karma, it seemed to provide an answer to many of life's more intractable problems. Why there was inequality, why there was suffering and how there was the opportunity for spiritual growth. The doctrine of reincarnation also implies the pre-existence of the soul and that concept made perfect sense to me as I had always found it hard to believe that I had only come into existence with my physical birth. I'm putting this in the fairly simplistic way I first considered it but that is not radically different to how I think of it now. I know one can argue endlessly over details, about what reincarnates and so on (it certainly is not the 'you' you currently identify with), but these are just details and don't detract from the general principle.

Michael and I arranged to meet again and I remember when I went back to work after that initial lunch I ran up three flights of stairs in excitement. I picked up my pen to write and then cast it away again. The work I was about to do seemed even more pointless than usual. A barrier had finally come down and light was streaming in. My lifelong intuition was correct. There really was a higher reality and this world was not all there was to existence. It's not an exaggeration to say that from that day onwards my life changed and did so for the better because it acquired purpose. For the sake of sceptics let me emphasise that my newfound enthusiasm for the spiritual did not come from the fact that it offered an escape from a reality I found distasteful but that it was a way into reality; a reality that I already knew existed but had hitherto had that knowledge denied.

Like most spiritual novices I imagined enlightenment was just around the corner. I began to meditate. Curiously, and I can't remember why now, I started to do this by sitting in a chair at my bedroom window looking fixedly out at some silver birch trees in the garden. I had no idea what I was supposed to be doing. Pretty soon I moved to sitting cross legged with my eyes closed and had some inner experiences of a quasi-visionary nature coupled with sensations of melting into light which naturally confirmed my suspicions that I was on my way. My understanding of the spiritual world was basic to say the least but my approach to it was sincere. I did seek a higher state of consciousness as a personal goal but I also had a genuine concern for what was right and true. Still, my approach was certainly unbalanced and misconceived, as is that of most beginners who lack proper guidance, and, although I continued to meet and talk to Michael, I had no direction. I read the books of Paul Brunton, which I still think are valuable works, and plenty of others which I can't remember now, some recommended by Michael and others that I found by combing through bookshops which research, incidentally, soon taught me that a large proportion of spiritual books just recycle other spiritual books. But I had no teacher so was free to make my own mistakes which I did. I threw myself into my new life with abandon, gave up almost everything all in one go (I even lived exclusively on millet for a couple of weeks after reading that Archimedes had done so!) and meditated enthusiastically.

I don't know if it was a result of this imbalance or part of the process of purification or maybe a bit of both but after a couple of months I began to experience some strange and frightening psychic reactions. One night I woke up feeling myself to be being sucked into a vortex of naked evil, a swirling, black whirlpool of malevolence that was wholly malign but in a quite dispassionate way. It had no personal feeling of dislike for me, it simply wanted to consume and absorb my psyche or so it seemed. Believe me, the description is a good deal less melodramatic than the experience was terrifying. The sensation continued in the daylight hours though thankfully in a somewhat abated form. I felt detached from reality but in a very disturbing way, as if my sense of self was unravelling, the centre about to explode, my identity on the verge of splintering and fragmenting. When people spoke to me it was as though they were doing so from the end of a long tunnel and I had difficulty concentrating on what they were saying. I wondered if I were going mad but, as part of me could watch what was happening as a detached observer, I concluded probably not. Nevertheless it was not pleasant and was made worse by the fact that I felt I couldn't tell anyone what I was going through. Michael had recently moved from London to Bath so couldn't help. I wrote to him but was unable to describe the process very articulately and there was not much he could say in reply. He did tell me not to be alarmed but to stop meditating for the time being and seek guidance through prayer.

After a few weeks of this I eventually confided in my parents and, because they didn't know what else to do, they arranged a visit to a psychologist. He had nothing very illuminating to say (I don't think my condition was in his textbooks) but he was a sensible person, and it helped me to talk to someone sympathetic. Shortly afterwards, coincidentally or not, I began to feel a little better, and gradually the disorientation started to subside, helped in no small measure I must say by the music of Mozart. This is actually an important point, I think. The order and harmony intrinsic to Mozart's music soothed my distracted state and brought balance back to a mind that had sometimes seemed to be spinning out of control. For those who are interested, the piece I found most therapeutic then, with its combination of Apollonian calm and outdoors courtliness (that's what it said to me anyway), was the Wind Serenade K361 also known as the Gran Partita. The serene adagio was particularly calming. I found I could listen to music from any period up to and including Mozart whilst in that fragile condition but anything later than that was disturbing to me with only a few rare exceptions, some of Debussy's piano pieces, for example. There's little doubt that the end of the 18th century was a significant moment in Western intellectual life in that it was the tipping point of a process that had begun much earlier, probably with the Renaissance, of removing God from His throne and installing Man in his place, and this is reflected in the arts. Of course, that process has been taken much further since then.

Once recovered, I felt I needed to come to a few decisions about my life. I had been pursuing a spiritual course but without any real direction. During the early days of my acquaintance with Michael, before he moved to Bath, he had made some suggestions concerning specific spiritual paths which he thought might interest me. I had been to a Buddhist meditation centre but a couple of visits convinced me that it was not for me. The people were pleasant but slightly too earnest. The practice was the fixed following of a particular method and the teacher just taught Buddhism, and Theravada Buddhism at that. There was no spark, no individual insight into a living truth beyond what the books and tradition said the Buddha had taught. I'm not decrying Buddhism. I felt this about every organised religion and most other spiritual approaches too. But I didn't want a guide who, while he may not have been blind, had more of his knowledge of the heavenly worlds from maps drawn by others than from visits he had made himself.

One of the reasons I felt no attraction to this centre or, for that matter, any other was that around this time I had an experience which, at the risk of hyperbole, had opened up my soul. That is how it felt at the time so that's how I shall describe it here. Experiences in meditation were one thing but this was of a much grander nature. It came unexpectedly and unbidden and it came like this. My parents' house had a large garden behind which was a park, and my brother and I used to go down to the bottom of the garden and climb over the railings into this park as that was the quickest way to get to the local shops. I set off on this expedition one morning when all at once everything changed. The change came with the suddenness of sunrise in the tropics. Reality became more real by a factor of several hundreds. All the things in the garden I knew so well, the trees, the flowers, the grass, the little pool surrounded by rocks, were transformed into almost living things, or, at least, they pulsated with an inner life. A great stream of love poured through me, and there was a sense of vastness coupled with one of extraordinary intimacy that was beyond anything I had ever imagined let alone experienced. As for time, well it really did seem to stand still or maybe it was, since there was a continuous movement like that of an ever-flowing river, that I had slipped into a dimension in which all time became now. Every fibre of my being thrilled with the sudden revelation that the universe was filled with meaning and joy, and that what the universe was, I was too. Yes, it was a spiritual experience but there was nothing abstract or insubstantial about it as that expression might imply to some people. It was more real than anything ordinary life could begin to offer, even in its most intense moments. I saw the material world as composed of dancing particles of vibrating light; nothing was hard or solid, everything was radiant, and I felt my body to be similarly constituted. As I realised the complete oneness of all manifested forms, the universe presented itself to me in the guise of a great rose with deeper and deeper layers of beauty hidden within its myriad petals. It was a revelation because it revealed the truth about things in their essential nature. There could be no possible doubt. I didn't try and understand it as there was nothing to understand. It was what it was and that was all there was to it.

The experience passed but the memory of it remained. As spiritual experiences go, it seems to me to be fairly typical. But its intensity and the overwhelming reality of it made it very hard for me to accept anything that did not measure up to it, which in part explains my reluctance to become involved with any spiritual group or organisation. Only in part, though. The main reason for this was a conviction I had always had, quite independent of any experience, that truth was not to be found in outer things or man-made forms of any type. This didn't preclude me from accepting a teacher but required it to be one in whom the truth shone without impediment. A tall order obviously in this imperfect world.

My other foray into the world of spiritual groups was a weekend retreat with the Ramakrishna Mission at a large country house they had in Buckinghamshire. Michael had had some connection with them in India and introduced me to them. I had read and appreciated The Gospel of Ramakrishna, who was obviously a genuine saint (though not without a few idiosyncrasies), and thought that a retreat with the order established after his death might somehow connect me to its spiritual source. Unfortunately not. The head swami and monks were certainly sincere men of spiritual integrity but the fire I was looking for was not burning there. No doubt I was expecting too much but I was looking for spiritual awareness of a sort that went beyond the religious sensibility and what I found was not that. There was undeniably much knowledge and genuine experience of the path but no internalised realisation, totally independent of any external support, of the kind the saint whose name the ashram bore had demonstrated. That is why, despite my appreciation of the monks' numerous qualities, it could not satisfy me. The reader may take this to be arrogance on my part but if you have a raging thirst you need more than a sip of water from the tap. You are not going to be satisfied with anything less than a full glass from the source.

So, there I was, restored to mental health but with no course on which to set my ship. I needed to find direction and a path. During my meditation practice I had continued with the job I had been doing when I first met Michael, mainly because I needed to earn a living. Now I felt it was time to leave even if it involved a jump into the unknown. Sometimes things happen on their own, others you have to make happen. Even if you don't quite know how, you can still initiate a process and see where it takes you. I left my job and booked a trip to Greece and Egypt.

I should say a few words about Michael. He had had an interesting life. At the time I met him he was 58 and had just come back from India where he had managed the Hare Krishna guesthouse in Bombay. As he was at pains to point out, he was never a member of that group but wanted a chance to go back to India where he had been conceived (though not born) and was stationed during most of the 2nd World War, for some of the time as A.D.C. to the then Viceroy. This, of course, was a few years prior to independence. His experiences in India spanned an interesting range and went from meeting Gandhi to being incarcerated for a few weeks in a Japanese prisoner of war camp just over the border in Burma. After the war he had gone to America, leading a rather worldly existence in New York high society, before returning to England and becoming, to his friends' astonishment, a Benedictine monk. During his time in the monastery he told me he had once witnessed an old monk praying in front of a statue of the Virgin Mary and levitating a few inches off the ground as he did so. When Michael expressed surprise (wouldn't you?) the monk said "It's nothing and I beg you, dear brother, do not mention it to anyone". An exemplary attitude to any psychic or occult side effects encountered on the path and a perfect example of Christian humility.

Michael always retained an affection for the Catholic religion (or, at any rate, the pre-Second Vatican Council version of it) but he left the monastery after a couple of years because he felt restricted by the way of life and the rigid belief system. He told me that when he mentioned that he believed in reincarnation to another monk that person did not deny it but said it was a belief he should keep to himself as it was not wise to have individual ideas in religion. The other reason Michael felt he had to leave was that after a while the monastic way of life became artificial, inhuman even, in his eyes.

Certain aspects of the monastic life are built on force (as in excessive discipline) and denial and this did not seem healthy to him. On a more practical level, he left because he developed what he called housemaid's knee from spending so much time in prayer so could not kneel with the other monks during the lengthy services. Was this a sign that it was time for him to move on?

From the extreme of monasticism Michael then swung back to worldliness again, becoming secretary of the Carlton Club, a political club in London though he wasn't in the least bit political, for more or less the whole of the sixties. There he led a hectic social life and met many of the eminent personalities, political and otherwise, of the day. From what he told me it seems that people's public image does not always reflect the private reality. Who would have thought it?

After that immersion in society there was a reaction and another radical change, seemingly a pattern of his life. In 1970 he left the allurements of the capital and went as far away as he could, moving to Penzance and working as an antiques dealer. He made new friends (he was always a gregarious fellow) but still didn't find any kind of real fulfilment, feeling after a while "like the tangerine at the bottom of the Christmas stocking" as he put it. The worldly and spiritual sides of his nature were constantly clashing but he always had the courage to follow his impulses and make new starts. Not being married or having children may have helped with that but it does require courage to uproot oneself, abandon security and start afresh. Easy at 25, not so easy at 50. So after a few years he sold his house in Cornwall and made another of his many trips to India, visiting the Ramakrishna Mission in Calcutta where he was initiated by a swami of that order. I don't think he took the initiation particularly seriously though I don't mean to imply that he took it lightly either. It was more a question of him always seeking some kind of spiritual home but never finding one until eventually coming to realise that he was not going to do so in this world.

He returned to London for a year or two where he had a little concessionary shop in Harrods selling crystals (unfortunately for him some time before the fashion for them took off), then made yet another trip to India, this time to the Hare Krishnas in Bombay to run their main guesthouse there. That didn't work out because he had been expecting a spiritual centre but found instead internal bickering and fights, not to mention a spiritual approach that he considered much too limited, so he soon left and went back to London where he met me.

Chapter 3

Setting Out on the Path of Return

In these pages I hope to distinguish between what I have learnt from experience, what I have been told by an authority I regard as unimpeachable, what I am aware of through the intuitive knowledge of the mind in the heart (a faculty which may be denied by many but which any spiritual aspirant knows exists), and what I have gleaned from books and the like. What I have read I may believe as it makes sense to me and gives an acceptable form to an idea I already have but I realise that any belief is at best a temporary approximation to be held lightly and discarded for a higher understanding when that becomes available. Too many people claim beliefs as personal knowledge or become stuck in their beliefs, unable to move on, and one must always be able to move on.

To further complicate matters, the spiritual field is rife with illusion and self-deception, much of which is the result of the mind projecting its own patterns on reality. When I was younger this greatly troubled my perfectionist self but I came to see that it could not be otherwise, given our current rather limited understanding of reality not to mention the tendency of the mind to interpret quite possibly genuine transcendent experiences in terms of what it already knows. Even so, the fact that there is so much half-truth and downright falsehood mixed in with spiritual truths as they are presented in this world can be very unsettling for the neophyte. Ultimately this requires one to hone one's own insight and search within (which is the only place true knowledge can be found) so the deficiencies of external presentations of spiritual truth can actually be used to one's advantage. Even so great an authority as the Buddha said that one should not believe anything that did not ring true to one's own inner sensibility, no matter who said it.

That's all a brief preamble to the next stage in my journey. A short while before my disturbing experience of psychic near disintegration described above, Michael and I had visited Glastonbury, well known then and now as the pre-eminent English sacred site. We climbed up the Tor just before dawn in time to see the sun rise at the top but to me it was something of a disappointment. The Tor had a wild grandeur that impressed but at that time I felt nothing you might call spiritual. I sensed that it had always been a place of power but not necessarily of holiness. On the other hand, the adjacent Chalice Hill when I visited it that full moon lit night seemed welcoming and benign. I envisaged the two hills as focal points for different kinds of energy which one might very loosely describe as feminine and masculine or maybe, in keeping with the times of my visits, lunar and solar, vague descriptions which I'm sure would exasperate a rationalist but which mean something quite definite to those symbol-ically inclined. These are the two primary forces of the universe, most perfectly depicted in imagery by the Yin/Yang symbol of Taoism whose two complementary halves encompass all dualities, the active and the passive, the light and the dark, the expanding and the contracting, the straight and the curved, the hard and the soft and so on. The list is pretty much endless. It occurred to me that the two hills might be physical manifestations of these forces, whose energies were there to be used by those with sufficient knowledge (through ritual, meditation and such like), though how they were used, energies being impersonal, would depend on the motive of the user.

Glastonbury was a significant step on my journey because it was during that visit that I first learnt that Michael was clairvoyant. I found this out when we went for a late evening walk through the garden of our guesthouse which was a spiritual centre of sorts. As far as I recall, he exclaimed words along the lines of "My goodness, this place is crowded!" Naturally, seeing no one there, I asked him what he meant to which he replied that the garden was full of nature spirits. The cynic will immediately presume he was making this up to impress a naïve youngster but the odd thing was that I too, normally no psychic, could see little flashes of light in the darkness of the garden. I suppose that's the power of Glastonbury, a place, like all true places of pilgrimage, where the usual barriers between heaven and earth can sometimes seem to be thin. To me these lights appeared to be no more than fleeting sparks darting this way and that but he apparently could see more clearly. On discussing his clairvoyance with him further he told me that he was sometimes able to see people's auras but had never made any attempt to cultivate this power, accepting it if it came but not seeking to develop it in any way. His attitude was refreshing to me. Of course, every spiritual seeker knows in theory that the psychic powers are pitfalls, potential distractions from the true business of ego transcendence, but it's easy to take that line if you don't have them.

One of the most fascinating things about Glastonbury is the range of spiritual atmospheres to be found there. The Tor carries the ancient pagan vibration and, to me at any rate, has a definite dark and light feel to it with the potential to bring forth either. This hill certainly has power and I can well see why there might be legends that it contains a dragon. Chalice Well is a place of healing where the troubled soul can find peace and refreshment. It has a tranquil atmosphere and a stillness that brings calm to anyone willing to open themselves up to its influence for a while. Then there is the abbey with its strong Christian feel and air of purity and sanctity that survives to this day despite 16th century desecration and 21st century spiritual tourism. The druids are supposed to have recognised Christ as the fulfilment of their tradition and early Celtic Christianity, as a combination of the two spiritual forces, bears splendid witness to that. Notwithstanding all it has had to put up with, there is still an echo of this happy marriage at Glastonbury.

Shortly after that trip Michael left London and went to live in Bath, something he had already planned to do before he met me. He bought a small flat in the centre of the town near those splendours of Georgian architecture, the Circus and the Royal Crescent, and started a business selling 18th and 19th century English porcelain in the local antiques market. I carried on meditating and went through the psychic meltdown I have related. Later on I was told that this was in part a process of purification, necessary to cleanse my psyche of much wrong thinking and toxicity, but had been exacerbated by opening up too much too soon as a result of my beginner's enthusiasm and exposing myself to forces I was ill equipped to handle.

My trip to Greece and Egypt was everything I had hoped it might be. A person of even moderate sensitivity can benefit by visiting sacred sites, and Delphi and Giza are undoubtedly those. It may be true that increased traffic to holy places has reduced the spiritual value to be absorbed there, almost as if quantity and quality were inversely proportional, and this is especially the case if those who come do so as tourists rather than pilgrims. Nevertheless the rose hasn't lost all its perfume, and power and virtue still remain. In 1978 Delphi and Giza were less frequented than they are today though I imagine that anyone who had known them thirty years earlier would have been taken aback by the changes that had occurred since then. Still, when I first visited the pyramids at Giza it was possible to be alone in the King's Chamber for a period which I imagine would be difficult now. This was once the heart of the Great Pyramid where the candidate for initiation would undergo the transformation of consciousness that would make him worthy to join the company of immortals. Or maybe it is just the empty tomb of a megalomaniac ruler. That's the official view, of course, but it's based on scanty evidence and contradicted by intuition. I also had the opportunity to climb to the top of the Menkaure pyramid when a local youth offered to take me up for one Egyptian pound. Halfway up he demanded two pounds and, when I refused, drew a knife. Too startled to do anything else I just laughed which seemingly endeared me to him so much that he immediately refunded all my money and invited me back to his house for tea and to meet his family. I don't recall very well now what the view from the top of the pyramid was like except that the sense of space created by the clear blue sky above and hot dusty desert below seemed to hollow out the mind, opening it up to the great emptiness.

Egypt was my first exposure to what you might call, stretching the boundaries a bit, the East and initially I hated it, wanting to get back to Greece as soon as possible. Not so much Alexandria, where I had first arrived on the boat from Piraeus and which was almost a European town, but Cairo with its noise, dirt and smells. Goats urinating in the street were not what I was used to back home in the suburbs of London. Within a couple of days, however, those things no longer troubled me in the slightest and the colour and character of the city became quite intoxicating. That's a common experience, I know. I stayed in a cheap hotel in Cairo and went out to the pyramids every day for about a week to explore the site and simply allow myself to be transported by the atmosphere of the stones and the desert. The pyramids and Sphinx are accepted by most people as one of the most extraordinary creations of humanity. What is disputed is their age and function. I could not possibly enter into the controversy over their antiquity but it is surely only a materialistic age with no conception of how the mythological mind works that can see the Great Pyramid as a tomb and not a temple of initiation.

What do I mean by the mythological mind? It is the mind that sees all of the world, indeed, all of creation, as a sacred symbol at once veiling and revealing the Deity. It is a mind that perceives unitively and in wholes rather than analytically in fragmented parts, and it sees time as unfolding cyclically instead of progressing in the straight linear fashion we are accustomed to think of it today. Early humanity perceived and knew. They may have had an incomplete understanding, or even no understanding, of what they knew, and that explains the path we have taken over the last few thousand years. But they knew. They knew that all things were interconnected and that they were part of the One Life that existed both within and beyond this world. They had a fragile sense of self but they participated in the wholeness of life. To a very large extent that participation was passive which is why we had to move on and seemingly fall back in order to progress. They were aware but not properly aware that they were aware. We need to become fully conscious of the oneness of life and active participants in creation. We need to become co-creators with God.

I had never felt particularly at home in 20th century Western culture but, living in that world and not knowing anything else except through books and art, most of the time it seemed as though that was all there ever really was. It alone was real and the rest was dreams from the past, over and done with and forgotten save in history books. It might have served its purpose at one time but was now outmoded and left behind in the light of our new and enlightened age. Standing in front of the Sphinx on the plateau of Giza where the sense of the infinite is very present, and visiting that embodiment of sacred harmony and proportion in stone which is the Parthenon, showed that idea to be false. All that was good and true of the past was still there, dormant maybe but ready to be re-discovered if approached in the right frame of mind. I am not suggesting anything so silly (and impossible) as a denial of the present and a retreat to a fantasy past but I do believe that anything in this world that was once a faithful attempt to reflect and give form to the good, the beautiful and the true still exists in higher worlds in its essential archetypal reality. All forms inevitably pass but the quality of anything that attempts to be faithful to the divine pattern remains. Ancient Greece and Egypt survive and not just in the museums.

On my return from Egypt I visited Michael in Bath and we decided that I should move down there to live with him, and that together we would lead a life dedicated to the spiritual quest. I thought for a long time about this as it represented a definitive break from the life I had been brought up to lead and was expected to fall back into, even though I had shown little inclination for it. I had recently been offered a good job in a branch of the Civil Service, the result of some exams and interviews I had done before going abroad, and would, for the first time, have had a career of sorts. This pleased and, I don't doubt, greatly relieved my parents who thought I was finally going to make something of myself so when I announced that I would not be accepting this job but instead be going off to live with Michael (whom they had not met), they were horrified. I didn't blame them in the slightest. To all external appearances this was a ridiculous and irresponsible thing to do but I knew it was the right decision even though I did not take it lightly. In addition I was aware of how tongues would wag if a younger man went to live with an unmarried older man. In spite of all that I had an overwhelming sense that I had to do this and this feeling of inevitability ultimately made the decision easy.

I went to live in Bath on 1st January 1979, a simple date to remember which is why I do. I had met Michael the previous June and, to my family, things had progressed very quickly. To me also changes had come rapidly but all the spiritual teachings I had discovered did not seem new to me. Quite the reverse, in fact. They seemed rediscoveries of things I already knew and which formed the deepest part of me. In that respect I was merely awakening to what I already was. I don't think this is unusual among spiritual aspirants, and, to those who recognise that we have an existence prior to birth in this world, there is nothing fantastic in such a notion. The soul exists on its own plane. It sends down a portion of itself to experience life in the physical world, the plane that is the furthest removed from God in His essence and where a sense of separation is possible. Only with this sense of duality can the individual come fully to know himself as an individual and go through the experiences that will enable him acquire the conscious oneness with God that is the goal of the spiritual life, a oneness that may be there all along but which is unrecognised. The incarnate soul forgets itself. The new personality, the mind, emotions and physical body, is, whilst the consequence of the past, to all intents and purposes a new construct. However it is the vehicle for something greater than itself. It is the means whereby the soul, the conscious self, may experience life in the world of duality where the 'I' exists in apparent isolation from everything else. I say apparent because, of course, God exists on all levels of life from pure unmanifest spirit down to fully manifested matter and all the planes in between. There is nowhere God is not but, to the unenlightened eye, the fullness of the divine presence is veiled by the energy substance in which it manifests in the material world. This is Maya, the feminine or passive pole of divinity, who is not illusion but appearance.

I am using the word God because I like it. For me it conjures up as much of its meaning as any word can, and more contemporary equivalents lack its resonance. I know that for some people it carries a lot of baggage, being identified with the Old Testament tribal deity, but I still think it is better than anything else. What do I mean by this word though? Well, who can begin to define God? There is a universal one life which is pure consciousness, pure intelligence and pure love. Yet though we can say this about it we must also say that, in its unmanifested state, it is beyond all attributes and qualities as we might understand them. In this state it cannot be conceived of as anything which is why it is sometimes described, perhaps confusingly since, being the source of all things, it is far from mere emptiness, as the void. When it manifests it moves from unexpressed being into expressed being and qualities and attributes have the potential to arise. You might imagine this as the void becoming the one and then the one, in the creative process, becoming many. However, before the one becomes many, it must first become two. God said "Let there be light" and there was light. This is the primary duality of unmanifest spirit becoming spirit and matter or essence and substance, God and Nature, if you like (if you accept nature as the totality of all the created worlds, subtle and gross, and not just the physical), and it is from the interaction between these active and passive poles of life, the one expressing itself through the other, that the whole of manifested existence arises. Note that there is no real separation between these two. They are not different things but different aspects of the same thing.

So does this mean God is impersonal or personal? Partisans of one or the other position often seem reluctant to accept that these are not mutually exclusive concepts but simply relate to different orders of reality. Occultism maintains that behind every cosmic energy there is a being embodying that energy, an idea roughly analogous to that of the classical gods. From this perspective the personal God could be seen as the being behind the entire manifested universe in all its dimensions, though not in a pantheistic sense as He is not only immanent in the universe, He also transcends and stands outside it as its creator. Beyond that is the unmanifest God or Godhead which has no form and no individuality, which is not anything. It simply is. The personal God is the highest form of manifested existence and that from which all else derives. Behind Him, however, (and He is conceived as Him not because He is male but because He is positive to creation which is negative to Him) is the impersonal absolute. This is a state of pure being which has no expression and no form. This pure being does not act and does not create but from it, as its manifesting aspect, emerges the Creator God who has individuality which is expressed in creation. If God could not say 'I' how could we?

Michael had once briefly mentioned that he was clairaudient and spoken to on occasion by disembodied spirits. He hadn't said much more than that and my curiosity had not been aroused sufficiently for me to pursue the matter further. That may seem strange but he had taken me to a spiritualist meeting shortly after we had met and I, as a high-minded 22 year old, had not been very impressed. I could believe that something was going on but it was all rather vague and did not seem to be at a particularly elevated level. I could accept that discarnate spirits might communicate through mediums but I also thought that many apparent spirits were probably just the cast off psychic residue of defunct personalities whose spiritual core had departed. Even if genuine, these communications always seemed to come from recent arrivals in the spiritual world who did not have much of real interest to say beyond the fact that they had survived death and were in a beautiful place. That was encouraging

29

but did not take one very far on the spiritual path. The personality may survive the death of the body but true spiritual insight can only come from those who have transcended personality. Curiously, at the séance I went to, the medium did say that my grandfather was present with his son who had died in the war and that they were guiding me. He also said that this person had been inspiring me to write poetry. My great grandfather had been a writer and his son had been killed in the 1st World War, and I was sufficiently intrigued to look through some tea chests of old papers at home where almost immediately I found a poem my great grandfather had written some eighty years earlier. It consisted of twenty six words, each one beginning with a consecutive letter of the alphabet, a-,b-,c- and so on. Oddly enough I had done exactly the same thing in my poetry writing days, so make of that what you will. My feeling, then as now, was that, true or not, it is of little significance, and I only mention to explain my attitude to Michaels's passing mention of his clairaudience, which he did not seem to set enormous store by either when he spoke of it.

I soon learned that there was rather more to Michael's clairaudience than I had first thought. Our life in Bath alternated between buying and selling antique porcelain by day and meditating for 45 minutes or so at night. I was now a little more proficient in meditation and could reach a point of inner silence on most occasions without too much trouble. My earlier approach of attempting to reach exalted spiritual states through meditation had calmed down and I was more inclined to regard it as a time to attune oneself to the stillness of the soul within. Nevertheless I still had not fully grasped that the spiritual life is not about inner experience but overcoming the ego even if, theoretically at least, I was starting to make that crucial distinction. I recall my favourite saying of the time was from *The Imitation of Christ* by Thomas à Kempis and went along these lines. "You are not making progress if you receive God's grace but you are making progress if you bear the withdrawal of grace with patience, humility and resignation". There's not much wiser counsel for the spiritual aspirant from any age. It warns one not to get carried away by mystical transports and, at the same time, emphasises the necessity of detachment from self and dis-identification from emotional states. Essentially it tells the seeker not to pursue experience. Likewise Ramakrishna, when told by his favourite disciple Vivekananda that his aim was to stay for long periods rapt in meditation, had said "You are a fool. There is a state much higher than that."

After a month or so of this way of life something occurred that confirmed I had made the right decision to come to Bath. Subsequently I found out that what took place did not happen before because I had to make the decision to dedicate myself to the spiritual path on my own, without coercion or undue influence of any kind. It had to be based on my own understanding without any external force interfering with me making the choice of my own free will.

We were meditating as usual when Michael suddenly and unexpectedly (he had not done it before) began to sound the OM, the Hindu holy word that is deemed to be the closest approximation we can know to the basic tone of the universe. It was loud, so loud in fact that one could almost feel the room shaking, and it was prolonged. It seemed to last for at least a couple of minutes. How does he have enough breath to do that, I wondered, while also being slightly concerned at what the neighbours might think. Coming out of the quietness of meditation it seemed like the thundering of a mighty waterfall crashing down onto rocks below. Then it stopped and there was silence again but the atmosphere had changed. This was not an empty silence but one impregnated with power, holiness even. I was astounded. I had never imagined that Michael could do such a thing. Then a voice spoke.

Chapter 4

The Masters

The voice that spoke was not Michael's. It had neither the timbre nor the accent nor any characteristic of his voice at all, despite the fact that it was undoubtedly formed by his physical vocal apparatus. It had an authority I had never encountered before and which he certainly did not possess. I simply have to state this as a matter of fact. I am aware that many will seek to explain the whole thing as an act of deception on Michael's part, either conscious or unconscious, whatever the latter might mean in this case. It's the obvious explanation and naturally that thought crossed my mind too. But going by the voice and the presence alone, and not even taking into account the teachings that came later, I know that is quite impossible. It was not Michael. There really was nothing of him in it.

I opened my eyes and looked at Michael. He was sitting bolt upright with his eyes shut. His face seemed to have changed slightly. It was immobile, hieratic, like that of an ancient Egyptian statue. It almost seemed to be carved out of marble, so motionless and dignified was it. I felt a sense of awe, not an accustomed emotion for me, in many respects a typical product of the irreverent sixties. Then the voice spoke again. What was said I don't remember exactly now. Soon afterwards I got into the habit of making notes when the talks ended but on that first occasion I just listened, feeling it would be disrespectful to write anything down. The being that spoke did not introduce himself or even say who or what he was. He greeted me calling me not by my name but addressing me simply as "my child". At no time did he or anyone else who spoke through Michael use my name. This name relates to my earthly personality and that is not who they are addressing. They are not concerned with the personality. They did not identify themselves by name for the same reason, and my experience has made me rather sceptical of spiritual beings that do. They have names, we all have spiritual names, but these are sacred things embodying what we are not just personal labels, and they are not to be bandied about lightly. More to the point is the fact that to focus on a name focuses on the individual and encourages personality worship, something these spiritual beings would wish to avoid at all costs.

The gist of what was said on that first contact was that they (it was almost always 'we', hardly ever 'I') were pleased Michael and I had made the decision to live together. They had sent him to me and me to him and would guide us both. The speaker said we should love each other and learn from each other. He was encouraging but made no promises. He did not explain much but seemed to assume I should know and understand what was happening. Oddly enough I did. It seemed to be the entry into the everyday world of something I had known on an inner level already and, though extraordinary, was somehow not unexpected.

He did not describe himself as such then but he was what is usually known today as a Master, a liberated human being who has realised his identity with God and transcended the need for earthly incarnation. Although he spoke through Michael in full trance he was no ordinary spirit and this was nothing to do with spiritualism as ordinarily understood. I must expand on this a little as it is commonly believed that the Masters do not speak through mediums in trance by the so-called direct voice method. They may inspire, they may overshadow, they may impress ideas on receptive minds but they do not speak through mediums in deep trance which is regarded as a rather crude and difficult means of communication. That is undoubtedly true. In general the Masters do not use this method and those who do are not Masters, whatever they may claim or be claimed for them. Nevertheless, although it is extremely rare, there are a few exceptions to that rule. This was one. Another indisputably authentic example I know of is the remarkable story told in the book "*The Boy and the Brothers*" and its sequel "*Towards The*

Mysteries"[1].

This is the story of an uneducated young man from the East End of London who was used by the Masters during the 1930s and 1940s as a medium for extensive communications which, in my opinion, are among the most profound and authentic spiritual teachings of the last century. As with any genuine teaching emanating from a true and pure source, it is not just the words that impress but the tone, the vibration as we call it nowadays, which has an impact that goes well beyond mere words. In our time so much that was hidden has been revealed, with once secret teachings readily available in your local bookshop, that it is not hard for any aspiring spiritual teacher to have the words. But only those who have truly internalised the teaching can transmit more than intellectual understanding. Only those who have walked the path, become the path and then completely transcended the path can convey the spirit and soul of the teaching as well as its outer form. These two books, simply written and with no mystery-mongering or sensationalism about them, do that as well as any other mystical book that I have come across, and considerably better than most. Their relative simplicity merely reinforces their deep wisdom. The author of the books was Swami Omananda, an Irish woman who in earlier life had been Maud McCarthy, a professional musician married to the composer John Foulds. She was the companion and protectress to the boy, as the medium was known, and in later life became, I believe, the first Western woman to be initiated as a swami. I've never quite understood why she wished to do that, given her contacts, but perhaps she felt she needed the grounding of an outer path. Quite possibly, as they lived in India for many years, that was necessary if they were to attract people to their ashram to hear the Masters.

This is the only published instance I know of and regard as genuine in which the Masters (as opposed to ordinary discarnate beings, high or low) spoke through a medium in full trance. There must surely be other occasions when they have used this technique but it is definitely rare though claims for it, unfortunately and confusingly, are not in this tail end of the Kali Yuga[2]. I don't know why they used that method to speak to me. Possibly it was because Michael was able to perform as a medium for them. I was given to understand that most mediums would not have been able to withstand such a powerful presence, certainly very different to the usual channelled entities. I should say that it was a strain for Michael and a sacrifice for him to allow himself to be used in that way. Afterwards he would be exhausted and in a highly sensitive state, hardly surprising when you consider that he had been taken out of his body which was then used by another being whose energies vibrated at a much higher rate. That is very unscientifically expressed, I fear, but the technical aspect of the whole process was not explained to me except in the most basic terms.

To begin with the Masters would come and speak to me virtually every night during meditation. Although it was not always the same individual (I could usually tell the difference, transcending ego does not mean losing individuality), there was a unity to them which went much deeper than any outer differences. Most of what they said related to what I had to learn in this lifetime, though occasionally they would broaden the discussion and speak in more general terms. Sometimes they would praise and often encourage but mostly they pointed out the areas I had to concentrate on in order to progress. They did not beat about the bush or express themselves in a roundabout way. They simply stated the truth and I recognised it as such even though it might have been a home truth. They were there to reveal the deficiencies in my character and the obstacles to spiritual progress and that's precisely what they did. All they did, though, they did with love.

It's hard to convey the quality of this love, so tarnished is that word today by misuse and trivialisation. In order to distinguish it from human love, spiritual love is sometimes described as impersonal but that does not mean it is without feeling. How could it? On the contrary, it is perfect feeling that arises from the sense of unity and is directed to all. What it is not is possessive, self-centred or attached. It asks for nothing and expects nothing. At the same time, just as Jesus and Buddha are said to have had their favourite disciples, so the universality of spiritual love does not preclude a special closeness between master and disciple. That does not mean that it is the personal self that the Masters love. They are concerned with spiritual growth and their love is for the soul which is why it might sometimes appear, from a strictly human perspective, as almost stern. Primarily, though, contact with them gives one the sense of being known completely and loved unconditionally.

Here's an extract from notes I took at the time. It's not a verbatim report but something I wrote up after the talk had finished. I did not have a tape recorder then but, even if I had, I doubt I would have used it. I can quite understand those who might think this attitude odd but, for me, to have recorded the talks would have meant paying less attention to them as they took place. To write them down afterwards was to impress them on one's memory but to have done so at the time would have divided attention and be somehow using the Masters for my own ends rather than, metaphorically speaking, sitting at their feet. If their utterances had been meant for a wider audience, that might have changed the situation but, in the context of a private talk, listening fully in the moment was the only option or so I considered at the time. And though I say that it is not a verbatim report, such was the impact of the Masters' words that in most cases I remembered them almost perfectly afterwards, and if I did not I would send up a little prayer for guidance and the right words would usually pop into my head so it is very close to being one.

February 15th 1979

The Master said he was pleased with my progress. He stressed the need to remain diligent and conscientious, and told me to keep on striving and forging ahead. My next trial would be in my relationship with Michael. Due to various experiences in his life, and the sort of life he has led, he has had to present a front to the world. This is necessary as, in his evolved state, lower vibrations could harm him. As I have not lead a sophisticated life, I might find this acting a role difficult to understand but it is with my assistance that Michael can find his true self. It is the will of the Masters that Michael and I help each other. I can help him find his true self through respect, understanding and love while he can train me in the outer spiritual path. The Master said it was not necessary to inform Michael of the contents of this talk as they communicated with him separately.

I have a few comments to make on this talk. First of all, there is nothing especially profound in it. It is tailored for a particular situation at a particular time. This is the hallmark of a good spiritual teacher. He does not need to dispense esoteric wisdom on every occasion nor does he offer the same remedy for all sicknesses. He may speak from the plane of non-duality but he is aware of the immediate needs of the individual he is addressing. He effortlessly encompasses both the relative and the absolute, and always with a sense of true priorities.

My second comment has to do with the relationship between Michael and myself. Although we had come together with a shared purpose, we were very different people. The thirty five year age difference was an element of that but, as the Master's words above imply, he had led a life that sometimes caused him to behave in ways that made my newly converted to the spiritual path sensibilities flinch. He could appear very worldly. He seemed to have a taste for small talk and trivia quite at odds with any kind of inner awareness, or so I thought, and he would sometimes speak in a way that would embarrass my young and idealistic self. This was a good lesson for me to learn detachment, refrain from judgement and mortify social pride but it was a hard one, and I would sometimes get quite cross with him for, as I saw it, betraying our purpose together. The Master's words made it clear that Michael had had to adopt a role that was not his own in order to get through life but, with the intolerance of youth, I found this hard to justify.

The Master spoke of a trial. The spiritual life is full of tests and trials which are there to prove us, using that word in its old fashioned sense. It is through them that we learn, and one of the very best fields for them is that of relationships because it is chiefly in relationships that our ego can be challenged. To retreat from the world at a certain stage of spiritual life is right and proper, as that gives us the chance to develop a solid foundation in a protected environment. But after a while any spiritual awareness acquired thereby must be expressed and tested in the world. That's the only way it can be shown to be real and not dependent on its outer surroundings. I had innocently thought that living with Michael would entail a steady progression upwards to spiritual heights without taking into account potential personality conflicts. This is a typical case of the ego wanting to be spiritual without realising that in order to be so it must die. My relationship with Michael brought out aspects of my character that needed to be corrected. That is inevitably the case with almost any serious relationship. I do not wish to imply that we were constantly arguing as that would be quite untrue. Nevertheless life was not always smooth and there were plenty of petty irritations to deal with.

My last comment on this talk has to do with the Master's final statement. Unlike most light trances where the medium is aware of what is said through him or her, Michael had no knowledge at all of what was spoken through him. He simply was not there. The advantage of this is that in no way did the medium affect the message. After coming out of trance he was completely ignorant of what had taken place. I would ask him if he wanted to know what the Masters had said but he never did. That was for me, he said. They spoke to him clairaudiently. When I asked him how this worked he would just say that he heard a voice, sometimes in his ear though seemingly at a different frequency to normal hearing, but on other occasions it would appear to be directly inside his head. He would know it was coming as there would be what he called a heightening of the atmosphere, words that do not convey a great deal but which were the only ones he had to describe the experience.

Michael was a totally loyal servant of the Masters and accepted them completely without feeling the need to question or analyse his encounter with them. That does not mean he was their dupe in any way. He recognised them for what they were. He had tested the spirits and found they were of God. He saw at first hand their overwhelming love and wisdom and became their devoted follower. This is not a very fashionable approach nowadays but devotion to the guru is a tried and tested approach to the spiritual path and quite legitimate if a) the devotion is genuine, and b) the guru is genuine. In this case both of these were so.

The first time I took notes after a talk had been a few nights previously. On this occasion I had been told that one of the higher Masters wished to speak to me. I know that the idea of hierarchy upsets some people in this democratic age and one can understand why. In human terms its potential abuses are obvious. The fact remains that in the spiritual world, hierarchy exists. It does not exist in the sense of intrinsic superiority or inferiority. Before God all men are equal. But we are not all equal in realised potential or spiritual unfoldment, and I for one am very grateful there are beings with greater understanding and awareness than myself. When the ego is transcended there is no risk of the higher attempting to dominate the lower or infringe free will. There is even a sense in which the higher is the servant of the lower as demonstrated so wonderfully by Jesus. Life is one but, in the context of unfolding spiritual being, there is a higher and there is a lower, and the medieval concept of the great chain of being stretching from highest heaven down to the lowliest state of matter is not just a poetic conceit. It is a real truth, and there are beings marking the links on that chain at every level.

The idea of higher Masters might also seem strange to those who imagine that liberation is the attainment of some absolute state in which the liberated being, having transcended duality and realised his or her oneness with God, can no longer grow as there is nothing to grow into, all relative concepts having been transcended. But oneness with God does not mean one has become the Creator. Life is never static. As long as it is manifest, it never ceases to grow and express itself in ever more perfect and magnificent forms, and the Masters speak of beings beyond them who are to them as they are to us. Life, it seems, truly is limitless and spiritual unfoldment a never-ending process. Having achieved everything achievable would be a sort of death and God is life.

February 10th 1979

I was talked to by one of the higher Masters. The feeling of power and majesty was almost overwhelming but he spoke kindly and unusually even gave his name though it was not one I was familiar with. He told me that the body is a frame and its functions are not to be feared. He said it was designed for beings of a lesser evolution than myself and was more suited to their needs. He said that sometimes it is the will and not the action that counts, and stressed I should avoid lassitude as I have important work to do. He told me to have faith, courage and determination and said that I was always protected by his helpers.

Once again a simple talk which I have transcribed here exactly as it exists in my notes of the time. I recall he said more but, unfortunately, I only wrote down a portion of what was said. The remarks about the body refer to concerns I had about sex, concerns which were theoretical as much as practical. Michael and I led celibate lives but, whilst that did not trouble me as much as it might have done some people, I was a still a normally constituted young man. Also, I was naturally curious to know what an enlightened approach to this often difficult subject might be. The attitude of the Masters was simplicity itself. They said that one should go beyond attachment to sexual desire as one should go beyond attachment to the body but, at the same time, sex is a natural function whilst in a body and one should not allow oneself to be tortured by suppressing that function. To paraphrase time-honoured words, the spiritual person must be in the body but not of the body. Look after the body, observe its needs but recognise it is not what you are and do not allow it to govern you in any way. Ultimately the sexual division and attraction reflects the original duality in manifestation of spirit and matter or subject and object, and to deny it is to deny life, love and creativity. That said, it reflects the divine duality in the body, and the body is a vehicle of manifestation for the spiritual person not an integral part of what he or she is.

What did he mean by beings of lesser evolution than myself? The plain truth is that human beings in this world are not all equally developed in a spiritual sense. Some of us may have had our origin earlier than others, and some may have become less mired in duality and made faster progress. However the Masters never said the slightest thing to flatter my ego (they were more concerned with flattening it) and were not doing so on this occasion. Here the reference was to anyone for whom this world and its attractions were no longer sufficient, and who, as a consequence, had set out on the spiritual path. It included all those who had started to turn away from the alluring dazzle of the phenomenal world, beginning to realise that they were more than the body and more than the mind. It is undeniably the case that the majority of people (and I include conventionally religious people) seem to go through life with very little awareness of the soul, but there is a substantial minority which is, I believe, growing all the time who are beginning to hear its voice and wake up to its call. This phrase applies to them just as much as it did to me. It probably applies to you who are reading these lines.

The Master used the now controversial word 'design' to refer to the human body but what else would you expect a being speaking from the spiritual world to say? However, while he did say that the body was **designed for beings of a lesser evolution than myself and was more suited to their needs**, one might wonder from the context whether he used that word to mean planned or intended so let us examine the question in slightly more detail.

The debate between those who hold to the strictly materialistic theory of evolution and those who favour so called intelligent design continues to rage with neither side much interested in compromise but might it not be that the truth contains elements of both? Or, putting it another way, goes beyond either? The scientific evidence for some kind of evolutionary process is extensive but it by no means inevitably leads to the extreme conclusions that neo-Darwinists have drawn, especially given the glaring absence of transitional fossils between species. It may well be that there are too many flaws in creation for it to be the perfect work perfectly executed of a perfect being but to believe that natural processes, unaided and undirected, could have brought forth life, consciousness, intelligence and all that is in the world in any period of time let alone a "mere" 4 billion years is surely only possible if you have already decided that to be the case. Or else been so bludgeoned by contemporary propaganda that you think there can be no sensible alternative for an intelligent person.

I was given no specific information by the Masters on this subject so am only offering my own opinion here which is based on a mixture of science, occultism and intuition, ingredients that make for an extremely dubious cocktail you might think. However, as none of these, as they stand, are wholly satisfactory on their own, it makes sense to learn from them all, and a theory I find persuasive is that the basic matrix for the life forms in this world was laid down by high spiritual beings under God (called *Elohim* in the Biblical account of creation) but that natural processes in the physical world, originally set up by these beings but then allowed to take their course, have also had some input in bringing about the rich variety we see around us, albeit with regular intervention from above at various critical points, the birth of humanity being an obvious but by no means unique example. And on that subject, it is a tenet of occultism and supported by the Masters that intelligent life has existed on this planet for considerably longer than is currently accepted by mainstream science. The absence of evidence for this is due to the fact that at one time the physical matter of which the Earth is composed vibrated at a higher frequency than now; that's to say, matter was less material, and the bodies of its inhabitants were correspondingly less dense so no trace of them survives.

Having said that, the most important thing to remember in the evolution/intelligent design debate is that we are not material beings. We are spiritual beings using material bodies and the origin of those bodies is very much a secondary issue.

This is a point worth emphasising given the prevailing opinion of our times. Human beings did not evolve out of the animal kingdom. They descended from the spiritual world. Moreover the human body may share a common template with that of the animal but it was also, to slightly paraphrase what the Master said without I hope distorting it, expressly **designed for (human) beings and suited to their (evolutionary) needs** so even the physical body cannot be said to have evolved in the way currently envisaged by contemporary science.

The story of human origins is obviously vastly more complicated than I have been able to describe it in these few paragraphs but they serve as a reasonable summing up of who we are and where we came from, given from the spiritual perspective.

Subsequently I learnt a little more about the helpers mentioned at the end of this talk. Some of them actually spoke to me through Michael. The change in vibration was noticeable. The Masters had a quality that truly was superhuman. There is nothing in this world that begins to approach it. The power, the authority, the wisdom, the love they emanated really was quite extraordinary. It was at the same time humbling and uplifting. When they spoke to me I felt that I was in the presence of a being that knew me completely and (still!) loved me completely but, as I have said, this love was not a human love with its desires, attachments, expectations and changeability. It was not personal but it was fully individual, lacking nothing in humanity but having nothing of the ego-based human. It saw all, understood all, forgave all.

The helpers on the other hand were more as you might imagine wise and kind spiritual counsellors in this world would be. They did not convey the impression of supreme power and dignity of the Masters, and I felt them to be more fellow disciples than spiritual preceptors. In fact it appeared that some (though not all) of them were in physical bodies and were coming to speak to me when those bodies were asleep. It is quite possible that they were not aware of this in their everyday lives. **"I come to you from a Zen monastery in the hills"** said one (I knew nothing of Zen at the time), and another mentioned being in the centre of Mongolia. They spoke in a good but slightly accented English that was different to the Masters' English which was unaccented and idiomatic though somewhat old-fashioned (in the best of senses), being quite without any contemporary colloquialisms. The helpers did not come often, and when they did I got the impression that it was because the Masters were occupied elsewhere but wanted me to be given some encouragement and simple instruction. **Tell him that the time has come to practise total surrender** said one. **Your guides have told me to tell you to meditate for longer periods. Concentrate on your breathing and keep your spine erect. Practise well and keep the Masters in your thoughts.**

The possibility of some of the helpers being in physical bodies raises the question as to whether the Masters themselves were. Liberation means that you transcend the need for physical incarnation. There is no longer anything that attracts you back to the material world as you have emptied yourself of all desires and attachments. However it is said that some liberated beings are born in this world from time to time. The Theosophists believed their Masters were in physical bodies but I can't comment on that. What I can say is that I am practically certain that the Masters who spoke to me were not. Such beings exist on spiritual planes in a form incomprehensible to us. Their mode of consciousness is not ours. Their means of communication is not ours. Indeed to communicate on our level through the relatively clumsy medium of words is to step down their teachings considerably. I was told they spoke to me as they did because of my novice status. They would not do so for long and in time to come they hoped to convey their messages through subtler, less direct, means. This would require two things on my part. A sufficient sensitivity to the soul, whence such communications originate, and the ability to bring down what exists at a level above mind to the mental level without distorting it through preconceptions and prejudices. So it demands the purification of desire, non-attachment to ideas and humility. No wonder they couldn't rely on such a method for me at that time!

I have mentioned the soul on a few occasions without properly defining it so let me now explain what I consider a human being actually to be. The traditional division of spirit, soul and body seems to me a good one though it needs a little expansion. By body one must include not just the physical form but the emotions, rational mind and ego too, in fact all that would normally be regarded as constituting the complete person. Yet, from a spiritual point of view, this is just the incarnate personality which is born, lives and dies. The soul is the individual consciousness that exists beyond that on its own plane whence a portion of it descends into matter whilst the main part remains where it is, rather in the manner of Krishna who, speaking as God (in whose image we are made), says in the Bhagavad-Gita "Having pervaded this whole vast universe with a fragment of myself, I remain". Our soul was created by God as a unique individual but it too has a beginning and an end, although its span is considerably longer than the single lifetime of the person-ality. It is the soul that goes through the cycle of incarnationary experience until ultimately it realises its identity with spirit from which it came and into which it is then reabsorbed together with the fruits of its labours in the phenomenal world.

If the soul is individual, spirit is universal. It is being. It is God. In truth it is the only reality. There is not my spirit and your spirit or my spirit and God's spirit. There is only spirit and nothing else. Spirit is beyond qualities, beyond definitions, beyond conception. It is the spark of God in us but this spark is in no way separate from the fire.

Each aspect of the human being exists on its own plane, in a world corresponding to its nature. We have to imagine the physical realm as the outermost plane of reality, the one at the furthest remove from pure spirit, where energy substance is at its densest and consciousness at its most limited. It is important to realise that, in an absolute sense, all is spirit, there is no separation anywhere in the universe, but in the context of manifestation, which is necessarily dualistic, or form and differentiation could not arise, the division of pure spirit into spirit and matter is a valid distinction to make. From this perspective, the highest level is unmanifested spirit. This is the divine state which is boundless and infinite where essence and substance are as yet undivided. As these separate and the basic substance of the universe, the stuff out of which the Creator creates, best conceived of in the form of light, is lowered in vibration, other planes are created until eventually we arrive at the physical where ideas that have become thoughts now become things. The intermediate planes represent stepping down of the formless into form, and correspond to spiritual and psychic states.

That's a very simple presentation of the facts as I understand them which I hope will suffice to give an idea of the basic anatomy of the spiritual beings we truly are.

Here are some more extracts from the Masters' talks.

February 11th 1979
The Master told me to overcome childishness and have a full sense of the wonder that was happening to me, not taking it for granted. I was told that although I was fast in some things, in others I was a "slowcoach".

February 12th 1979
I was told that progress had been made for me by the Masters but obstructed by myself. Henceforth I should not depend on them for support but make my own progress. Put yourself in other people's

**shoes and understand their position, he said. I was instructed to
let these words sink into my consciousness.**

The Masters were direct. They were never unkind but did not mince
their words either. They either assumed or required a level of
maturity on my part sufficient to accept what was told me without
seeking to make excuses for myself or hide the truth from them.
Quite frankly not only did I realise from the beginning that this
would be utterly futile but I never had any desire to do so. When
confronted by a being in whom ego is non-existent and who is trans-
parently an ocean of love and wisdom, your own ego is immediately
quelled. When you know you are an open book to somebody, in
whom you have complete trust and with whom you could not
possibly hope to compete, there really is no point in dissembling or
trying to deceive either yourself or that person. I knew the Masters
knew me better than I knew myself, that much became rapidly
obvious. I accepted what they told me. I didn't accept it indiscrimi-
nately and they would not have wanted me too. They never gave me
orders or tried to override my free will. But they assumed I understood they knew what they were talking about, and I did, so I
accepted what they told me without internal resistance. That does
not mean I didn't think about it. But if they said something that
didn't immediately make sense to me, I would mull it over and try
to understand it rather than automatically rejecting it and thinking I
knew better (though see further on for a slight reassessment of that).

It seems that just a few weeks into the extraordinary thing that
was happening to me, I was beginning to take it for granted. I don't
know if this is human nature or just my nature but I was brought up
short by these two talks. The first talks, most of which I no longer
have notes for, were of an introductory nature but now things were
serious. If I had imagined that all I had to do was bask in the aura of
an enlightened being who was privileged to be able to come and talk
to me, I now realised that there was a serious purpose behind these
visits. I had work to do. Spirituality did not consist in believing in

the reality of spiritual things and waiting for change to come about as a matter of course. It required getting to work on the lower self. I could no longer just passively listen without acting on what was said. I had to apply the teachings.

I think one of the things that distinguishes an experienced spiritual instructor from others is the knowledge of what to say and when to say it. Lesser teachers will have a more formulaic approach but the true teacher approaches everything on an individual basis. This is so obvious it should hardly need saying but I have come across a fair number of aspiring spiritual teachers who appear not to have grasped that simple fact and who have a single answer for every question. Could they have been seduced by the glamour of being seen as the wise one? It may just be inexperience but it does sometimes seem as though such teachers have more concern with themselves as teachers than with their pupils' actual requirements. This was decidedly not the case with the Masters.

Nor did they ever talk about the goal of all this. True teachers do not. They teach the path not its destination and you tread the path for its own sake not for what you might get out of it. I don't recall the Masters ever mentioning enlightenment or liberation though it's possible they may have done so in passing. But it was never seriously discussed and that's because, for the serious seeker, it's just not so important. That may be hard to believe and I don't deny that, in the early stages, it is legitimate to have such a goal but, if that continues to be your purpose, you won't get beyond a certain point. The Masters never even talked about why I was treading the path. It was assumed I was because that's what human beings are supposed to do. That is our duty and our destiny.

It's never pleasant to be called childish. And yet from the perspective of the Masters we are all, even the most sophisticated of us, children. That's just a fact. There is no condescension involved, their only feeling towards humanity being one of love which is extended to all humanity without exception. But to one who has seen through the illusion of the personal self, identification with that self is the mark of ignorance. That having been said, while I was quite content to be addressed as "my child" by the Masters, to be described as childish is a different matter altogether, implying, as it does, the failure to have gone beyond a stage one should have left behind long since. Dealing with a spiritual novice can be a tricky affair but the Masters always knew when to praise and when to scold. The sense of self-satisfaction I had started to feel at having been seemingly chosen in this way had had a large bucket of ice cold water poured all over it.

February 13th 1979

A Master who had not spoken to me before came. He said that the greater progress I made the more I would be assailed by evil in all its forms. He told me to banish all evil thoughts and press on in love and faith. Guard against evil was his message.

Here's a challenging thought for the modern mind. Dark forces exist. The atheist and materialist will ridicule such an idea as hopelessly unenlightened and superstitious. Equally many people who belong to the so called New Age movement, and who like to think that the spiritual rose has no thorns, will reject the notion. It is true that, in the final analysis, evil is ignorance and has no fundamental reality but all traditional religions recognise the existence of spiritual powers of darkness, even Buddhism which seems to be the religion most likely to attract the Western intellectual. Do not think that these are just personifications of impersonal forces or misdirected energies within the human psyche. There are on the astral plane, the commonly used term for that psychic world between the purely spiritual and the physical, beings who have abused their free will to such an extent that they have fallen into darkness. Evil is not part of God's reality but its possibility arises because of free will. Free will gives a soul the opportunity to be consciously, rather than automatically, one with God. In effect, it gives a created being the chance to become a god. However it also means that a soul can go against

God's will, deny oneness and separate itself from reality.

I was never told that I had to fear evil, merely to be aware of its existence. To fear something is to give it power and truly it has no power unless you give it such. Nor was I told that I should fight it and for exactly the same reason. Fear and conflict trap one on the level of duality which is the only field in which evil can have any sway. When I was told to banish all evil thoughts I was effectively being told that if there is no evil in you, evil cannot touch you for "unto the pure all things are pure". I think Christ's instruction to his disciples to be wise as serpents and harmless as doves sums up the attitude all aspirants should have towards evil to perfection. Be vigilant as to the possibility of evil but do not react to it on the level of ego. If you fight it, you strengthen it and you let it into your heart. You respond to it on its own level and address it in its own language. You acknowledge its reality. What then should you do if you encounter evil in the world? What do you do if you go into a dark room? You turn on the light. That is just what you should do with evil. You turn on your light. You demonstrate truth.

Why is one **assailed by evil** as one makes spiritual progress? There are two possible answers to this question, one that might be acceptable to the contemporary mindset because it doesn't conflict with what we consider to be rational, and one perhaps slightly less so. The acceptable answer is that it is a test. This is the Satan as Saturn theory, Saturn in astrology being the planet that tests. As you advance on the path you are given tests to bring to the surface unresolved problems in your psychology. The human ego is highly adept at hiding away, denying or disguising what it doesn't like about itself. A test, by applying pressure to weak points, reveals that which is concealed. Only then can it be dealt with. So, looked at in this way, a test is designed to make you stronger.

This explanation may have the virtue of logic but it is not actually the only or even the true reason why one is **assailed by evil** as one makes spiritual progress. A test would not have to take this form. The real answer will be less palatable to 21st century tastes (prejudices?) as it smacks somewhat of old-fashioned religion. The real answer is that the forces of evil do not want humanity to become spiritually aware because every person that does so represents a loss of their power. They have set themselves up against God and they desire to influence as many other souls as possible to follow that path. Each soul that escapes their net brings their eventual downfall that little bit closer. This is because these beings have separated themselves so comprehensively from their divine source that they can only continue their existence by influencing human beings to give way to negative emotions such as anger, pride, fear and hatred, the energies of which they can then absorb. Like attracts like and they cannot sustain themselves with energies of a higher vibration because they are unable to respond to them. I am aware this idea might sound as though it comes from the wilder reaches of science fiction. That's as may be but I can testify to the existence of these beings as there were a few occasions on which what one can only call an evil spirit did indeed possess Michael. Normally he would be well protected from such eventualities (which apparently were a possibility due to his mediumistic nature) but very rarely something profoundly unpleasant slipped through, manifesting itself with shouting, swearing and even attempted violence until it was ousted. Similar incidents are described in *"The Boy and The Brothers"*.

February 14th 1979

The Master told me that I had moved on to a higher stage. He warned me that from now on I must guard against great joys as well as great depressions and should keep an even keel at all times. He said I should also guard against negative entities which will attack when I least expect it in ways that I least expect. He told me to listen to Michael and remain with him for the present. It is they, the Masters, who have arranged this life together and though I may not understand it all now, things will become clearer later on. Michael is as he is because the Masters have arranged it for the purposes of teaching me. All is proceeding well and is

guided and arranged by God and His Masters who look forward to being reunited with me. He said it is not wrong for me to talk to Michael about aspects of his personality I think could be improved on but do it for his sake and the love of God not because I want to change him or am irritated by him.

As already mentioned, although I was very fond of Michael and we got on well most of the time, we were quite different characters in a lot of respects. He was certainly more extrovert than me and his seeming worldliness would, on occasion, irk me to a degree that I was quite unable to rise above. Arguments would ensue. What I can see now (actually I knew it perfectly well then but was unable to act on that knowledge) was that my observations might have been right but my reactions to them were not. This is what the Masters meant when they said that Michael was as he was for the purposes of teaching me. That does not mean it wasn't in his nature to behave in a certain way but this aspect of him could be used, and doubtless even exaggerated, by the Masters to bring out and challenge my own intolerance and sense of superiority. I could also be embarrassed by what I perceived as Michael's tactless and undiplomatic behaviour in front of other people so here was another lesson not to be concerned about how I appeared to the world. But I was lucky. There's a story about a Sufi who was instructed by his teacher to crawl through a crowded market place barking like a dog in order to overcome his sense of self-esteem. At least I was never called upon to do that.

We have the experiences we need in life. The purpose of life in this world is spiritual growth and everything is geared to that end. This ranges from one's daily encounters and relationships to deeper matters up to and including suffering, much of which comes to us because on some level we have called it to ourselves. This is often very difficult for people to accept and it is easy to misunderstand so let me go into that idea a little more. First of all, I am by no means saying that those who suffer deserve to do so. I do not believe that suffering is ordained by God (I think we can say that there is suffering in life because there are human beings in life) but, looked at from the perspective of the absolute, suffering is part of our experience of life because of our identification with form and our attachment to the ego. The experiences we undergo seek to break that identification and false attachment, and so enable us to see the truth about ourselves. This may not require suffering but, if we are honest with ourselves, we must admit that it is often only when forced to do so by a degree of discomfort that we will really break away from our self-centredness.

Goodness knows this does not mean one should not have compassion for those who suffer or ignore suffering in others just because, in some ultimate sense, much of it might be self-inflicted. Nor does it in any way imply that we should not attempt to alleviate suffering wherever we see it. Suffering may be part of the cycle of human life as it exists at present but we are here to break that cycle. What it does mean is that we should recognise the truth about suffering which is that arises because of incorrect identification with the lower self. This is what the Buddha taught 2,500 years ago and nothing has changed since then.

Suffering and karma are interlinked. The idea of karma has entered the Western mainstream now but it was always clearly implied in Christianity as reaping what you sow This has tended to be perceived as something of a threat in the past but karma is not punishment. Nor is it simply the inevitable result of the transgression of an inflexible law though it does have an element of that to it, especially if you think of the universe as a mirror that reflects back to you what you put out to it. However what we may regard as the negative aspect of karma is really an opportunity to learn from our mistakes by experiencing the consequences of those mistakes. Being on the receiving end of our own incorrect actions is surely the fastest way to find out that they are incorrect and move on to a higher understanding. To those who say that, if we don't know we are experiencing the results of our own actions, how can it benefit us, I would reply that we don't necessarily have to know consciously. If the flaws that caused us to err are still present within us then experiencing the effects of choices made by succumbing to those flaws will help us to correct them. Besides, the teaching that we reap what we sow is always there to enlighten us if we are willing to receive it.

Karma is meted out with mercy as well as justice and, despite appearances, it is said (in the Qur'an and elsewhere) that no one is given more than they can bear. You may dispute that but we do not know what we agreed to before we were born as it was the soul that made the choice of what to experience. The soul may wish to press ahead with its development in which case it may choose to experience the results of many wrong choices made in the past in a relatively heavy dose. It may wish to burn off a quantity of bad karma in one go, freeing it up to move forwards on the spiritual path unencumbered. We do not know. Let me make one further remark on this subject to illustrate the fact that God's mercy will always precede His justice. If a person has completely transcended the psychological state that caused him to make wrong choices, it will not be necessary to experience all the karmic consequences of those choices. But until one has reached that state, the law of action and reaction being equal and opposite operates, and we are fortunate it does because without it we would find it much harder to outgrow our weaknesses.

When told I had moved on to a higher stage I was naturally pleased but let me refer back to my previous comments under February 12th. I was yet to appreciate the Masters' expert use of the stick and the carrot. Sometimes we are brought up short by an admonishment, sometimes we are encouraged, sometimes we are praised to see how we will react to that praise. Will it enthuse us for future exertions or will it go to our head? I may be reading too much into what was a simple statement but it is the task of a good spiritual teacher to play the student rather like an expert fly fisherman plays a salmon, letting him run at this point, pulling him back at that. Eventually we end up caught and in the net which for us, unlike for the salmon, is release rather than capture.

It may seem curious to be told to **guard against great joys** but the reason for that is implied immediately afterwards when the Master added **as well as great depressions**. It is not the joy that is the problem but the reaction to the joy. To experience great joy on the spiritual path is not unusual, especially in the earlier stages when, to follow our fishing analogy, the hook is baited. But the attempt to hold on to that joy and the desire to experience it again once it has passed, which it always will, come from the ego and will lead to a reaction. Equally, to succumb to the, also not unusual, feeling of emptiness and spiritual desolation so vividly described by medieval Christian mystics is to fall back into the lower self with its desires, fears and attachments. We have to live in the moment if we are to live in truth, neither desiring joy nor fearing depression. Balance and detachment are absolutely essential if one is stabilise oneself in the spiritual self.

Here's an example of this. It took place a couple of months later when Michael and I visited the gardens of Stourhead in Wiltshire. It was a beautiful late spring day, the rhododendrons were out and the gardens were at their best. Walking along the paths by the lake, surrounded by flowers and with birds singing, I suddenly felt myself to be uplifted to a higher plane. I am not speaking metaphorically here. That is literally what I felt to have happened. Light was streaming from all around. There was an extraordinary sense of great height to everything external, with my inner perception also undergoing a kind of elongation that stretched and expanded it, introducing new dimensions into my mind. Behind the birdsong and soft lapping of the waters of the lake against the shore, I detected that deep silence that existed before the birth of the worlds. I was not conscious of my body and had no sense whatsoever of myself as a separate being. There existed at that moment nothing but the divine presence and it was everywhere.

Then Michael made a flippant remark. I tried to ignore it but he persisted, demanding a response. It was not his fault. How was he to know that I had been swept up by the angels? He was just having a walk in the park but to me his apparent insensitivity destroyed the atmosphere and my mood deflated like a pricked balloon. I fell into frustrated resentment knowing this was wrong but quite unable to control my emotional reaction. What should I have done? I should have saluted the experience and let it pass. Instead I sought to cling onto it and suffered the inevitable consequence of trying to hold onto what lies beyond self with self. It should have been enough to know that this state existed and was real but I wished to possess it. You cannot possess spirit.

February 16th 1979

The Master said he was pleased with my quick response to the message of last night. He told me that I must have more control over my moodiness which was due to the fact I was in a young body. Rather than being swayed by moods I should ignore them. He said that this would be the last talk for a while as Michael was getting too weak to be used as a medium for a while. The Masters would guide and protect us as long as we did their will which was to live together in love and harmony. He would watch over our progress and come back at a later date. He said at this stage I should regard the Masters not as individuals but as messengers from God. He sent his love and blessings and the love of the higher Masters.

May I say here that I am setting these notes down just as I wrote them at the time. The Masters always expressed themselves in a clear and concise way but that does not necessarily come through in my notes, jotted down quarter of an hour or so after the talks had ended. I did remember very well what was said and most of the words are theirs but not all are. The sense is exact though.

When the Masters first spoke to me they would talk and then ask if I had any questions. There were inevitably many things on many subjects I would have loved to have asked them but I knew they were not there to satisfy my curiosity and so I restricted myself to what seemed pertinent to my immediate task. After a while they would come and straightaway ask if there was anything I wanted to question them on, demonstrating the truth that it is the student who should initiate proceedings. "Ask and you shall receive" we have been told. Normally it is the second part of that saying that is emphasised but, in my view, the first is equally important. The initial seeking must come from within us. The degree of our readiness to be instructed is indicated by the questions we pose. The inner need to know something which prompts a particular question shows the ripeness to receive the answer, and though a spiritual teacher may start off giving basic teachings, there comes a stage after which he can give no more unless they are drawn forth by the disciple.

I bring this up here because, although I was not yet setting the talk's agenda, I was beginning to do more than just thank the Masters at its conclusion. As I recall I had asked for a little more information about who they actually were. I knew they were liberated spiritual beings, and on a couple of occasions a name had been mentioned but this was only in passing and, as it was no name I was familiar with, I was not even sure what it actually was. I've previously said that names are not important and can tie one to the personal, distracting from the essential message, but I must confess to having been a little curious! Still, I got my answer and it was one I fully expected.

When a person, particularly a young person, is first exposed to the truth of the mystical life, and has certain experiences which confirm that truth, it is not easy to keep a proper balance. Possibly if we lived in a culture that did not either deny the reality of the spiritual world or else, as in institutionalised religion, put it in a bottle with a cork in it, that would not be the case. But given that most people in the Western world, and increasingly the Eastern one too, are brought up with little or no idea of who and what they really are, the discovery of the soul and the enormous vistas that discovery opens up can easily sweep one off one's feet. Add to that the feeling that one is now in possession of a great secret and the result can be a heady brew. This is akin to, though a more intense form of, the conversion experience.

I was in the middle of this stage and I was burning with zeal to devote myself wholeheartedly to the spiritual life. However I also had to live in the world. The tension between the two was not something I had mastered hence the moodiness. It is a common error during the earlier stages of the mystical path to separate the spiritual and material worlds and see them as mutually antagonistic. At certain times it may even be necessary but to continue to do so beyond a particular point is to maintain the illusion of duality. It is essential for the spiritual aspirant to learn to tread the middle way, finding the correct balance between outer and inner. I realised the wisdom of the Master's words that I should ignore moods and that they arose from identification with emotional states rather than the point of stillness within but I was still at the stage of seeking pleasure and avoiding pain, and had yet to understand that a true spiritual awareness lies beyond experience.

It should be noted that the Masters tended to prefer me to find things out for myself. They would guide and indicate the way but they would generally do this by means of hints rather than saying anything directly; hints I could then find deeper levels of meaning to as I pondered their words. This is because it is their aim to develop wisdom which, unlike knowledge, cannot be taught but must arise naturally from within. When I was told to ignore moods I was not just being told to control myself (though I certainly was being told that). I was also being taught about attachment and non-attachment. Finally I was being asked to consider what I really was and where a true and unconditional happiness might ultimately lie.

I should probably make a brief comment on the phrase "**as long as we did their will**" in that last talk as it might raise a few eyebrows nowadays. It is really no more than an example of their slightly old fashioned form of expression which to me had a dignity much lacking in modern ways of speaking. Although they spoke with authority, at no time did they seek to impose that authority. There was never any question of compulsion or expectation of obedience. I was perfectly free to do as I wished as was Michael. All they were really saying was that if we accepted them as our teachers we had to allow ourselves to be taught. And please note what their will was. To live together in love and harmony, hardly an authoritarian command.

Chapter 5

What are Masters?

The Masters once told me that we live during a period of great vulgarity, greater, in fact, than at any time in the history of our planet. These are strong words but they are the ones they used and it is not hard to see what they meant. You might argue that this is the result of the prevailing atheism. Deny God and you cut off access to the highest with inevitable consequences. Then again you might say that it has come about as an inevitable by-product of the spread of democracy. People are freer today than ever before and there is less repression both within the individual and within society as a whole which is surely a good thing. That would be true but does it justify the more negative aspects of what has come with it? Then it could be said that the vulgarity of today isn't greater. We are just more aware of it because technology in the form of television, the Internet and so on enables us to be so. That view might have some truth to it but is largely a clever excuse to deny the obvious. Technology might make us more aware of it but it also spreads it.

I am inclined to think that the Masters know what they are talking about on this subject. Our view of the past comes entirely from history books, historical documents and artefacts, archaeological digs and the like, all second hand, all interpreted through the refracting prism of our own thoughts and contemporary preconceptions and prejudices. The Masters have full recollection of the past and, what is more, can re-experience it as though it were the present at any time they wish. We conjecture. They know.

An example of the vulgarity the Masters referred to, and one pertinent to our subject, has followed on from the popularisation of spiritual truths. Making what was once hidden and esoteric potentially available to all must be regarded as an advance and would not have happened if a sizeable proportion of humanity had not been ready for it. But it has its risks. Popularisation often goes hand in hand with debasement, and it has frequently done so in this case. Profound mystical insights of the past are brought down to the level of catchphrases and mottoes, in the process robbed of much of their grace and power. Sacred truths are bandied about like shiny trinkets in the marketplace and as a result made to look superficial and tawdry. No longer are we exhorted to go beyond ourselves to reach the holy but encouraged to try to bring the holy down to us. Yes, New Age, I am looking at you.

The New Age movement may have started off as a movement of great potential but it rapidly degenerated into a concern with the psychic rather than the spiritual, and was soon infiltrated by the forces of glamour and deception, both obvious and subtle. It has its good side but it has often cheapened sacred teachings, sometimes to the point where no sensible person would wish to have anything to do with them and certainly to the point where they cease to be operationally effective. This is not new, of course. Writing in 1889 in her book *The Key To Theosophy* Madame Blavatsky made the following by all accounts typically robust comments.

"Great are the desecrations to which the names of two of the masters have been subjected. There is hardly a medium who has not claimed to have seen them. Every bogus swindling Society, for commercial purposes, now claims to be guided and directed by 'masters', often supposed to be far higher than ours!"

Theosophy is regarded as a major source of what eventually became the New Age movement and some might argue that it was responsible for some of the desecrations to which Madame Blavatsky herself refers. To its credit, though, it did introduce to the Western world a vast amount of hitherto esoteric lore, concepts of reincarnation and karma, an occult version of the history of the world that made more sense than either the prevailing Christian creationist one or the recently put forward totally materialistic one, satisfactory descriptions of the geography of the inner planes and the anatomy of the inner man. And, of course, the idea of the Masters themselves.

One of the concepts that has been debased since it was made public by the Theosophists is precisely that of enlightened beings guiding humanity with an abundance of channelled communications supposedly coming from a variety of exotic personages claiming spiritual eminence (see Madame Blavatsky's comment above), and even a number of spiritual teachers in this world identified as Masters who plainly are not. It may be that sometime in the future the Masters will manifest themselves openly in the world, such at any rate has been the rumour for a hundred years or more, but they are not doing so at the moment. Some of them may be in physical bodies but they are not the teachers encountered in the world today, the very best of whom are still not fully enlightened souls despite the claims and assumptions of their followers. That is not to say there are not some wise and saintly teachers to be found but, in my view, even such undeniably great souls as Ramana Maharishi and Krishnamurti were not incarnate Masters in the true sense; though no doubt those two were approaching that status. As for the many lesser mortals who are proclaimed or who proclaim themselves to be Masters, they may well be genuine spiritual teachers (they may not be but that's another story) but that's by no means the same thing. I do not say there are no Masters in physical bodies. It is possible that this is necessary to maintain some kind of spiritual balance in the world. I do maintain they are not to be found amongst the teachers active at present, none of whom have reached that level of enlightenment.

So who are the Masters then? I have said that they are liberated beings, souls who have destroyed the sense of self and overcome all personal karma and attachments that would bind them to earth. For them the mind is not the focal point of consciousness any more. It is merely that which gives form to consciousness. No doubt their ranks are filled with many of the great mystics and saints of the past (which does not contradict what I have just said, since they are unlikely to have been Masters during those lifetimes) but to seek to identify them as such misses the point. Nor can they be regarded as Christians, Hindus or Buddhists or identified by any earthly appellation, all of which they left behind long ago. They are individualisations of the Absolute, as we all are, but they are fully conscious of and at one with their source so the emphasis should not be on them as individuals. When questioned as to their identity they simply say it is not important and that they are merely different aspects of the One Life. In fact, the word they most often used to speak of themselves was brothers.

Do not take that to mean I am saying all enlightened souls are male. I personally have no experience of their female equivalents, unless you count my vision of the goddess, which I don't, and, for whatever reason, these are decidedly thin on the ground in the literature except, I have to say, in that of the more spurious kind. However there have been plenty of female saints and mystics, and many of the most significant occultists in the West over the course of the last century have been female, so if they exist on that level they are bound to exist on higher levels too. More to the point though is the simple fact that, just as spiritual realisation is beyond self, so it is also beyond gender. A realised soul will function outwardly as male or female but to identify oneself as such inwardly would be to limit oneself, and to attain realisation one must shake off all limitation and identification with form. This is why the arguments about whether God is masculine or feminine are so silly. Obviously He encompasses both in His manifested aspects and is beyond either in His essence. Is it necessary to add that English linguistic convention requires me to use that pronoun for which no satisfactory substitute has yet been devised?

Earlier I said that what took place when the Masters communicated with me through Michael was not a form of spiritualism or, by implication, since it is just a new word for the same thing, channelling. One reason for this assertion has to do with the nature of the spiritual source. The vast majority of channelled messages come from what are known in occultism as the psychic and mental planes, and they come from beings who exist in those worlds and who have not transcended duality. They may have more knowledge and metaphysical understanding than most of us still incarnate on this physical plane do but they have not attained Christ consciousness. They have not attained liberation which means liberation from form, from self, from duality. Confusingly some of them may believe they have and others may just claim they have so how do you tell the difference? The planes beyond the physical are home to a huge variety of souls with many levels of consciousness represented and the only means of determining that level is through the use of one's own intuition. There really is no other way to do this. Common sense and reason certainly help but they are not the infallible guide that the fully functioning intuition is. This may mean that we fall victim to deception but that is not necessarily such a bad thing as it is through tests or opportunities of this kind that we can come to develop spiritual discernment. As a rule of thumb to be going on with, though, I would say that in virtually all cases you can safely assume that channelled communications are not from the Masters whatever the communicators might say about themselves. Why do I say that with such confidence? It is because the Masters work with the soul not the manifested personality and, except in the rarest of cases, their contact and communication is on the spiritual plane. That does not mean that what those who do communicate through channelling have to say is without value but it does mean that it should be treated with caution and that discrimination should be exercised at all times. Always couple an open mind with a healthy scepticism and realise that a channelled message may well contain a mixture of truth, half truth and error. It's up to you to sort out the wheat from the chaff.

Quite apart from the question of the source there is the problem that all channelling is coloured by the personality of the channeller. His or her ideas, beliefs, opinions and prejudices all affect, sometimes quite radically, the message. They may subtly shade it or they may completely distort it but they will certainly affect it to some degree. This was not the case with the communications through Michael as his body was used but not his mind. He was, the Masters told me, quite literally taken out of his body, which they occupied for the duration of the talk, and he did not influence that talk in any way. I realise that I can offer the reader no proof for this assertion but can only report what I was told and what, as a witness to the proceedings, seemed to me quite evident. I am also aware I may appear to be withholding from others what I demand for myself when I claim that I spoke to the Masters but many other people who make similar claims are deluded or deceived. But I must speak the truth as I see it. To encounter the Masters is to love them and (quite foolishly, since they are far above such concerns) to wish to protect them from the many distortions and travesties carried out in their name. But much more importantly, for the sake of spiritual aspirants who might be put off the whole idea of spiritual Masters because of the nonsense the subject can attract, I would like to add my voice to those who would put that subject back on a more serious footing, one more in keeping with its essentially sacred character. I may not succeed in this but any deficiencies on that score are entirely mine and not the responsibility of those who spoke to me whose words, I hope, as I record them here in bold type, have still enough authority to bear witness to their authenticity.

You find as you tread the spiritual path that you encounter countless illusions, distractions and blind alleys that must be negotiated, even if it is only in the sense of seeing through them, before one can emerge into the open and see clearly. There are false trails, will 'o' the wisps and lights that beckon only to reveal themselves as one approaches as unsubstantial and ephemeral flickers. This can seem a bit discouraging after one has set off full of high hopes and enthusiasm but we are attempting to unravel a very twisted thread on this journey, that being none other than the thread of our own selves. The distractions that exist externally are merely the outer manifestations of what exists within our own psyche. As we are informed by the *Tao Te Ching* "Great Tao is very straight but the people love byways". It's important to be aware of the existence of these illusions and counterfeits of truth but also to know that if one succumbs to them, it is always because of some shortcoming in oneself. Without exception it is because of some desire they satisfy, some fear they appear to assuage, some prejudice they confirm, some false hope they offer or some boost they give to the personal ego.

Before moving on from this brief discussion of the Masters, I would like to make one last point. Ultimately the Masters are an illusion. Yes, they are our guides and companions but as long as we in any way depend on them, or even regard them as something outside ourselves, we are living in duality. Truly there is no them and us, there is only the One Life. That is why they will always at a certain stage depart and leave us to our own devices. They are always there, **closer than your jugular vein** as they once told me, but in the final analysis each soul must tread the path to God alone. If we are to attain spiritual mastery ourselves we must, metaphorically speaking, "Kill the Buddha". This does not mean we do not need spiritual teachers but if we are to realise God within ourselves we must not seek Him in any outer person, place or thing. There will always come a point when the guru is an impediment to truth and for this reason he must eventually withdraw if the disciple is to win his spiritual spurs and take his place beside his teachers as their equal.

Chapter 6

"Forget the Personal Self."

February 17th 1979
The Master returned and said he was pleased with the progress and study I had made. He said that I must acquire an attitude of calm far beyond my years, and that this should go with a complete acceptance of people, things and situations. He told me that Michael and I could teach each other but that this should always be done with love and kindness. I should not take these words for granted but think on them and regard them as the essence of a spiritual person's behaviour. We must join together in order to complete our mission on Earth. The time had come for me to act of my own accord. "Forget the personal self and merge with the universal self" he concluded.

There's not a great deal to say about this talk which for the most part is quite straightforward. An attitude of calm is a standard requirement for anyone on the spiritual path but was particularly necessary for me at this time as my emotions were being brought out and stirred up in a number of unexpected (to me) ways. Serene detachment might be relatively easy in the ordered atmosphere and security of a monastery or ashram where there is little in the way of outer disturbance to threaten it. It is not so easy living in the world and surrounded by people largely unsympathetic to an approach to life at variance with theirs. I found myself regularly unsettled by people who challenged my new outlook on life and by circumstances that in some way or other disturbed my inner equilibrium. In other words, I did not have inner equilibrium! To a casual acquaintance I might have appeared a picture of calm (such in fact was my reputation, I was surprised to hear later) but behind the

façade my peace was far too dependent on a lack of outer disturbance to justify that description.

Perhaps this makes me sound rather thin skinned but in my
defence I should say that I was only twenty three years old and as
sensitive as anyone would be who is beginning to open up to the
realities of the spiritual world. Imagine a lifetime of cloudy skies
suddenly rent apart to reveal the bright sun beyond. Unless one is
very grounded it is difficult to stay balanced and doubly so when it
clouds over again. Nonetheless, regardless of any difficulties, I had
to learn that a high degree of sensitivity is no excuse for loss of self-
mastery. It may make an attitude of calm harder but that's what one
has to acquire if one is to progress in any real sense and not just
remain paddling about in the shallows of spiritual life.

I was told I should have **complete acceptance of people, things
and situations.** This does not mean failing to recognise what is
wrong or abandoning discrimination between the real and the
unreal. In the sense the phrase was used by the Masters it is really
about accepting free will and allowing people to be themselves
rather than trying to force them into any particular mould of one's
own liking. In my particular case it required recognition that the
people and situations I met were the ones I was supposed to meet.
Not necessarily the ones I would most like to meet but those from
whom I could draw most benefit if I set aside personal preferences
and had the sense to cooperate with the flow of life rather than resist
it. Indeed, taken to its logical conclusion, this instruction meant not
resisting anything that might cause one psychological pain or
suffering. All resistance is of the self. *All* resistance is of the self. This
is one of the hardest lessons to learn but one of the most liberating
when it is learnt.

Just to be clear. Non-resistance refers to an inner attitude. It does
not mean standing back and ignoring wrongdoing. Jesus, who can
serve as our exemplar in most things, may have allowed himself to
be arrested, knowing that he would be crucified, but he also chased
the money lenders out of the temple. In general, though, it is plain

from the scriptures that he confronted falsehood not by resisting it directly but by speaking, living and demonstrating truth, and this should be our approach too with regard to the many things wrong in this world.

Forget the personal self and merge with the universal self. Here we have a summing up of the totality of spiritual teaching in a single sentence. One might go so far as to say that if all the scriptures of the world were lost, their essence could be reconstituted by meditation on those words. If a seeker after truth travelled the globe in search of the greatest guru he could be told no more than this, and if he put it fully into practice he would become a great guru himself. Is it not a strange and wonderful thing that the wisdom of the world can be condensed down to ten simple words? This is the truth and the rest is commentary.

The Universal Self is God, not necessarily God as conventionally understood but God as the One Life from which we came and to which we shall return. Not that we are ever separate from it (that could never be – the One Life is all there is) but, by identifying with the personal self, we separate ourselves from it. Without being individual we could never know the universal but when we restrict ourselves to the individual we enclose ourselves within the boundaries of the personal. This is the source of illusion which is error of personal thought, and sin which is error of personal will. The remedy to both these ills, which can be seen as simply two facets of the same thing, is to **forget the personal self and merge with the universal self**.

I found it slightly odd that I had been told there would be a break in the talks but then there was one the very next night. It may be that Michael's strength was sufficient to permit one more visit from the Masters before the alluded to break, during which time he could recuperate and build up his energies. I was always aware that to be used in this way did take a lot out of him, leaving him thoroughly drained on each occasion. It was not just physically exhausting. It was emotionally upsetting as well, and though he never complained or even spoke of it in any way, the Masters made clear to me that the process was a difficult one for him and potentially a risky one too. I need to put on record my gratitude for the sacrifice Michael made even though I know he made it gladly as it was a way he could serve the Masters.

Whatever the reason for the Masters' return that night, the fact is that henceforth the talks did become less frequent. Up until then they had taken place more or less nightly and if I haven't included them all here that is only because there was a fair degree of repetition which may have been necessary for me to hear but would not be so interesting to read. Now it seems that the basic foundation had been laid and I had to build on that myself.

There were two aspects to my training during this period and they might be described as inner and outer. First there was the meditation which I practised for about an hour and a half a day and which seemed a natural part of spirituality. At the time I took it to be the heart of what I was doing, the moment when I withdrew from the external world and focussed all my attention within. This was also the time when the Masters came and spoke to me. Then there was my relationship with Michael which continued to be a testing ground. This was less obviously part of the training process but, as I came quite quickly to realise, was actually just as much so. After all, it is perfectly possible that a meditator can experience states in which the "I" appears to be extinguished but, on returning to normal everyday consciousness, remain the ego-bound person he was before. Such an experience is not necessarily going to alter who you are. I'm not saying that meditation has no greater benefit than the transitory peace it may bring during the time of its practice but if you engage in it for what you hope to get out of it, seeking results, seeking reward, without at the same time sincerely trying to cleanse the soul of sin (I am using deliberately provocative language here – without a frank acknowledgement of one's basically flawed nature, one does not get very far on this path), then, for all you might experience, you will remain in the petty world of self. I had to learn to conquer tendencies to anger, irritation and superiority, and all these failings were provoked and brought out in my day to day life with Michael. That is not to say we were constantly arguing. That did happen, and more often than it should have done, but by and large we got on well. Nonetheless I have to admit that I experienced many annoyances and embarrassments in the course of my relationship with him. These were not his fault but due to our rather different temperaments, and I mention them only because of the broader relevance they may have in the context of other people's experiences. Anyone who accepts serious spiritual training rapidly finds out that it is not what they might have expected. Faults you have kept down for years are dug up and brought to the surface. Fears you have avoided must be faced and overcome. Nothing can be hidden and nor would you really want it to be. Unpleasant as the dredging up process can sometimes be, it is vital if real progress is to be made.

As the Masters hoped, Michael and I began to find common ground and to learn from each other, he to be more inward and reflective, me to be more outgoing and less self-absorbed. Well, we made a start. To an outside observer we were certainly an odd couple. There was the wide difference in our ages and there was the difference in our tastes and characters but we had begun to discover a unity of purpose that we had hoped for when deciding to live together but at first found hard to attain. During the twenty one years we lived together the temperamental differences would remain but they became much less of an issue as we learnt to appreciate each other's point of view, and our mutual love for the Masters overcame any stumbling blocks the differences might have caused.

The Masters themselves did not return for another ten days but midway through that period one of their helpers came and spoke to me during meditation. He actually told me his name, which was unusual. Not the name, which was Rachman, unusual in itself, but the mentioning of it. He said he was a messenger from the higher Masters and was protecting me. He told me to beware of evil and guard against it, and warned me that my emotions would be brought out and churned up as part of the training I was under-going. As I have already said the differences between messenger and Master were quite marked. Rachman appeared as a kind friend and wise adviser but did not possess the same Himalayan authority as the Masters.

Ten days later the Masters came back and here is a record of what they said then.

February 27th 1979

The Master said that they were pleased I had pierced Michael's "outer skin" as he had been prevented from making progress for many years because of this. I was told to teach him with love, always avoiding impatience or a superior attitude. When I asked what sort of things I should say to him, he replied "You must act for yourself. Rely on your instinct". He concluded by sending greetings and blessings from the Most High.

February 28th 1979

A different Master told me that Michael and I were now more evenly balanced and that if we pursued our course with common sense and love our second test would soon be over. He said "Be complete in knowledge and understanding and you will become aware of the Masters' general plan for you".

Michael's outer skin was the manner he had adopted to protect his sensitive nature from being overwhelmed by the world. Many of us do this to some extent but, either through necessity or fear, some do it more than others. This "skin" had started out as a buffer between him and the outside world but there came a point when the adopted personality began to assume a life of its own. Long habit gradually made the artificial nature Michael had created to hide behind acquire a sort of reality, and although it was always only the uppermost layer of his being, it was where he tended to live for a lot of the time. It was certainly the personality he projected. When, despite searching for a long while, a person cannot find their place in this world because nothing in it can answer the questions they have within them, they may just resign themselves to getting along as best they can. This may mean, as in Michael's case, acting a part, and if they become too identified with that part they can sabotage any chance of progress for that lifetime. This appeared to be the risk for Michael and was why his outer skin, as the Master called it, needed to be pierced.

What exactly did that involve though? As far as I could gather (and, although I was the agent for this, I was something of an unconscious agent), part of it entailed demonstrating that one could lead a spiritual life independently of any organised religion. Michael had always had a pull to the mystical life. His period as a Christian monk and his time at the Ramakrishna ashram in Calcutta testified to that. But he could find no real answers to the questions posed by his soul in organised religion. At the same time, he was brought up in a conventional world where authority and the established order ruled so was reluctant to believe that an individual path was fully justifiable. He could not resolve the contradiction between his inner knowledge that organised religion was a stepping stone that could take you so far but no further and his conventional conditioning. I, being younger and of a generation that treated convention with rather less respect, could, with the Masters' help, enable him to see that the true path was the inner path, and that this could be followed within or outside a religious framework. In fact, given that all religions, much separated in time from their source and much distorted by input from the human mind, have the potential to bind and limit as much as they do to release and liberate, an individual path can be the higher option. Indeed, I would say that, as one advances on the path, it is often the only option, for those who attain must ultimately do so on their own without being followers of anything in this world, and that includes spiritual teachings. Do we not have the supreme examples of Gautama and Jesus here, both of whom ploughed their own course, independent of the religion they had been born into? I do not say we can all attain to those heights in this lifetime but part of the purpose of those great lives was to lay down a pattern for all men and women to follow.

I need to sound a caveat here and a strong one at that. Religion has produced many saints, though genuine ones, I don't think it can be denied, more in the past than now. The individual way can be fraught with pitfalls and requires a greater degree of spiritual attunement and purity of motive to be successful. Witness the many unbalanced people with their extravagant claims and swollen egos in the esoteric and occult fields. The advantage of religion is that it provides a structure, an order and a discipline, more or less vindicated by time, in which the aspirant can grow, protected from his own imaginings and potential excesses. The disadvantage of religion is that it is basically man-made. No religion is of God though every religion claims to be so. I do not say that religions do not have original inspiration from God (that's what distinguishes a religion from a cult) but the inspiration and the form that inspiration takes are not the same thing. And any form, even the purest, is a limitation. It is not Truth which, by its very nature, transcends all form. Besides it is undeniably the case that all religions follow the natural cycle of birth, growth, maturity, decay and death just as much as anything else does in the phenomenal world, and they are all, without exception, in the latter stages of that cycle now. Certainly there are lesser cycles within the greater one and religions can be revivified on occasion. The fact remains that there is no religion that is not in decline nowadays, and consequently they have much less to offer the contemporary person than at any time in the past. It would be absurd to claim that there is not a great deal to be learnt from traditional religious teachings but full affiliation to an organised religion and complete adherence to its dogmas and doctrines will tend to limit one to the mental plane. One must go beyond the mind to reach the soul.

I know many people will disagree with my assertion that all religions are in decline. They may claim that the body only awaits a new spiritual spark to ignite the spirit within and restore it to its former glory. But religions are not eternal. They exist in time and space as much as anything else does and many old religions have faded away. Possibly we do now need a new revelation, a new religion, more suited to our present day mindset, but even that would have to be transcended in the end for, I repeat, any form, even the purest, is a limitation.

None of this makes the difficulties of a path outside the established frameworks any less real, particularly if one has no external guide, and I would certainly not recommend it for everyone. At the risk of appearing to contradict myself within a few lines I would even urge a person to be quite sure that this is the path they are called to pursue and not to follow it unless they feel almost impelled. It should not be a matter of choice but necessity. **Rely on your instinct**. That is the best advice on such a matter. I only wish to give general principles here. Human beings are not mechanical devices so there are no hard and fast rules that apply to everyone under all circumstances.

Rely on your instinct. The instinct referred to here is not the vague hunch one often associates with that term. Nor is it the thinly disguised personal preference we might occasionally deceive ourselves into believing comes from beyond the self. To say it is the voice of the soul might seem a poetic metaphor but that is precisely what it is. It is an awareness of the real, the spiritual intuition that is latent in everyone but only properly develops as we move beyond identification with the rational mind and the separate self and begin to transcend ourselves. This may initially be through music or art or the contemplation of symbols, religious or otherwise. It may be through a spiritual practice such as meditation or it may be through a widening sympathy with our fellow human beings. As we are all limited by ego to some extent, we have to be careful to exercise discrimination as to what is true intuition and what comes from one of the many layers of the personal self. But eventually this intuition will completely supersede the analytical mind and be our primary means of knowing. Then we will realise it to be the direct insight into truth that comes from being one with truth. You know because you are.

When the Master told me to rely on my instinct this is what he meant. He wanted me to trust my intuition but there was a secondary meaning to his words as well. Certainly I should allow myself to be guided by my own soul. By listening to it, its voice would become more audible, but he was also implying that he would speak to me that way too. This is the Masters' preferred means of communication. They speak soul to soul, at a level beyond words, beyond mind and beyond the personal self, all of which distort true communication. How could I tell what came from my own intuition and what came from the Masters? It would not matter. There would be no need to discriminate on that score as there would be no fundamental difference. At the intuitive level truth is one. Now, introductions having been made, the Masters were not going to speak to me on quite such a regular basis through Michael. Instead they hoped to be able to start communicating through the correct spiritual channels, in other words, through the higher self.

Chapter 7

The Sea of Blue and Gold

March 3rd 1979

I was greeted by a Master who said he came from a far off place. He told me to love and support Michael and said that colour would be poured down on me. He said that one day I would understand "the mysteries of your cosmic law". He sent love and blessings and told me that the truth would be revealed to me to the degree that I kept on making efforts.

March 5th 1979

I was told that the Masters and guides were pleased that we were making efforts to understand each other. Love was growing and progress would follow in its wake. He said that communication was becoming difficult and would cease for a few days.

March 10th 1979

The guide came for just a few moments. He said "We are pleased with your efforts. Work and love and at the end you will join us again, triumphant. See the colours and believe."

March 13th 1979

The Master told me he came to me in a sea of azure blue and gold. He said that for now life must be strict and outwardly dull but if we made a strong spiritual effort together we would one day enter into a glorious future.

I have put these talks together as they are connected by their brevity, their encouraging tone, their exhortations to make efforts and the fact that all except one mention colour!

The far off place was the higher planes rather than a physical location. I have said that the Masters who communicated with me were not in physical bodies though some of their helpers were. However I had the definite impression that certain amongst their number would have to descend further down through the planes than others. I recall that this particular Master did actually sound as though he was speaking from a long way off in the sense that there was a remoteness about him, as though he had attained to a state far removed from the human condition. Perhaps that is why he said **"your cosmic law"** which phrase did strike me as out of the ordinary even for the Masters. When a few days later he told me that he came in a sea of azure blue and gold, he projected an image into my mind of an ocean of fiery light in which intense colours of radiant hue flashed and danced. The blue and gold he brought poured down from on high like a waterfall of light, and this vision of almost living colour brought home the reality of the higher planes to me more vividly than anything else I had thus far experienced during the course of my encounters with the Masters.

Light is universally regarded as the first manifestation of God but what we perceive as light in the physical world is dim and faint compared to the glorious radiance of the spiritual realms. It is the same with colour, light's raiment and its primary offspring. What we see in this world, however beautiful it may be to our earthly eyes, is but colour as a faded shadow of its true self. Even the flash of a kingfisher's jewelled wing as it enters the water or the magnificence of a burning tropical sunset are but dull, lacklustre tones compared to colour as it exists on the higher planes. For those who have perceived something of these higher aspects of colour, its exquisite, self-luminous beauty is beyond description. Words are quite inadequate but they are all we have and at least can point in the right direction. However there is more to colour than just beauty. Each colour is the embodiment in light of a certain quality, and meditation on a particular colour can attune one to the quality it represents. For instance, rose pink symbolises self-sacrificing love whilst orange energises and green has a calming and healing quality though one should in no sense be limited to these definitions. I have mentioned that Michael could sometimes see auras, the energies of which manifest as colours to the clairvoyant eye. He told me that he was able to interpret what he saw in both psychological and physical terms but tended to avoid using this gift as he felt it was akin to reading someone's private letters. Despite that reticence he did on rare occasions make a remark to me about a person specifying either a character trait or indicating possible health problems. With regard to the former he might be accused of being wise after the event since we usually knew the person anyway. But he did once mention to me that he was concerned about an acquaintance's heart and wondered whether he should say anything. Not knowing the individual well enough to make such an unconventional and unverifiable statement, he kept silent. Shortly thereafter that person did actually have a heart attack although fortunately it was not a serious one.

Combinations of colours can also have a symbolic meaning to the receptive mind which is why the Master specifically described himself to me as coming in a sea of azure blue and gold. Here the spiritual depth and serenity conjured up by the blue come together with the radiant enlightenment qualities of gold to convey to the imagination an effect of transcendent realisation. Do you think it without significance that the far off sky is blue or that royal crowns are made of gold? Is it just because of the shorter wavelength of blue light or the fact that gold is a scarce and valued metal? Those might be facts from a prosaic quantitative point of view but there is a symbolic meaning as well for people who do not limit their minds to the horizontal conception of life and who can see that nature is a book to be read and that the world, together with everything in it, bears witness to what is beyond itself.

The emphasis on effort was marked at this stage of my journey. It should be obvious that to accomplish anything of either a physical or spiritual nature one must make the attempt to do so but you might also consider that this contradicts the important spiritual teachings on effortlessness. These teachings, though, relate to matters such as living from moment to moment and working without attachment to results, so this is a contradiction which really only exists on the linguistic level. Once you realise that effortlessness in the spiritual sense applies to motive and desire, not application or action, it is easily resolved. You must make efforts if you wish to progress but they should not be initiated by the ego wishing to gain something. You must work if you are to attain enlightenment. It is perfectly true that you don't go to it, it comes to you, but still you must work for it. You must prepare the ground. It will not happen just by wanting it to. So you must work but you must work in a spirit of non-attachment and without being motivated by desire. I suppose what I am saying here amounts to this: you must work for love of God rather than desire for heaven.

It was around this time that I had what is now called an out of body experience. I put it like that because I had not heard the term back then. Nor in fact had I heard of the phenomenon. I had practised meditation for around nine months and often entered into a great peace, occasionally even feeling my sense of self to be dissolved into a sea of light. But actually leaving the body was not something I expected to happen. So you can imagine my surprise, tinged with no small degree of alarm, when, as I lay on my bed one night, a ringing noise started up in my ears. This got increasingly louder until it started to resemble the roaring of a plane's engine as it was about to take off. Then there was a rushing sensation within and I felt myself being sucked out of the top of my head. That's the best way I can describe it unless I resort to an un-poetic simile involving a vacuum cleaner. There was a tremendous feeling of being pulled upwards but internal resistance too as if a natural protective force in the body wished to arrest the process. For a moment it seemed as though it might do just that but then with a great burst I shot up and out through the crown of my head. Whoosh! My surroundings were unaltered and I was still completely myself but the sensation of physical freedom was tremendous. No longer bound by gravity, I floated up to the ceiling of the room from where I could see my inert body lying on the bed. Simply by wishing to I moved over to and then straight through the window and was able to see the night sky and houses outside from an unusual vantage point. At that stage I should probably have remained calm if I wished to continue with the adventure but I became (reasonably, I think) rather excited by what had happened. It is this, I believe, that caused me to be pulled back into the body after only a couple of minutes of escape. I re-entered my fleshy abode, my heart thumping.

As I am not trying to convince anyone of the truth of anything I say in this book I will content myself with a simple description of what happened and not try to forestall rationalist objections other than to say that at no time did I fail to have complete continuity of consciousness. I was lying on my bed but I was not asleep and I did not dream. The next day I spoke to Michael about what had happened and he told me that he had had similar experiences in the past. His had been more extensive as he had travelled around the house he was living in at the time but he had still remained in the counterpart of this world rather than ascending any higher to astral levels as, according to the literature on the subject, is possible for the experienced practitioner. He added that while he had not consciously left his body since those experiences about twenty years ago, he assumed that that was what happened to him every time he went into trance although he had no recollection of it.

The next time the Masters came I asked them about this episode and what I should make of it. This is what they said. **Do not be concerned. Such incidents may well occur during the course of your training but are of no consequence.** That was all they had to say on the subject. I saw at once that it was true. Spiritually speaking, such incidents **are of no consequence** and are actually more likely than not to be a distraction. That is why the Masters also said that I should not be concerned if they repeated themselves. I had initially thought that 'do not be concerned' just meant 'don't worry' but then realised that what it also could mean was 'do not give these incidents any importance'. I didn't and they did not repeat themselves. I am not belittling them and they are of interest from the angle of whether non-corporeal existence is possible but they do not have any spiritual value and nor do they even prove the existence of an afterlife so, to those who might wish to pursue the possibility of astral projection, I would say why not save your energies for more constructive pursuits?

March 26th 1979

The Master spoke to me and said that he was watching my progress with love and interest. He said that Michael was their mouthpiece and they taught me through him. I could teach Michael best through the progress that I made and through what I radiate not what I said. He told me that there would be a time for me to talk later but that now I must listen, as an untrained colt can win no races. He stressed that I should guard my behaviour as lapses in that regard might severely retard progress. I asked if constantly thinking of beauty was an unwise habit and he replied that this was natural in a spiritual person but that I should project beauty and not dwell on it. He told me to meditate on this. He repeated that he came to me in a sea of blue and gold and that I should meditate on those colours to gain strength.

I must once again remind the reader that when these talks took place I was only twenty three years old. Idealistic and, as is the case with most people of that age, somewhat self-absorbed, I found it hard to accept that one could be taught spiritual lessons by teachers who were not great gurus which Michael fairly obviously was not. I had many illusions that needed to be shattered, one of which being that I could teach others before I had learnt anything myself. I was impatient and I thought too much about my own feelings. In other words, I was young. Later on I came to appreciate that the Masters not only spoke to me through Michael when he was in trance but could impress him when he was fully conscious as well. Certainly the communication would not be on the same level of wisdom as it was filtered through Michael's mind and understanding but the essence of it was the same. I should have known that then but I was still at the stage when I rejected or looked for an excuse to reject a possibly unwelcome message if the messenger was less than perfect. I thought I knew better than Michael in many respects, and it's possible I did have a better intuitive grasp of spiritual matters than him. But I lacked his worldly experience, I lacked his humility and, most of all, I lacked his capacity for love. It is that which made him such a good and faithful servant of the Masters.

The Masters were never shy about making strong statements. To say that lapses in behaviour (by which they meant giving in to behaviour motivated by the ego) might severely retard progress is guaranteed to give the recipient of such a remark pause for thought. It might seem an extreme comment for a spiritual teacher to make but then these teachers were by no means all sweetness and light. They were not there simply to offer spiritual platitudes but to hammer the recalcitrant ego into shape. Or rather to hammer it out of shape. Jesus famously said that he did not come to bring peace but a sword, meaning his job was not to make people feel better. He taught radical transformation and that involved cutting away all untruth. In like manner, the task of any spiritual teacher is to break down as well as build up. He must plant the seeds that will eventually flower into holiness but he must also totally uproot the ego. He cannot simply trim back its more wayward branches.

I had always been moved by beauty and in the days before I found the spiritual path it was a veritable lifeline to a young person who felt he was stranded in a world of darkness. Does that statement sound a touch over the top? From my present perspective I can see it does tend in that direction but it was how I truly felt when growing up. After starting to meditate, this sensitivity to beauty increased, developing almost to the point of an inability to tolerate its absence. I realised that this was not a desirable position in which to be, hence my question. The meaning of the answer, **that I should project beauty and not dwell on it,** was not immediately apparent to me but I gave it some thought and soon understood that it meant that it was the task of the spiritual person to give out beauty to the world from their own inner awareness and not be attached to it externally. He or she should not depend on beauty for spiritual nourishment but should be able to realise it within themselves and then project it back out into a world hungry for spiritual truth, whether it knows that or not. Beauty is truth, truth beauty. Spiritually aware people must be channels through which truth and beauty can pour into the world, and the more they realise beauty within themselves, the greater their projection of beauty can be.

The next day the Master returned and spoke a little more on the subject of beauty. Now when I look at what he said it seems quite obvious but I recall that at the time it was almost shocking to my purist sensibilities. I was looking at things from a very dualistic standpoint in those days. Here's what he said.

March 27th 1979 (1)
The Master told me that beauty is everywhere. It varies in degrees according to its closeness to God but there is God in everything and that means beauty. Do not love one thing and despise every-thing else because it does not match up to what you love. Accept everything on its merits, not judging it or comparing it with more evolved things or the higher planes. Be detached from your surroundings and feel the humility of accepting gratefully whatever God offers you.

I was taken aback by this because I was so attached to my concept of beauty that to be told that it was in everything seemed somehow to be desecrating it. The point now seems self-evident but I remember at the time feeling quite upset by it. I may have understood it theoretically but still found it hard to accept.

Is it true though? Well yes, of course it is. I only ask the question because there are some possible misunderstandings that I should address. Human beings are very capable of distorting anything if it suits them. The way scripture is bent to suit individual agendas and prejudices is proof enough of that. So the first thing to make clear is that the Masters' words do not mean that somebody regarded as physically beautiful is closer to God than someone not so fortunate, if fortunate is what that is. I don't suppose that anyone of sound mind would really think such a thing but the remark that **it varies in degrees according to its closeness to God** could be taken to imply that if one so chose. There is an inner beauty which does indicate spiritual attainment but physical beauty is dependent on other, quite different, factors, chief of which is probably karma. That said, beauty of feature and form on the higher planes most probably is determined by the degree of spiritual realisation. This is not a sensual beauty though.

Next, the Master said that God is in everything, which is obviously the case, but does that mean that everything is of God, the good, the bad, everything, everywhere? This is an important distinction to make because the answer to that question is no, it does not. Human beings are co-creators with God in this world, that is part of our function, but we can create in harmony with God's laws or out of harmony with them and according to the dictates of our own ego. Only in the former case will the products of our creation have genuine beauty. There can be nothing that is not God but if we distort God's light, what we create is not of God and will not have true beauty even though it may have a certain amount of interest. This is not to deny the individual in art but the individual must be attuned to the universal, to some degree at least, if its creations are to be truthful, and without truth there is no beauty.

Following on from that, the words that **beauty is everywhere. It varies in degrees according to its closeness to God but there is God in everything and that means beauty** could be taken to justify the assertion of many modern artists that there is beauty in ugliness. However if we look a little more closely at those words we find they do not fully support such an interpretation, not in the way it is often understood anyway. The key point is that there is a difference between ugliness and deliberate distortion. There certainly can be beauty in what we might call ugliness if it is natural but there is no beauty on any level in the perversion of reality which is the stock in trade of much modern art. And, on that point, it has often seemed to me that the principal purpose of a great deal of modern art (usually, though not always, undeclared if not unconscious) is the attempt to disprove the existence of God and assert the primacy of the ego. That is why in future times it will come to be regarded as a curious aberration created by people who had forgotten or denied who they were. What the modern artist frequently fails to understand is that truly great art neither seeks to reflect human life nor delve into the subconscious, which from the spiritual point of view has no funda-mental reality anyway. It points away from all that to the eternal. The real purpose of art is to express primordial truth.

I don't intend this to be an attack on all modern art. Much of what passes under that name merely reflects the confusion in the artist's own mind but it is perfectly valid to try to find new forms in which to express the formless, and there are many creative people who are making genuine attempts to find something new to say which will increase our understanding of what it is to be human. Ultimately, however, if this either denies or misconceives transcendent truths or distorts universal archetypes it cannot be said to be art in the highest sense. The greatest art instils a sense of wonder and humility in those who participate in it (I use that word because viewing or listening to or reading a work of art should be an active process). The greatest art is sacred.

I may seem to be contradicting the Master's words here, that **beauty is everywhere……. there is God in everything and that means beauty** but these need to be understood in the context of which he spoke them. I was yearning for the beauty of the higher planes, of which I had a distinct recollection, and because of that I was failing to appreciate the presence of God in all creation. But, as the Master reminded me, God is in all creation. Even if He is more fully present in the higher dimensions of the created universe, which are, as it were, more transparent to His presence, still there is nowhere where God is not.

Unusually, the Master came back and spoke to me again that same evening. As I recall he came at the beginning and then at the end of our meditation, possibly because Michael was particularly robust that day. I must emphasise that the process was always a strain for him and, with the objectivity that maturity brings, I'm a little ashamed of how I took his sacrifice for granted during those days. Once again, I make the excuse of youth.

March 27th 1979 (2)

The Master returned and said he was glad to see that I was now taking on responsibility and acting for myself. Progress was being made and would become apparent in the future. He told me to give love and support to Michael, and to realise that if I felt antipathy or irritation towards him this was the evil influences at work and should be ignored. He repeated that I should meditate on blue and gold as this would purify the mind and take it to a higher level where such influences could not operate. He went on to say that apathy is one of the besetting sins of many on the spiritual path and one I should at all times guard against. I must not become bored with the routine of our daily existence but continually make efforts to keep things fresh by putting myself fully into spiritual life.

It is a sobering thought that our emotional reactions may not always be entirely our own. If we entertain negative feelings of any kind, that provides an opening for what the Master called evil influences which may then enter our mind and affect us to the degree that we allow ourselves to follow their promptings. The remedy for this is to ignore all negative feelings. If they arise, do not permit them to gain any purchase in the mind. Do not indulge them. Do not seek to justify them. They may provide a temporary rush of energy but do not be seduced by that into thinking that they somehow bestow strength. The truth is quite the contrary.

We cannot be influenced by anything to which we do not respond. The responsibility therefore is completely ours. We have to open the door before these influences can enter into us but if we succumb to negative emotions then that leaves the door ajar and entry is possible. I know this goes so completely counter to the view of the world that many people have that they will just reject it out of hand - or would do in the unlikely event that such people would ever read a book of this nature. On the other hand, there are some, more open to investigating these pages, who could react to this statement in a frightened or superstitious way, thinking that they might be helpless victims of dark powers. Let me assure them that that is not the case. We should recognise that there are spiritual shadows in the universe but these are powerless to affect us without our complicity. I was able to observe this process in myself, seeing how a small irritation, unless it was rapidly nipped in the bud, could easily grow and develop into something quite out of proportion to what had started it off. I am not claiming that this proves the existence of forces of evil but that is not really the point. In a sense the existence or non-existence of such things is incidental. The main issue here is that any negative feelings should be ignored. It does not so much matter how they arise or increase. What matters is to realise that if you identify with them they have power over you and grow. If you ignore them then they lose energy and die.

I think that the reason many spiritually inclined people are prone to what the Masters called here apathy and at other times spoke of as lassitude is twofold. Such people often tend to be more contemplative than active types and, although a contemplative attitude is definitely an advantage on the spiritual path, it can also result in a certain inertia which might be justified by saying that truth is found in being rather than doing. So it may but that does not mean that being is just doing nothing. It is all too easy to excuse laziness, and even fear of action, on the grounds that one is remaining centred in the watchful state of the non-attached observer but one has to be ruthlessly honest with one's motives for such an attitude. I recognised the tendency to indolence in myself and, like many others for whom **apathy is one of the besetting sins on the spiritual path**, have had to stay alert so as not to give way to it.

Another common reason for apathy in a spiritual person comes from a pronounced distaste for the world as it is. You might think this would have the reverse effect and drive someone to act to change things and it surely does in many cases. But there are others who feel overwhelmed by the sheer scale of the problem and the seeming impossibility of ever really changing anything, and who consequently shrink from the attempt. After all, history is not very encouraging. There have assuredly been many changes brought about by the actions of great men and women over the years but, by and large, human nature does seem to be the same mixture of self-interest and corruption tinged with a touch of idealism and a dash of altruism it always has been. Two and a half thousand years of Buddhism in the East and two thousand years of Christianity in the West have not changed things significantly, have they? Well, first of all, maybe they have. How can we tell? And secondly even if they have not, that is no reason not to keep trying. The combined efforts of centuries may one day lead to a tipping point and humanity may eventually change its path. It certainly will not if those who have some inkling of the truth keep quiet. Anyone who has even had a small glimpse of spiritual reality has a duty to share that. They may do so very imperfectly but that doesn't matter. The important thing is that they do it. I'm not saying this to justify the many spurious, deluded, hypocritical charlatans and egotists one finds in the occult and mystical fraternities, but I do say it to galvanise the true seeker who might shrink from sharing his or her insights on the grounds that they are incomplete or not yet perfect. If you wait until they are perfect, you will wait forever. If you are sincere and have a genuine love for God, truth, call it what you will, then share what you have found. Do it humbly and do it in the full recognition that there is always a higher presentation of truth but do it.

Chapter 8

Thoughts on Homosexuality

Michael had never married and it did not take me long to work out that he was probably homosexual. I was initially slightly concerned that this might have been the reason for his interest in me and that the spiritual talk was just a pretext. That, of course, would have made him a rather deceitful person. But he never made the slightest attempt to switch our conversations away from spiritual topics to anything that could be remotely construed as romantic. As far as I could see his interest in me was what he said it was, a spiritual one, but I wasn't naïve (or maybe I was just fearful) and, in the early stages of our relationship, I remained alert for such a possibility.

Occasionally I did let my fears get the better of me. Once, before Michael moved to Bath, we had arranged to spend some time together but I had taken fright and not turned up at our pre-arranged meeting place. I had spent the previous evening with a friend and told him about my new acquaintance. He had rather over-reacted and said that Michael was probably a black magician and I should be very careful. This had set off superstitious alarm bells in my head and the next day, when I should have been meeting Michael, I stayed at home. A little reflection made me feel very ashamed of myself. As I say, Michael had never made any suggestion that he was interested in a romantic relationship and, in the twenty one years I knew him, he never did. The reason is, he wasn't. He had not mentioned that he was homosexual but why should he? He came from a generation (he was born in 1919) that had lived with a great deal of intolerance and the fear of scandal and, worse, prison. Later on, when he did tell me that he was homosexual, he said that this had been a problem for him as well when he met me. Not because he had mixed motives in wanting to get to know me but because of the assumption that I and others might make that he did have mixed motives. And inevitably people did assume that. Even when assured there was no romantic element to our relationship, they were still quite sure there must be in his case even if it was sublimated.

I once asked him why he had approached me in the bookshop. After all, many people would assume that if a homosexual in his late fifties starts talking to a young man in his early twenties there is only one thing on his mind. I fear his answer would hardly reassure them. He told me that he had seen me surrounded by a blue light and clairaudiently heard a voice saying. "**Speak to him**". He had gone up to me with no idea of what he was supposed to say and just began talking about books with not the faintest notion as to where that might lead. The fact that I had not immediately rebuffed him and had seemed interested had been encouraging but he still had not known what, if anything, was supposed to happen next. It was probably as odd for him to be talking to someone like me as it was for me to be talking to someone like him. He told me that later on he was told that he and I had a connection and that it was the Masters' wish that we got together, but he was not told much more than that and he did not mention any of this to me at the time. I asked him how long he had known of the Masters and he told me that they had contacted him only around the time of our meeting. He said nothing of this to me for fear of seeming to influence me in any way. As I have already said, I had no knowledge of them until we were living together.

Michael's homosexuality had not been easy for him to live with. Not just for the obvious reasons for anyone living in the 1940s and '50s but it also caused him a moral dilemma because of his spiritual beliefs. He knew it was a natural part of him but did that justify it? Should homosexuals remain celibate and channel their sexual feelings into spiritual aspiration or creative endeavour? Or could they live just as anyone else? Nowadays we think we know the answer but I wonder if we really do. Our current attitude, whilst a vast improvement on previous centuries' ignorance and bigotry, is still based on a humanistic view of life not a spiritual one. Even most modern spiritual groups in the West (other than fundamentalist ones) largely adopt their view of homosexuality from the materialist, humanist one, but that does not take into account spiritual reality so perhaps it is incomplete.

The metaphysical position is that there is a unmanifest, unacting Supreme Principle that, manifesting, gives rise to the primal duality of spirit and matter, here to be understood as essence and substance, which are the active and passive components of the universe, and it is through the union of these two polarities (which are not separate but different aspects or modes of the same thing) that creation takes place. From the highest level of manifestation downwards, this complementary duality and its creative potency is reflected, and it translates in gender terms as male and female. Therefore it has to be said that, if human beings are to reflect divine order and live in harmony with divine law, they should conform to this archetypal reality. If they do not, they are not living in accord with what is real. That is the ideal based on metaphysical principles.

However we live in a fallen world, a world very much out of kilter with divine law. I once asked the Masters for their view of homosexuality and this is what they said. I must warn the reader that this is an occasion, by no means unusual, when they did not answer my question directly but used it to point to a deeper truth.

"Is homosexuality wrong or is it perfectly acceptable, spiritually speaking?" I asked.

"Homosexuality is an imperfection but you live in an imperfect world. To us what matters is what is in the heart. That does not mean that love excuses all, at least not what passes for love in your world. With true love there is always discernment. Does that surprise you? Nevertheless it is the case. It is desire that makes love blind."

"Can you have love without desire?" I asked.

"Of course, my child, but I am not saying desire itself is neces-

sarily wrong. It is the attachment to desire that takes you away from the truth."

There we are. I hope that makes the position quite clear! Here's what I think it means though I should say that what follows is also based on remarks the Masters made to me at other times. Homosexuality is not in line with divine truth but nor are many, you might even say most, other aspects of human behaviour. If one is born homosexual (for whatever reason, it may be a karmic debt or opportunity, it may be the first incarnation in one sex after a number of lives in the other, it may be due to some imbalance in the soul, there are a variety of reasons based on past life behaviour), it is incumbent on one to seek to learn the lessons of that experience. This is not necessarily best done by rationalising that there is no difference between homosexuality and heterosexuality. That may well just be an avoidance of the lessons your life as a homosexual is giving you the opportunity to learn.

At the highest level of our being, we are pure spirit and there is no masculine or feminine. There are no distinguishing characteristics at all. At the level of the individual soul, we do have a masculine or feminine polarity but it is not exclusive as each contains the other as in the well-known Yin-Yang symbol. Please note that at this level there is no sexuality, as we think of it in physical or even emotional terms, it is more a question of quality. Occult tradition states that human beings were created in pairs, one male and one female, but this does not mean that the female soul will always incarnate in a female body or vice versa. Here is one possible reason for homosexuality. However the fact that there is an explanation for homosexuality does not mean it is a natural condition, spiritually speaking. It is still an abnormal state not a reflection of truth and should be recognised as such. Equally, though, the fact that it is an abnormal state does not mean that the condition itself should in any way be condemned. To be frank, there is not much about our world that is normal today when looked at with the eye of spiritual understanding. What it does mean is that our approach to it should take into account the reality of the situation and not be formed by prejudice or ignorance.

I would like to take Michael as an example of someone who dealt with the fact of being a homosexual in an enlightened way. It was not easy for him and it took a while but out of the attempt to understand came some sort of resolution. To begin with, he did not deny what he was. This probably does not need saying nowadays, such have been the advances in our understanding, but for someone of his generation it was often hard to acknowledge the reality of their own nature, such were the pressures of society. Having accepted his situation, he still had to deal with it.

It is an irrefutable fact that the sexual act between two people of the same sex cannot create new life. If you do not believe in the spiritual basis to life this may seem irrelevant (I should add that whether you believe or not does not alter the truth) but if you do, and comprehend the implications of the famous Hermetic maxim "As above, so below", you must regard it as significant. Basically, you must regard the sexual act when performed between two people of the same sex to be a misdirection of energy. There is no doubt that a great deal of heterosexual sex is also a misdirection of energy, especially if engaged in for purely sensual gratification, but it does at least have the potential to direct divine energies in the correct manner.

So does this mean homosexuals should not practise their homosexuality? Ideally, yes it does. Hard as it may seem, it does mean that homosexuals should try to realise that it is not necessary to express sexuality physically. Indeed, to learn to rise above identification with oneself as a sexual being may well be one of the reasons some people are born as homosexuals. That is a lesson all must learn eventually. This may be one of the means whereby it can be learnt. You might say this is impossible and unfair and cannot apply to everyone but why are you saying that? Is it because you do not wish to accept the truth? Is it because you are too attached to your desires? Besides, I said that this is the ideal. It is something to have as a goal. The powers that be are not inflexible taskmasters, unable to tolerate the slightest error or weakness. As they said, **homosexuality is an imperfection but you live in an imperfect world.** They do not expect us to be perfect and they understand that life in a physical body is not easy. They watch over us with unconditional love and they know that we will stumble and fall many times as we make our way back to God. We gain experience through experiment and that is only to be expected. However their love is for us as spiritual beings not earthly personalities, and it expresses itself as a desire for us to grow as spiritual beings, not to be happy and content as earthly personalities. Thus they have boundless compassion for our weaknesses and failures but that does not stop them from holding fast uncompromisingly to the truth.

How does this apply to Michael and his experiences? He had certainly had full homosexual relationships in his life. He was a loving person and he had sought love. However he told me that he always knew that something was not quite as it should be. You might say that this was just misplaced guilt caused by the conditioning of the world in which he lived, particularly as I have previously spoken of his somewhat conventional attitude in many matters. You might say that but I think you would be wrong. A spiritually sensitive person will always have an intuitive awareness of what he should or should not be doing. Michael never denied his homosexuality or tried to change what he was in any way, but he began to wonder how it should be expressed. This lead to him exploring spirituality and his eventual decision to become a monk. I must repeat that he was not in flight from his homosexuality but it was the cause of him thinking more deeply about what he truly was.

The donning of a monk's habit is certainly not recommended for everybody and it didn't suit Michael for long but it was a step on his voyage of self-discovery. He came out of the monastery and gradually found a way to resolve the dilemma caused by his homosexuality through spiritual practice and going beyond the need to express his sexuality in a physical way.

I've gone into this at some length because it was a part of my experience with Michael and because I regard current attitudes towards homosexuality as well meaning improvements on the past but still limited, especially for those who are intent on making spiritual progress. I believe that many homosexuals are similar to Michael, souls who are further along the path than average who have to deal with certain imbalances in their nature (as do we all, this is only one of many) in order to move forwards spiritually. This they will not be able to do unless they have a clear understanding of their situation. To accept it as perfectly natural and normal might actually be spiritually counterproductive. To channel sexual desire into its higher aspects of creativity and spiritual aspiration is much more likely to bring about spiritual growth and help people move forwards on the path. "Why not do both?" it might be said. This may be feasible up to a point but there comes a critical stage on the path when if you really wish to progress you must decide whether you will live in harmony with spiritual reality or not. So I am not saying it can never be part of any individual's life destiny to experience the physical aspect of a homosexual relationship but I am saying that eventually they will need to go beyond that.

I can imagine various objections to the above, one of which being that it is just a rationalisation of an innate prejudice that I may have. My position is the metaphysical one and if that is admitted, the rest, I would submit, follows. Of course, you may deny a spiritual reality to life but perhaps that it is your prejudice. Then again, it could be argued that what I say might apply to people who have spiritual beliefs but why should it apply to those, probably the majority, who do not? Why should they not be treated just like heterosexuals instead of being discriminated against in this way? To this I would reply that, as the Masters said, **homosexuality is an imperfection**. It is not the same as heterosexuality, which reflects reality, and cannot be viewed in the same light. I would also add, as the Masters did, that **what matters is what is in the heart.** What is true is true but no-one is judged or condemned for not living up to the highest truth.

After all, who among us does? At the same time we should know what the highest truth is.

Individuals all differ and this subject is assuredly more complicated and nuanced than I have been able to present it here. I have treated it from the spiritual perspective but many people will reject that and, ultimately, each individual must decide for him or herself how best to act. It is good to have the right information on which to base your decision though.

Chapter 9

"Remember the Creator."

March 28th 1979

A Master who had not come before and who radiated great love came. He said that where he was all was poetry, music and colour as the vibrations were much higher than on the earth plane. I was going down a river and there would be eddies, currents and even waterfalls but one day in the not too distant future it would flow into the sea of tranquillity and I would know peace. He told me to love Michael as he was their messenger and worked unceasingly for me. The Masters were always with us and sent love from their sphere from where I had come and to which I would eventually return. I asked him how I could become more detached and less upset at the lack of beauty in the world. He told me that I must not let beauty possess me or seek to hide under its wing but I should salute it and be grateful for it, letting all feelings of possession and upset roll off me like water from a swan's back. I should not hide from ugliness but face it and seek to understand it. I could never lose beauty but beauty could lose me if I let myself become attached to it. He ended by saying that beauty had sent me to earth to do my duty and I should do it gladly.

April 3rd 1979

The Master told me that I was in a most critical period on my path to the heavenly plane which was my home. He said that the Masters constantly rained down beauty from these planes onto me to give me inspiration and support but I must not allow myself to get carried away by this. The force was strong and could be unsettling but I must learn how to deal with it in a mature and balanced way. He told me to imagine an armour of light around me that

would protect me from the evil influences when they attacked, which they frequently would. He emphasised that I should love Michael as love was essential for progress. He said do not think of love as a feeling desirable for a spiritual person to have but as the reality of the higher worlds without which no-one could gain entry.

I well remember the impression made by this Master when he spoke to me of the higher planes on these two nights. He had not come before and he had about him a loving tenderness which drew from me a devoted response. Previously some of the Masters had emanated a majestic power and authority while others had seemed the embodiment of profound wisdom. Of course, all the Masters possessed all of these qualities to a high degree but they each had a certain keynote to their presence that was quite noticeable despite their essential oneness. This clearly demonstrated that the realisation of universal consciousness does not eradicate the individual. I think this is an important point. The reason Jesus and the Buddha elicit such love is because, while manifesting the universal, they are not remote, withdrawn, distant, impersonal, unapproachable but fully, uniquely and lovably individual.

The three primary attributes of God are spoken of in most traditions as love, wisdom and power, these corresponding on the human level to feeling, mind and will. Occultism talks of seven rays or divine qualities of which the principal three are described as Will, Love and Intelligence which obviously refers to the same thing. All souls are said to come into being on one or other of the rays which stamps them with its imprint. Hence the different characteristics, or points of emphasis, of the Masters who would have developed to the fullest extent the potential of all the rays, insofar as they relate to the human kingdom, but retain a focus on one in particular.

The subject of the seven rays is a fascinating one and some occultists go into great detail about the supposed attributes of these rays but I have to say that, although this kind of research may be very interesting to pursue, it can easily become a sidetrack to the true spiritual path. Indeed it is fair to say that a more realistic objection to occultism than the traditional religious one, that the occultist is illegitimately delving into the unseen, is that it belongs to the form side of life, and true spirituality is about transcending form. It is surely significant that neither Jesus nor the Buddha nor any other great spiritual teacher was concerned with what we call the occult. No doubt they had intuitive and experiential knowledge of the hidden side of nature but they did not focus on that at all in their teachings. I am aware that many occultists regard themselves as initiates in possession of higher truths, and I don't deny that they might have great knowledge, even power. But I've come to think that occultism can be an all too alluring diversion for the intellectually inclined. It exists in the realm of thought and multiplicity. Spiritual truth is simple as the Masters never tired of telling me and as they demonstrated in talks like these two. They undoubtedly possessed great occult knowledge but that was not something they appeared to regard as particularly important for the spiritual seeker. Their attitude would have been summed up by the words of Jesus when he said, "Seek ye first the kingdom of heaven and all thing will be added to you" or in their own words which described **love as the reality of the higher worlds without which no one could gain entry.**

Here's a thought. What is love? I make no apologies for returning to this subject regularly in the course of these pages. Never was a word so trivialised by overuse and to such an extent that even that statement is becoming a cliché. But still we don't seem to get very far in our understanding of it. I have to admit I occasionally found the Masters' constant emphasis on love to get a bit, dare I say it, dull. Yes, I know that God is love, please tell me something new that I don't know. But did I really know it? Do you really know it? We are not told that God loves. We are told God is love. There is a world of difference between the two. Love, divine love, is not a feeling. It is a fundamental state of existence. As the Masters made clear, love is

the reality of the higher worlds but we cannot truly know love in this sense as long as we have our current focus on self. You might say that one could not know love at all without self, and it is true that the possibility of love does come from the existence of the individual, but it is the identification with self that stops the flow of love and reduces it to the personal level. Divine love has no opposite and pours forth constantly. It is not dependent on anything. It is not conditional on anything. It does not require anything. We think we know love but we are really just paddling about in rock pools on the shores of the great ocean of love that the Masters bathe in perpetually. And yet even though we confine and limit it by our self-identification, even though we tarnish and corrupt it by our attachment and desire and possessiveness, love is our true nature. We are built of love and we know in our hearts that life and love are synonymous.

During this period it was as though my vibrations were being speeded up, if I may put it that way. Actually it's probably not too far off from the truth. Anyone who has been through spiritual training will know what I mean. For those who have not, think of it as a stepping up of responsiveness to spiritual energy which heightens your awareness and, at the same time, your emotional sensitivity. And that is the problem. Your feelings are being intensified just when you have to learn to detach yourself from identification with them. I was going through a process, common on the path, of being opened up and exposed to the glories of the spiritual world while having to live and function in this one. But that is the test. It is easy to be emotionally balanced when you are unchallenged but you have only learnt your lesson when your feathers remain unruffled even in a force 10 gale.

We all come from the heavenly planes so we are not human beings so much as spiritual beings in human bodies, which is why the evolution/intelligent design debate has always seemed to me rather to miss the point, as I mentioned in an earlier chapter. We were created in the spiritual world and that is our true home. We may descend to the earth to further our unfoldment but this is not where we belong. As a result of my contact with the Masters, I was becoming much more aware of the reality of this, and their warning that I should try to remain on an even keel was a necessary one, as an awareness of otherwordly origins can be unsettling to an immature mind. Similarly the advice not to resist ugliness was important for me to hear then, since that is what my attachment to beauty was making me do. Instead of appreciating beauty and then moving on, I was letting my feeling for it make me reject all that did not match up to its standards, and this rejection was inevitably resulting in pain and frustration. Following the Master's instruction, I did **seek to understand ugliness** and what I understood was that in truth there is not beauty and ugliness, there is the real and the unreal with the latter being what derives from the separate self. It was easy to see that one should not compare but take everything on its own terms (those are the sort of everyday words uttered by wise grandmothers everywhere), less easy to understand that the unreal was, well, unreal and only given reality by our focussing attention on it. By reacting to ugliness as ugliness, in other words, by resisting it, I was in a sense validating it.

April 4th 1979

I was told that it was very important that I always remembered the Creator, keeping Him in my thoughts at all times. Throughout the day I should constantly visualise a white light surrounding and protecting me. This is a very crucial period for me and I was vulnerable to attacks from outward evil that would affect my thoughts if I let it. If antagonistic thoughts did arise I should dispel them by concentrating on the Masters. I had to do my work in the market but should remain unattached to it. What we needed would be provided. When surrounded by many people during the day, I should endeavour not to let their vibrations affect me, something I could do by centring myself in the Masters and focussing on the white light surrounding and protecting me. I was told that I should listen to Michael as he was being directed by the

Masters.

I'm going to play devil's advocate for a moment here as I am sure that some people reading these transcriptions of the Masters' talks might say to themselves. "Hold on a minute. The situation here is that we have an older man claiming to go into trance as the medium for supposed spiritual beings who tell the young and inexperienced person with whom he is living to love him and listen to what he is saying as he is being directed by higher powers. This is deeply suspicious. In fact it's a plain case of dishonesty and manipulation". That's an entirely logical and reasonable point of view. It's also entirely wrong.

I may have been young when this took place but I wasn't a fool. I was quite aware of the possibility of deception. My intelligence and powers of observation were not lulled into insensibility because of the extraordinary nature of what was happening to me nor did I suspend judgement because I felt flattered at being spoken to like this by exalted spiritual beings. In fact that only caused me to be more alert to the chance of some kind of fraud, conscious or unconscious, on Michael's part. For that's what it would have amounted to. He would have had to have been a fraud and one of a fairly nasty kind. My six or seven month acquaintance with him up to the start of the talks made that seem very improbable and my twenty one year friendship with him thereafter showed it to be completely impossible. As for him doing this on an unconscious level, I suppose I can see the theoretical possibility but then his unconscious must have been of a superhuman quality. The Masters could see into my heart. They answered unasked questions. They revealed to me things about myself that I wasn't aware of but could see were absolutely true. Their authority, wisdom and love were not of this world. Their voices were not Michaels's and nothing like Michael's and their vocabulary was not his either. On top of all that the power of their presence left no room for disbelief or uncertainty. The sceptic may be convinced either that Michael was a fraud or that his unconscious was somehow involved or that, given something of a supernatural nature might have been going on, it was deceptive spirits amusing themselves and feeding off the attention they were given. All of these things do happen, there's no question about it. In the end, however, to have been a witness to these proceedings was to have any doubts dispelled like dew before the blaze of the early morning sun and I can only hope that something of that comes through in these pages.

The Masters told me to love Michael because without that kind of fraternal bond between us our life together would not have worked. The love they required us to have was one that demanded mutual support and unity of purpose. It was a spiritual fellowship, a recognition that we were fellow disciples of the same Masters. They told me to listen to Michael because he was older and more experienced than me and because he was being directed by them in how to handle me, and I can see that I needed careful handling at that time. I had to be guided, encouraged, prevented from getting swollen-headed, kept in the world, detached from the world, opened up, protected and goodness knows what else. Anyone who thinks spiritual training is a soft option knows nothing about it. I resisted and rebelled much of the time. In time honoured fashion I wanted to run before I could walk. I thought I knew better and I was impatient.

The sorts of things Michael had to tell me were not radical and certainly not things of a personal nature. They were more to do with keeping my feet on the ground, living in the world and not becoming over-balanced on the spiritual side with a consequent rejection of anything material or worldly. It seems absurd to recall now but he had an innocent liking for Gilbert and Sullivan which I thought quite inappropriate in a spiritual person who should stick to Bach, Palestrina, Indian ragas and the like. I exaggerate but only a little. As the reader might have guessed, I was in danger of becoming a bit of a spiritual prig and it was part of Michael's job to earth me. In fact, the Masters described it in such a way on more than one occasion. In my defence, though, I must add that behind my apparent puritanical attitude was a love of purity and truth which often seemed to be in danger of being trampled underfoot in the world. I felt I had to stand up for what I believed in but secretly I was frequently motivated by fear of losing it myself. I still feel one must stand up for the truth but now I realise that one must also learn to have perfect trust in God who knows full well what He is doing.

It's such a simple thing to be told **always to remember the Creator**. Too simple for us moderns sometimes, especially for the metaphysical snobs among us for whom it is non-duality or nothing. It's really rather strange that the idea of God has become almost part of the second division of spirituality in some circles. If there was ever anyone who had realised the absolute non-dualistic truth (rather than just identifying with a mental concept of it), it was the Masters but they did not disdain the personal God. I have come across numerous people who, when they learn of Vedanta or Zen Buddhism or some other non-dualistic system which teaches (correctly) that the human spirit is one with the transpersonal universal spirit, seem to forget or ignore that there is a personal God too and that, although that may not be the absolute highest state, it is still infinitely higher than their little selves. In fact, insofar as the manifested universe, of which they are a part, is concerned, it is the highest state. This is because these people have become idolaters of Brahman, the Absolute. They have formed a mental construct and confuse that with the reality. They mistake the idea for the truth behind it and then base their thoughts, words and actions on conformity to the idea. If your behaviour is in any way considered and not totally spontaneous then it is false. You are acting a part. There is a division between you, the subject, and your thought, the object, and that means you are not living in reality. Here the Masters, recognising the tendency in us moderns to dispense with God in the name of a supposed higher spirituality, issue the necessary corrective, reminding us that God is real and it is through love of God and constant remembrance of the Creator that one rises out of the world of self-centred thought into true spiritual awareness. If you think you can transcend the personal by denying the personal, you will end up in a mind created thoughtform of genuinely empty emptiness, not the true metaphysical Void beyond mind that may be no-thing but encompasses and gives rise to all things.

I am well aware that people point to Buddhism as a religion without God and think that because the Buddha denied God you do not need God in order to walk the spiritual path. Buddhism is certainly a non-theistic religion but the Buddha did not deny God. He simply chose not to talk about Him, and he did so because he wanted to bypass the numerous concepts about God existing at that time and reach the reality beyond them. He came at a time when Vedic religion and ritual had ossified to the point of complete conventionality, and he had to break through that fixed mindset in order to present a new and practical approach to the realisation of non-dualistic truth. For this he chose not to name or attempt to define that which is beyond name and definition. Others may name it whilst still knowing perfectly well that it is beyond any limitation that the naming of it might imply.

The Buddha pointed to the supreme reality beyond God in His aspect as Creator and he referred to this simply as the Unborn, Unmade and Uncompounded. He had realised the truth behind this description but it would be monumental arrogance on our part to think we can dispense with the Creator merely because we incline to the belief (which might be true but in our case is still just a belief) that the ultimate ground of existence is pure unqualified being which is beyond even Him. Those who reject God in order to attain the transpersonal Godhead will be left with neither, as fundamentally the rejection of God is an act of ego however much we may dress it up in intellectual rationalising. Of course, ultimately speaking, God as Creator is associated with the world of form and we must transcend identification with form in all its aspects, including the aspect of mind, in order to know and to be truth. But we do not do that by denying or rejecting it. When Jesus, speaking as the universal Christ, said "None cometh to the Father except through me", he was making a similar point. Western imitators of the Buddha need to understand that there is no enlightenment without oneness with God and there is no oneness with God if you deny Him. Indeed there is no oneness with God if you do not love Him. How could there possibly be?

To say that God has a personal aspect does not mean He is a person. What we can say is that the Impersonal Absolute, which as pure being has no form, individualises as God with form and this whole manifested universe is an expression of that individualisation. God both transcends the universe and is present within every atom, and, in a similar way, He can be said to have personhood as the Creator even though, in His essence and ultimate state, He is the Unborn, Unmade and Uncompounded. This personhood can be known and it manifests itself to us as His loving presence.

By remembering God you are not forgetting Him. By making a conscious effort to lift yourself up to His presence, you are creating a channel through which something of the divine presence can enter into you and begin the process of transformation. If you find it helpful to use an image as an aid to remembrance that is fine, as long as you bear in mind that the image is not the thing. It is a vessel which can act as a holder of the divine light but is not itself the source of the light. I once asked the Masters how I could **remember the Creator.** After all, if you're not careful you can end up just thinking the word 'God' in your mind, which is of some but perhaps not very much use. They told me to try to **imagine His presence in your heart**. It is the creative imagination that is the key. That does not mean that what you imagine is imaginary. God is there. Through your imagination you are permitting yourself to perceive that. You are opening yourself up to what lies beyond yourself.

Once again the Masters warned me about attack from evil forces and this time gave me a technique to protect myself. I know it's hard for those conditioned by contemporary ways of thinking to believe in such things and you can rationalise it away by saying that all evil is ignorance which, as far as it goes, is perfectly correct. After all, if any being knew the truth it would know that by harming another it harms itself. It would know that there is no separation, and the basis of the illusion of evil is belief in the illusion of separation. But spiritual powers of darkness, fallen beings if you like, do exist and they do seek to divert human beings away from the light because the more humanity walks in the path of light, the less power these dark forces have. They gain power by absorbing energy but they can only absorb what you might think of as contaminated energy, energy lowered in vibration from its original purity by negative emotion. So they seek to create antagonism by adversely influencing the mind. If you are aware of this you can recognise it for what it is, not identify with it and pay it no attention. Or else you can dispel it by calling on a higher power, **by concentrating on the Masters.** The visualisation of a white light will create a protecting barrier, what the Masters called an armour of light, which will make it harder for evil influences to gain entry. This works by creating a field of energy of a higher frequency than that of the evil forces and one that they therefore cannot penetrate. Of course, there may still be chinks in the armour, depending on the strength of your visualisation and your own imperfect thoughts and emotions so it is wise to guard against these too.

In case this sounds a little alarmist let me once again assure the more nervous amongst my readers that there is no cause for concern. Nothing in the universe can affect us unless we let it. These forces may exist but they are powerless against a pure heart and can only influence us if we choose to allow them do so. Do not fear evil and do not seek to fight it but be aware of it and manifest the truth.

If you doubt this, and regard talk of evil forces as superstitious fairy tales that should have been outgrown by any rational human being long ago, please ask yourself whether that view might be based on intellectual arrogance. Possibly you are a materialist who acknowledges the existence of nothing beyond what can be perceived by the physical senses or scientific instruments, a very curious and limiting point of view based on a preconceived idea and a denial of your own humanity, or the fullness of it anyway. If you acknowledge higher dimensions to life and think of yourself as a spiritual person but still cannot accept the existence of evil, possibly because you believe everything to be part of God and there can be no evil in God, then you must ask yourself why there is evil in the world and why all religious teachings acknowledge its existence. Jesus cast out evil spirits, Buddha was tempted by Mara. You may dismiss these as myths but if you examine religious history you will find countless other examples. It is certainly correct to say that everything is a part of God and there is no evil in God but it must also be acknowledged that God gave created beings free will which gives them the possibility to reject Him. When free will becomes self will then evil can arise.

April 6th 1979

The Master told me that I had made good progress recently. Henceforth I should be strict in my diet, eating plain foods (no richness), and milk, fruit and nuts. It was important during this period to remain in good health so I should not neglect that. He said that I could rely on my instinct which was highly evolved but then added that I was sometimes a little self-important. I should work hard and remain united with Michael. He said that because of the progress made the Masters were able to come closer to me and as always he concluded by sending love and blessings.

April 7th 1979

The Master said that Michael and I had earned peace and rest for a while before we embarked on the next stage which would involve rigid discipline, hard work and learning, reading and meditation. He said that it was most important for me to be true to my conscience and to follow my instinct which was on a high level. When I asked how to concentrate he told me to concentrate on concentrating and added that I should not be airy-fairy. I had

asked to come back to the world and I must come down to earth if I was to be of service in the future.

Practical and theoretical spirituality can be rather different. We seek out profound philosophies and arcane esoteric lore but then are told to work hard, eat properly and look after our health!

I had asked about concentration because I found it difficult, which for most of us it is. I recall that initially I did not find the answer at all satisfying but then when I considered the matter more fully I realised that it was the only possible answer. There are no shortcuts. You learn to do something by doing it. There is no other way. How prosaic that sounds but how true.

Please note in both talks the slight praise immediately followed by the mild censure. As is the case with any teacher, the guru's job is to encourage but also to point out weaknesses and sometimes, it seems, to do both in the same breath. I was pleased to be told that my instinct was on a high level but the moment for self-satisfaction came and went rather quickly.

I have one more remark to make on this pair of talks. The Master really did use the word airy-fairy.

Chapter 10

What is the Soul?

In the previous talk I was informed that I had **asked to come back to the world.** In the orthodox Christian view that has formed so much of Western thought there is, despite possible hints in the New Testament, no concept of the pre-existence of the soul so such a statement would be instantly rejected. For those schooled in the scientific materialism that has been an increasingly dominant force in the world since the 17th century, there is not even a soul as such so the (to that way of thinking) far-fetched idea of asking to come back to the world would be seen as quite preposterous. Only in Eastern religion would this idea find a degree of acceptance but even there the soul is usually regarded as a largely passive partaker in the inevitable cycle of births and deaths, bound to the wheel by karma and necessity.

The Masters took reincarnation for granted. For them it was a fact and they spoke of it as an assumed reality. This does not mean that they were Hindus or Buddhists or that they belonged to any particular school of thought. They did not identify with any earthly religion or philosophy. They never expressed an opinion or a point of view. They had no opinions or points of view. They simply saw things as they were. For them the intuition had become the fully functioning direct insight, the knowing by being of an enlightened soul. So for them reincarnation just was what is, namely the means whereby the soul gains complete knowledge of itself, and, through the experience of limitation, eventually realises ultimate freedom.

With regard to my opening paragraph, it is true that reincarnation is much more generally accepted in the West today than it was in the past but it is still not very well understood. For instance, what reincarnates? To understand that we have to understand a little spiritual anatomy and know that a human being consists of spirit, soul and personality. Broadly speaking, this translates as the divine spark within us, our individual consciousness and the thinking, feeling and physical self with which we are familiar. Spirit cannot incarnate directly (that is, in its pure state it cannot descend into the dense vibrations of the physical universe) and must do so through its vessel or intermediary created on a lower plane for that purpose, the soul. The difference between these two can be a little difficult to grasp but I can sum it up best by expressing their respective realisations as "I am Life" and "I am one with Life". Thus spirit exists on the plane of absolute non-duality, beyond all form and distinction where there is not my spirit or your spirit, there is only spirit. On the other hand the soul has its home on a spiritual plane of what can be thought of as subtle form where qualities and attributes make an appearance, and where there is my soul and your soul but with no sense of separation between them. For the soul, there is you and there is me and we are one. For spirit there is no you or me, there is only oneness.

To experience life in the material world (for whatever reason - the repayment of karma, the opportunity of growth, the chance for service or all of these), the soul must descend from its relatively high state into duality, taking on a new mind and body, the nature of which will be determined by its karma. Once incarnate, in the vast majority of cases, it forgets its true self (functioning as it does through a newly formed physical brain), and may experience at best only occasional flashes of its true nature. From what the Masters told me not all of the soul descends into incarnation. Indeed the greater part may remain on its own level. This makes intuitive sense. Are we not sometimes aware of a greater self existing behind our everyday awareness? It is probable that only as much of the soul descends as is necessary for it to complete its life mission successfully. Incidentally, when I talk about the soul descending, I am obviously not talking literally but the idea of up and down is time-honoured and symbolically satisfactory.

So, to answer our earlier question, it is the soul, or part of it, that reincarnates. The personality with which we identify, the name and form which we believe to be us, exists for one lifetime only. It may persist for a period after death but eventually the experience it has gathered is absorbed by the soul and it is returned to the elements from which it was formed prior to birth. Nothing good is lost, self-awareness is not lost, the fruits of its labours are assuredly not lost but the form our personality took dissolves and returns to its source. Therefore I, Mr X, cannot say that I was Mr Y in a previous life. The soul that incarnates as Mr X may also have incarnated as Mr Y but that is not at all the same thing.

An obvious question to ask at this point is why the spirit need incarnate. If it is perfect in the first place why can it not simply stay on its own level and avoid the world of suffering? The answer is that spirit may be perfect but God seeks ever greater levels of perfection. He seeks to become more than He is. This is why He creates and that is why he creates self-conscious individuals out of Himself. He multiplies Himself. That is the answer on the macrocosmic scale. On the level of individual souls, incarnation is part of the process that makes the pre-lapsarian Adam into the risen Christ. It is the means whereby created beings may become gods. Only in the world of form, matter and duality, the world of time and change, can the soul gain the experience it needs to develop its nature so that ultimately it too can become a fully conscious creator. We descend into the darkness of matter to gain experience and we become released from the necessity to incarnate in matter when we have consciously transcended the duality that is inherent in the material world. In so doing we unite the whole of creation, unmanifest and manifest, spiritual and material, within ourselves. To sum up, Adam was unconsciously one with God. We are consciously separate from God. Christ is consciously one with God.

The "I' that had **asked to come back to the world** was the soul. It is the soul that dwells **where all is poetry, music and colour**, a description which is to be understood as referring to a state of consciousness as much as a place. This is not the Summerland of popular spiritualism which is an idealised and mentally created version of Earth existing on the astral plane, the common term for the psychic realm of immediate post-mortem experience where the personality exists in much the same form as it did on Earth, albeit free of physical limitations. As a world of form, the astral plane is considered esoterically as part of the material world. It is, in its way, a thought-formed extension of that world, though without the apparently impermeable solidity of physical matter. It is not **the heavenly plane** of spiritual oneness which is our true home from whence we descend and to which we return after our brief immersion in physical matter.

Death releases us from the physical body. That is all it does. Where we go after death depends on our state of consciousness. Eventually we will return to the soul for a spell prior to taking a new birth on the physical plane (except in the rare cases where the soul has achieved liberation) but that will take a longer or shorter period which is determined by the speed with which we are able to shed the emotional habits, mental conditioning and personality identification of the preceding lifetime. Spiritualist literature speaks of opportunities to reassess our past life and doubtless these exist. We are presented with the truth about ourselves but the only judge is our self. We cannot escape the consequences of our actions, and probably of our thoughts as well, but there is no punishment and no hell, not as traditionally depicted anyway. Planes of darkness and isolation do exist but these are reflections of darkened and self-centred consciousness and those who find themselves in such places do so because of their own state of consciousness. In the post-mortem world like attracts like and the outer reflects the inner but God is merciful and no-one is left bereft of help (though some may reject it), whether it be by angels or ministering guides whose task it is to rescue and redeem the fallen.

There are multitudinous spheres of consciousness in the world beyond the physical plane, there being considerably more vertical extension to the world than horizontal, but spiritual geography can be roughly summed up by envisaging an ascent through planes of form, mind and abstract thought onwards to planes of colour, light, undivided consciousness and then the formless oneness of pure spirit. The soul may be conceived of as existing at a midway point on this scale above form and mind but below spirit. It is the seat of individual consciousness, built up through long incarnationary experience to become a thing of power, wisdom and beauty but it must eventually be renounced (some traditions actually speak of its destruction) before liberation into spirit can be attained and the individual merge into universal oneness thereby enriching both itself and God which at this point is almost the same thing. This merging does not imply the loss of individuality but its transcendence.

The spiritual seed incarnates in the fertile soil of the earth in order for it to develop and grow. It rises upwards, stretching towards the light, unfurling its leaves. It blossoms and flowers and eventually reaches the point at which its fully ripened fruit can be harvested. Then comes the final moment when the fruit must effectively be destroyed so that its virtue may be released. The grain is ground to make bread. The grape is crushed to make wine.

When we walk down the street every person we met is God. This is not an easy concept to grasp. The reality seems so very different. But here is the truth. The Unmanifest Absolute manifests as God, and the Creator God creates to become more than He is. It challenges the imagination to conceive how the infinite and eternal can become more than it already is but it is so. In order to create, the Undivided One divides becoming spirit and matter which are the Father and Mother of the Universe. Out of the substance of the Mother, the Father forms all the worlds, both outer and inner, from which you might correctly infer that every particle of creation has divine consciousness within it. Out of His own essence, God creates self-conscious individuals (souls) who are the means whereby He experiences the world from within the world. These souls, through their experience in matter, grow and evolve until they finally transcend their limited sense of individuality and realise their true divine nature. From God's point of view we are created with self-consciousness because otherwise creation would be static. There could be no growth and no expansion. From our point of view we are self-conscious because otherwise we could not freely participate in creation. We could be known but not know.

So in one sense every person truly is God. In another sense, though, nobody is God until they have realised themselves to be so which they can only do by ceasing to be themselves. God gave us a self so that we could know Him. We must voluntarily give back that self before we can know Him. The gift of self-consciousness is a risk. It can lead to unimagined glories. It can lead to darkness, fragmentation and isolation. The choice is ours. At this stage in planetary history it might appear that fragmentation is winning the day, but it could be that the downward forces are being brought out and given their head in order for them to be dealt with. A great cleansing needs to take place but it can only do so when everything is expressed and out in the open. This too is a risk. If the process goes too far it could gain a momentum which would make it unstoppable and could only end in destruction. But if God, through the men and women sent into this world (because that is how He acts, through us), can cause enough people to turn from darkness to light, then this critical mass will raise up the entire planet. It will reorient the human race from the path we seem set on (which at best can only result in a transitory and superficial happiness) to one that leads to what is truly our heart's desire, whether we know it consciously or not. There are souls at many stages of consciousness in the world today. It might be thought that the general level is not that high, but I think it is higher than it could appear to the jaundiced eye as the general trends tend to mask the truth on an individual level. In any case, every soul at whatever stage is a child of God and can only find true fulfilment through obedience to its divine nature. This may manifest itself in different ways but no human being can find an authentic and lasting happiness except through reaching beyond self.

Chapter 11

The Routine of Spiritual Life

The talks from the Masters continued on a near nightly basis and, as there is a certain similarity to them at this point, I shall set a few of them down here without comment until the end. It may be that the reader will find them a little repetitive but the basic truths of the spiritual life are few in number. We may easily grasp them with the mind but they need to be thoroughly absorbed and meditated on until they become part of the fabric of one's being, and not merely known, however well, on a factual/intellectual level. That is actually one of the problems of our time. Spiritual truths are widely known by many people who have not internalised them. They may think they have, they may have been following the path for years, even decades, they may even be teachers, but it remains external to them, just words and thoughts which they may know as well as any university professor knows his subject but which have never caught fire.

April 9th 1979.

The Master said that he was gratified by the fact that my intuition had picked up their messages and that I had passed them on to Michael. He said that henceforth Michael would have to change completely his mode of living. He had led a full and active life with many experiences but now that must change and we must both settle down to a life of quiet discipline with as little as possible outside disturbance or distraction. When I passed on to Michael what had been impressed on my intuition I should always do so with patience, love and understanding. He had his lessons to learn. That was my lesson and this was the means whereby I could learn it.

April 11th 1979
I was told not to dwell on the past or anticipate the future but live in the present. This was a time of great learning and change and I should not be frightened by things that might happen as I was guarded and protected.

April 13th 1979
The Master said that he came to encourage me and to tell me that he was pleased with my efforts. Michael's life and mine had converged on a similar point and we should work together in love and harmony. We had been together in the past and would be again in the future. I asked if it was wrong of me to try to ease Michael away from the Catholic Church and he replied that he had told me before to trust my instinct. He said that the Catholic Church, like any outward form of religion, was good for souls on a certain level but it was time to lead Michael away from it into a new and higher understanding of life. He told me not to be intolerant but to do this with love and patience.

April 16th 1979
I was told that my life must continue in a routine, in fact, until I left my physical body. The Master said that they always knew what was in my mind but it was up to me to broach a subject if I wanted to discuss it. They impressed things on me but it was my responsibility to act on them. When I speak to Michael about things that I thought important I should at all times do so calmly so he would know that what I was saying came from deep intuition and not petty caprice. No-one can accept something that he is told angrily even if in his heart he knows that it is true. I asked about our work in the market and how we should approach it. The Master said that I should not ignore what happens in the market but must not get upset by it either. Simply point out calmly where I thought Michael had erred without seeking to hammer home my point. Say what I had to say once and then move on

without expecting an instant result.

Our daily work in the antiques market had caused a little friction between us. When I had first joined Michael in his business I soon picked up a reasonable knowledge of early English pottery and porcelain. I appreciated its delicate beauty and liked the connection to the past that working with it brought. I also enjoyed the buying side of the business and was even moderately good at it. I had a reasonable eye and didn't mind a haggle. We had no car so mostly went to local markets at unearthly hours to buy, though sometimes we travelled further afield if a colleague was going on a buying trip and had room for us in his car. All of that was fun. I did not much like the selling though. Michael, however, was a born salesman. He loved engaging with the public and looked on it as a challenge to convince someone to buy something they didn't know they wanted. I would frequently cringe inside when I heard him trying to force through a deal, and whereas I would always tell a customer if a piece was damaged or restored, he would not mention anything unless asked. I thought this dishonest and we had, shall we say, words about it on more than one occasion. He would justify himself by saying that he had written on the price label 'a/f' which stood for 'as found', implying it was being sold in the same condition in which it had been bought, whatever that might be, and it was up to the customer to see that and ask about it. I pointed out to him that was ridiculous as most people would have no idea when 'a/f' meant, and anyway were we not supposed to be leading a spiritual life and so shouldn't we be whiter than white in our business dealings? Hence my question to the Masters and hence their reply.

Michael had a lesson that you cannot separate your spiritual and your so-called normal lives, but I had a lesson to transmit what I knew without attachment to it. I had to learn not to let wrongdoing upset me, and I had to learn to teach without demanding an instant result that was personally gratifying. There's no doubt that when I reprimanded Michael for his over-enthusiastic salesmanship I was motivated more by irritation and embarrassment than a real concern for his spiritual welfare. I wanted him to do things in the right way for my sake not his.

I really would not have put it past the Masters to have engineered these situations. Many times I have seen evidence of their power to cause change in the outer world, and I don't doubt for a single second their skill in bringing human failings to the surface and forcing a resolution. They *can* do more or less anything they wish. What they will never do is infringe free will. God did not just create humanity with free will. The specific point of this creation was free will so no spiritual being will ever go against the free will of another.

The talk of April 11th was longer than the section I have selected but I include that bit because it contains one of the cardinal rules of the spiritual path. The rule not to live in time. Pure consciousness lives out of time since it exists above the phenomenal levels of change and becoming. Time is allied to the passing of mental states so if the mind is still there is no awareness of time, there is only the present moment and that is all there ever is. This is the *ABC* of spirituality, known by thousands, taught by hundreds, lived by few. In *'The Boy and the Brothers'* and *'Towards The Mysteries'*, the books I mentioned earlier, which I regard as coming from the same source as the Masters who spoke to me[3], there are four basic rules given on how to lead a spiritual life. These are:

Be simple.
Live from moment to moment.
Blind the eye of attachment.
Be individual without being individualistic.

I was never given rules as such but the Masters would constantly mention the first three of these as essential to spiritual progress, and the fourth was also implied by them on various occasions. To take just the first in the list, they always emphasised the virtues of simplicity. That's not to say one should be simple in the sense of abandoning intelligence but one should be uncomplicated, more non-intellectual than unintellectual. Our mentally based culture fails to see that normal thought divides and complicates but there is a mind in the heart which sees directly and with complete wholeness. To access this mind in the heart requires one to have the openness of a child as in the famous words of Jesus, to have an attitude of faith and mental innocence. Many spiritual seekers delve into all the minutiae of esoteric and metaphysical philosophy and lose sight of the essential because of an obsession with unearthing, understanding and, most of all, possessing all the details. They need to let go of all that and embrace simplicity without the fear this might mean foolishness or ignorance. Where there is thought there is always ego but with true simplicity there is none. To be simple means to be spontaneous and natural – it's as simple as that and perhaps in keeping with the subject I should leave it there.

Be individual but not individualistic. This might seem an odd thing for supposed teachers of non-duality to say but the Masters' version of this sometimes misunderstood doctrine was not one that denied the individual soul. Life is one but God created us as individuals and it is as individuals that we win eternal life. Those who deny that the self has any kind of reality at all are confusing levels. Life may be one in absolute terms but the absolute is not all there is. If it were then nothing would ever have arisen and although some philosophies do indeed preach that nothing has ever arisen, they are only able to do so because it has!

The remarks about the Catholic Church relate to discussions Michael and I had been having about organised religion and its place in the mystical life. Although not born a Catholic, Michael had converted in order to become a monk in the Benedictine order and he retained a soft spot for that way of life even though he had abandoned it because he found it restricting. But he still tended to idealise religion and overlook its faults whereas I was more inclined to view as it was, and as it was now rather than as it might have been in the past in a possibly purer form. Although he had turned away from it himself, Michael still considered that organised religion continued to have a role to play in modern spirituality, but I thought that one needed to go beyond it and that it would bind its members as much as it would release them. I did occasionally go to church with Michael and could respond to the ritual and traditional element, but my feeling was that Catholicism, or certain aspects of it at least, tended to crush the human spirit with its authoritarian dogmas and conviction that it alone offered a path to salvation. Like so many human institutions (and, despite its beliefs to the contrary, that is basically what it is), it mixes good with bad but it has always seemed to have had as much love of power as it has love of God. History shows that very clearly. No one could ever deny the holiness of the great saints of the church or the devotion of many modern day practitioners or the beauty of the liturgy or even the profundity of many of its teachings, but I believe with the Masters that there is **a higher understanding of life.**

There is a school of thought whose adherents are known as Traditionalists which maintains that membership of an orthodox religion is essential for spiritual progress, and that anything outside of that is a false path. I think that the Traditionalists, especially the founder of the school, René Guénon, have made many extremely pertinent criticisms of the modern age (which anyone of insight must surely see is completely out of step with reality), but I disagree with them on this. I share their concerns with the materialistic tendencies of modern science and the many counterfeit forms of spirituality that have arisen to fill the gap as religion has declined and which are, as they correctly observe, psychically rather than spiritually based[4]. However, even if you disregard the point that truth is beyond form and any religion is necessarily part of the world of form, the fact remains that religions, whether divinely inspired or not, are as subject to the corroding and corrupting influence of human thought and ego as much as anything else. Certainly the Traditionalists believe in what they call the transcendent unity of religions, and they are also clear that exoteric religion, i.e. the outer practices and beliefs, is not enough. There must be an esoteric understanding as well, an appreciation of the metaphysical truths that lie behind and unite all religions despite their outer differences. That is well and good but to restrict the living and eternally self-renewing spirit to channels through which it has operated in the past, none of which is less than 1,500 years old, particularly in this time at the tail end of the Kali Yuga (as the Traditionalists themselves would be the first to point out) when all spiritual forms are decaying, is odd to say the least. It is clear that most, if not all, of the cults and sects that have arisen over the last century or so are man-made diversions of very little worth, but we should remember the words of Jesus, that "the spirit bloweth where it listeth" meaning that the spirit of God can never be pinned down or limited to any particular container, none of which could ever hold more than a tiny part of it. Surely the fact that none of the great revealers of religion of the past rested content with the religions of their day tells us something too. Did Mohammed, did Jesus, did Buddha? Assuredly not; rather they were all renewers and revitalisers of the timeless spiritual impulse. You might argue that they were sent with a special mission from God and that what might apply for them does not apply for us but I would counter that they were exemplars too and that a major part of their special mission was to demonstrate to us how we should be. They themselves said as much.

So much the Traditionalists say is good and true, and they are an excellent corrective to the materialism, both as usually understood and the spiritual variety, of the modern world. Guénon's identification of it as a world concerned with quantity rather than quality surely hits the target smack in the centre. No one reveals with such clarity as him how the modern worldview is based almost entirely on the horizontal axis of reality and totally neglects the vertical, transcendent, one with often disastrous results. Even so, the tendency that some Traditionalists have to reject almost everything that the modern world has brought is a shame since it probably restricts their influence to those who already agree with them. For instance, their criticism that science is responsible for the atheism and materialism we see all around us is a valid one up to a point, but no-one could deny that science has also swept away much of the superstition, obscurantism and ignorance of the past as well as revealing an enormous amount about the physical world. Moreover, the levelling of humanity that has come about since the 18th century may have reduced much human behaviour to the proverbial lowest common denominator but the social reforms that were responsible for it have introduced a far greater degree of fairness and justice to the world than ever existed in the past. Do the Traditionalists really think that the elitism of the past and suppression of the masses was something that could or should have lasted indefinitely? I'm quite sure they do not but one might get that impression from some of their writings.

Notwithstanding their claim to see things just as they are, there is a strong Islamic influence on the Traditionalists and I think this is evident both in their rejection of reincarnation and their over-concern with orthodoxy. But, despite my stated reservations, I would encourage anyone to seek out their literature, especially the books of René Guénon which, in addition to their superb metaphysical insight, offer surgically sharp dissections of the flaws of the modern age, whether it be the limitations of the scientific approach or the narcissistic shallowness of New Age spirituality. Perhaps in these works more than anywhere else the basic flaw of the modern world, that it denies a transcendent reality and so has lost all sense of the sacred, is plainly spelt out. Read them with discrimination though. They are a very necessary counterbalance to prevailing opinion in the modern world but they in turn need to be balanced by a little of that prevailing opinion.

April 17th 1979
The guide sent his love and blessings. He told me not to get

complacent about these simple words and regard them as spoken in a perfunctory way as they had great force. He said that I should now prepare for my future work. People would come to me and listen to the knowledge that I would be given by the Masters. I should help them as much as I could but never regard myself in a superior light because of that. I was only giving what I had been given. I could not work alone for quite some time but should work closely with Michael. He said that one day this form of communication would cease but they would transmit messages in another way though he could not give full details now. Later on I was told that everything I did here had a bearing on my training. The exercises, the companionship with Michael, even the cooking and the selling. He said it did not matter so much what I said in selling as things would be sold anyway but it was important that I talked to people and gained self-confidence. Reading aloud was also important, to teach me how to speak properly and give my voice the correct modulation. I must learn to speak with authority, not feebly but forcibly.

April 18th 1979

The Master advised me to keep a balanced approach to both joy and misery and not to get carried away by either. He told me to be like a steady boat, calm and unswayed by happiness or suffering, taking each as it comes and not being attached to the one or rejecting the other. I was young in earthly years but I must face life with greater maturity than would normally be expected of someone of my years. The Masters came to talk to me as often as they did to keep me "on the mark" and I must remember all the work they are doing (though gladly) on my behalf.

April 19th 1979

I was told that when my lower self is to the fore Michael's lower self will be too as the Masters have unified us for the purpose of teaching. So if I succumb to moodiness or irritation then precisely those things in Michael that cause me to react like that will be accentuated. The very things that annoy me will be strengthened if I allow myself to get annoyed by them but the converse is also true. If I conquer my moodiness and do not get annoyed by anything or anyone then those things that do upset me will disappear. I am too critical but I must learn to criticise only myself and love everything without a sense of superiority. The Masters have linked us and what one does the other will follow so if I wish Michael to act according to his higher nature then I should act according to mine. The Masters said I was fortunate in this as I was being given the opportunity to see myself reflected in a mirror and so could correct my errors more easily.

There is some quite profound teaching here. I have written of how certain aspects of Michael's behaviour would irk me and how I would react to these with irritation, annoyance and (yes, it must be admitted) sometimes superiority. I have also stated my belief that the Masters could manipulate Michael's behaviour if they so chose. This last talk went further when it was made clear that our spiritual teachers can create situations in which we ourselves bring out in others whatever it is we most dislike. It is actually a truism of the spiritual life to say that we will often encounter what we fear or what causes us pain, in effect what we seek to avoid. How else could we learn to overcome our fears than by facing them? This talk spelt that out as plainly as could be. The Masters were confronting me with my prejudices. They were offending my desire to appear loftily superior in public and they were doing it by causing me public embarrassment, which is precisely what happened in the antiques market when Michael would behave in a worldly, silly or mildly dishonest way as he often would. On these occasions, instead of reacting with patience and tolerance, which is what I knew I should have done, I would get angry with him, not necessarily outwardly but from the Masters' point of view if something is expressed or unexpressed makes no difference. If it is there, on any level, it is there. The ego is devious. I would justify my reaction by telling myself that Michael's behaviour was wrong and there is no doubt that it was but that was totally immaterial. My reactions to it were equally wrong. Here is a classic case of looking at the splinter in someone else's eye rather than the mote in one's own.

Knowing that I was wrong to react to the provocation and that it probably only existed to test me did not always help. You can know something intellectually but that in itself does not stop the irritation arising (to take this example) if one finds oneself in a situation that draws it forth. You cannot pretend it is not there if it is. You cannot suppress it as it will simply reappear in another form. So what do you do? I think the answer is to replace darkness with light. We all experience anger and annoyance for one reason or another but those on the spiritual path have to find a way to overcome this if they want to move forwards. They will be tested. You who are reading this will be tested. So what do you do? The response of the Masters to this question came in an earlier talk. They did not advise control or self-discipline (though nor would they have approved of a lack of these either) as that would have been a force based approach. Their approach was subtler and went deeper in that it did not seek to confront one energy with another similar, equal and opposite as in the irritation and the attempt to suppress it, but to replace a lower energy with a higher one. Their counsel was to **visualise a white light surrounding me. If antagonistic thoughts did arise I should dispel them by concentrating on the Masters.** In other words, raise your vibrations and do it principally through the imagination rather than the will. Of course, if all else fails then deep breathing and counting to ten will help as well!

The reason the Masters came to me was to train me to help others. That is what they told me. They did not say how, when or to what extent this would happen but that was the main reason they spoke to me. I imagine they were putting forth a lot of time and effort into the complicated process of talking to me in the way they did which would be hard to justify if it were only benefitting a single person. I am not saying that helping me was purely incidental but I'm sure it was not their sole purpose. But were they training me to be a spiritual teacher? That's what one might assume from the foregoing but I don't think they were in the traditional sense in which that word is understood. The concept of a new or Aquarian age has been hopelessly compromised by those of more enthusiasm, psychic over-sensitivity or just plain fantasy than spiritual perception but behind all the clouds, smoke, glamour and illusion it is possible there could be something real. In this new age, the old way of looking at teacher and disciple might need some adjustment. This does not mean that hierarchical differences are to be completely negated or ignored. These are a fact of nature and a reality in the spiritual world. What it possibly could mean is that the traditional guru/chela relationship might change and a new one come into being that operates as much along horizontal as vertical lines. In other words, is less authoritarian and functions more with the teacher being a sort of first among equals in a group of people who are learning and growing together. In this scenario the teacher does not sit on a pedestal as the all-knowing one but is a wayshower who clears a portion of the path for others to follow and then extends a hand back, consolidating his own position as he does so. Hesitant steps are already being made along these lines and if, as always happens, the old is being cast off before the new is properly formed, this might still be the start of what will become the norm in the Aquarian age.

Now I have no idea what the Aquarian age, if it exists, might entail and if anybody tells you they do I would advise you to treat them with caution. Nevertheless it does seem that something new is struggling to be born in the human mind. In astrology Aquarius means various things but equality and freedom are seen as two of its primary concerns. These have become increasingly important over the last fifty years, sometimes to excess but that's inevitable in a time of adjustment as we react to new energies in an unbalanced or unenlightened way. Translated in terms of spirituality, they imply a need for seekers to become more individual, wanting to know things for themselves and to depend less on an outer authority. This is good and necessary if we are to progress as a race but it has its attendant dangers too as, although one might fly higher, one might also fall further if one forgets the injunction to **be individual without being individualistic.** Virtues overemphasised can swiftly become faults and the ways of the future should build on the past, having learnt the lessons of the past not ignoring them. That is why, with an individual approach, an attitude of humility is so essential. To follow an individual path requires going beyond oneself as an individual and if that does not happen then the path will lead not up but down.

It is interesting that the Masters regarded many things not normally thought of as especially relevant to spirituality as having a bearing on the growth of the soul. As they said, **the exercises, the companionship with Michael, even the cooking and the selling** were all part of my training. They were not perhaps a major part but they had a role to play, which implies that many of the things we do in the course of our everyday life have the potential to be spiritually instructive if we react to them aright. In my case the exercises were just a few simple yoga exercises that I did as part of my evening routine and which I found helpful in establishing a harmonious atmosphere prior to meditation. A sort of tuning up, if you like. I recall that the Masters also encouraged good posture as something that was not only physically beneficial but even had an effect on the way one thought and acted. Hold yourself upright and you will find it easier to be an upright person. Similarly they considered the way one spoke to be important which is why they had advised me to practise reading aloud. By **correct modulation** I assumed they meant enunciating words correctly, unhurriedly and with clarity. At any rate that was the way they spoke. Their vocal delivery was strong, measured and assured, almost solemn on occasion but never in the slightest bit stiff or pompous. They didn't rush and they didn't hesitate. In the beginning was the Word. Sound creates but it must be uttered correctly to have its proper effect.

I don't remember what the cooking involved but it certainly was nothing special. Just the preparation of ordinary vegetarian meals but done with as much care and attention to detail as one could come up with at the end of the day. All little things but all part of a general attitude of mindfulness that is a prerequisite for anyone on the spiritual path. Isn't hewing wood and drawing water an integral part of Zen training? This was our equivalent.

The remark that it did not matter **what I said in selling as things would be sold anyway** echoes an earlier comment (on April 4th) that **I had my work to do in the market but should remain unattached to it. What we needed would be provided.** It is hard to have faith that if one sincerely dedicates oneself to the spiritual life then one's material requirements will be provided for. After all, there are plenty of impoverished good people in the world, are there not? We do not know what an individual's karma is or if even a nominally good person is in fact living a life in accordance with the laws of God and the requirements of their own higher self. We do not know if they have in effect "let go and let God" and submitted their life to the will of a higher power. However the Masters did quite categorically say that **what we needed would be provided** and that has been my experience over many years. That doesn't mean you can put your feet up and things will drop into your lap automatically. You still have to make some sort of effort (**I had my work to do in the market**) but if you truly dedicate your life to God then what you need will be provided. Of course what is provided is what you need and not necessarily a great deal more but what more do you need than that? Nowadays it seems to be becoming rather fashionable to say that it's all right for a spiritual person to be well off as long as he is not attached to his wealth. This is no doubt true and I am in no way decrying material comfort or saying that poverty is a prerequisite for spirituality. It is plainly evident that poverty can grind you down so there is no time for anything more than seeking to make ends meet. But might the, on the face of it, correct statement that there is nothing wrong with having money, it's the attachment to it that is wrong, sometimes be used as an excuse to have your cake and eat it? We may think we are not attached but is that really true? The Masters did tell me, and it's quite obvious anyway, that the more one has, the harder it is to give it up. Remember the story of the rich young man in the Bible who was undoubtedly devout and sincere in his desire to follow the spiritual path but who, when it came to it, could not renounce his riches.

So what you need will be provided. What you do not need you must be prepared to sacrifice. You may not have to but you must be fully prepared to. Sacrifice is an interesting word by virtue of the fact that its root meaning is to make holy. Sacrifice is certainly a fundamental requirement of the spiritual life and is called for at every level right up to the final one where it is the self that is sacrificed. The attitude behind sacrifice is as important as the deed itself. If something causes you pain to give up then you have not really given it up. You have not outgrown the desire for it, the attachment to it. Obviously this does not mean that one should not be prepared to give things up even if that does cause pain but it points to the fact that mere outer renunciation is not enough. The reason behind this requirement for sacrifice is that if you hold on to outer things then you cannot have God. Ultimately everything other than God is an outer thing, even your own soul, which is why, ultimately, you must give that up too. This is symbolised in an extraordinary powerful way by the crucifixion of Jesus. Here was man made perfect but he had one further step to take before reaching the final goal. The crucifixion is about much more than physical death. It is about the death of the 'I', the giving up of ego completely, and in the end this is the only true sacrifice, the one that all earlier ones have simply been a preparation for.

Chapter 12

The Role of the Spiritual Teacher

The Masters' purpose in coming to me was twofold. On the higher planes, which are our true home, we are part of what are known as group souls, which we can think of as extended spiritual families, these being bound together by their origin just as earthly ones are. Of course, the real origin of every human being is God and there is fundamental unity between every human being but, on the level of the created soul, these spiritual families exist. We do not all come into being at the same time or from the same spiritual source by which I mean that our primary keynote or quality may differ. The occult teaching on the seven rays is helpful here as long as one thinks of it symbolically and remembers that all seven rays stream forth from the one light. So, our divine source is God, our spiritual source, the source not of our being but of our individual soul, we can think of as being from one of these rays or archetypal forms of God, His different qualities as expressed in and through creation. This, to an extent, explains certain affinities between people.

I am touching briefly on this intriguing but rather complex subject of group souls only to point out that one of the reasons for the Masters' interest in me was that they and I (or some of them and I) formed part of the same spiritual family. Need I add that I am not claiming this puts me on a similar footing to them? An earthly family contains members of many different age groups and so it is with the spiritual version. And once again I must emphasise that the fact of group souls does not minimise in the slightest the essential unity of human beings. Not all the Masters who came to me were necessarily part of the same soul family as each other but they were all, as they frequently said of themselves, brothers, all one, and we are all brothers and sisters too.

So one reason the Masters came to me, or were able to come to me, was what you might call similarity of vibration, though naturally I had to be ready for their approach at both inner and outer levels too. The other reason, as I have stated, was to train me to share what I had been given, and I would like to devote the rest of this chapter to the subject of spiritual teachers.

To be a spiritual teacher is a noble calling and one to which an increasing number of people are drawn. This is all to the good as there are now more spiritual seekers than ever in search of guidance and direction. The trouble is that, whereas in other fields there are recognised authorities to confirm that an individual is qualified to teach, in this field, outside the main religions, there are not and this can cause problems.

Anyone desirous of teaching has to ask themselves why they want to teach. To put it bluntly, is it love of their fellow men and women or is it love of self, the desire to be the enlightened dispenser of wisdom? Very possibly there are elements of both in many cases. People are only human after all. Which is precisely the point. Spiritual teachers are only human. Even the greatest have their foibles (Ramana Maharishi apparently believed that his cow had attained enlightenment) and most of them are not the greatest. Most teachers (genuine ones, that is) are human personalities with some knowledge and experience of the soul. They are not the superhuman enlightened souls they are sometimes posited to be (those that say they are are the least likely to be so) but regrettably the idea has arisen in some circles that the spiritual teacher necessarily is enlightened and this has only added to the glamour that surrounds such people. Perhaps this comes from the Eastern idea of the omniscient God-realised guru as religious teachers in the West were not generally thought of in these exalted terms but maybe the concept of a spiritual teacher as someone with a little more experience and wisdom than most but by no means, on that account, perfect is the more realistic one.

There are spiritual teachers for all levels of student which is as it should be since the best teachers are often those who are not too far ahead of their students. Unfortunately some nowadays like to present themselves as having realised ultimate truth when they have simply had an experience of the soul which, let me remind you, is not the same as spirit even if it is frequently assumed to be so. Moreover to experience something is not to be it. That does not stop many seekers after truth who have experienced a partial awakening or contact with the soul imagining they have reached full enlightenment and are now qualified to lead others to the Holy Grail. That is far from the case. The eminent English mystic Wellesley Tudor Pole added a touch of realism to this topic when he made the point in his book 'A Man Seen Afar', written in the 1960s but no less applicable now, that a great many holy men and spiritual leaders were through the 1st gateway of initiation but no further.

I am not qualified to go into the subject of initiation at any great length. The Masters did mention it but only in very general terms, possibly because it is a subject in which too great an interest can lead to concern about spiritual status which can only have a detrimental effect on a student's progress. However there are, according to Theosophical and other teachings, five of these major openings up of awareness before one reaches the stage of adepthood, roughly corresponding to the episodes in the life of Christ (which, on one level, was a public re-enactment of the ancient mysteries) represented by his birth, baptism, transfiguration, crucifixion and resurrection. These are inner events quite distinct from any initiations given by gurus or occult organisations which may or may not have value. It seems perfectly reasonable to assume that the majority of spiritual teachers operating in public at the present time are those who are there to cater to the level of the average spiritual seeker of the moment, and it is the coming to birth of an individual Christ consciousness rather than its full efflorescence which is the goal for most contemporary aspirants. This marks that moment when the spiritual current is firmly established in the heart and one can rightfully be called a spiritual person not just someone who believes in or aspires to spirituality. It is the end of one path, the path of spiritual disciplines and meditation viewed as something to be practised by the goal-seeking separate self, but it is the beginning of another in which one does not so much tread as start to become the path.

Let me elaborate a bit on that. There is a certain sense in which there is no such thing as a spiritual person. Spirituality can only truly exist when there is no 'I' trying to be spiritual. This does not mean that in the early stages of the path, when you step out of the worldly current and start swimming upstream to the source, you should not try to cultivate the spiritual qualities. You absolutely must. You have to start from where you are and that is a very necessary first step and one that may last for a long time. However, from a higher perspective, this stage is only a preliminary one that must eventually lead to the realisation that the self can never be spiritual. Spirituality can only be when you transcend the illusion of a separate self. This might seem impossible and, in fact, it is impossible for the separate self but "with God all things are possible", and the paradoxical impasse is resolvable when you realise that all you need do is stop resisting oneness and maintaining the illusion of separation. In a practical sense you may do this by living out of time and **always remembering the Creator,** that's to say by practising the presence of God, keeping your source and true being in the forefront of consciousness at all times. This is becoming what you are. A word of warning though. To attempt to effortlessly be what you are before passing through the earlier stages of aspiration, purification, spiritual effort and discipline, what you might call the monastic stage in which the spiritual and material worlds are seen (falsely but usefully for the time being) as separate, will almost certainly only result in an imitation of being what you are by the ego. A dualistic counterfeit frequently seen nowadays in those who try to copy their concept of what is. You must purify the self before you can transcend it. The ego is an illusory construct fabricated by the mind but the unpurified ego cannot realise this fact except intellectually. The path must be trodden, every last step of it, before you can truly see that there is no path and that your point of arrival is no different to your point of departure. And this is why we need spiritual teachers.

I am not saying there are no teachers nearer the goal than might be implied by the quote from Tudor Pole above. However I would counsel against expectations being raised too high so as to avoid possible disappointment or, worse, disillusion. There are certainly some wise and saintly teachers in the world but most are not at that level and it is a sad fact that there are many charlatans, deceivers, self-deceivers, egotists and spiritual businessmen too. There are the relatively sincere but deluded and there are the just plain corrupt. Some of these may be perfectly able to give teachings which seem to echo those of the great Masters and saints, but the vibration behind these teachings is not the same and so the inner effect is not the same either. So choose your teacher wisely. It is often said that when the pupil is ready, the teacher appears. To make sure it is the right teacher who appears, be sure you are properly ready. Readiness means a pure desire for God. I use the word desire because in this case and coupled with the adjective pure, it is an appropriate one. It means that the heart wants answers as the dry earth wants rain. The pure heart is not in search of joy and happiness. It wants truth and truth is its right. If you follow a false teacher it is because of a falseness in you. That might sound a little harsh but it is a fact though, if you prefer, you could call it unripeness. Those who are attracted to such teachers are so because of what they hope to get out of them. Their desire is not pure but this is more than likely a stage through which we all must pass as we travel from ego to egolessness so there is no shame or cause for despair if you find that your esteemed guru has feet of clay. Learn the lesson that you must look beneath the surface and do so with eyes not blinded by want and then move on.

How can you identify a true teacher? I have already given one answer to this question and that is to make sure that your desire for a teacher is true. What do you want from the teacher? Your motive must be honest, your heart sincere. If that is not the case you are more than likely to be led astray and fall for the glamour of a false teacher. A true teacher will not promise you anything. He will not seek to mystify neither will he exhibit psychic or occult powers of any sort. He will not spin you yarns about your or his past lives or tell you that you are one of the chosen on the threshold of greatness if you follow him. All of these are fairly obvious things to look out for but even so a powerful personality can sometimes overwhelm despite one's better judgement sending out warning signals to beware.

A true teacher will be humble. Possibly, though not necessarily, he will even be unassuming. He will not be concerned with personal prestige and I won't even mention money. He will not promote himself or regard himself as the source of his teachings. He is an intermediary, no more. His task is not to make his disciple dependent on him in any way but to bring that disciple into closer relationship with his own soul. This he may or may not do within the context of traditional religious teachings but if he does, he will not be limited by them. If he does not, he will not despise them. The true teacher is not concerned with the personal self, neither his own nor his student's, but that does not mean he rides roughshod over it either. He simply goes beyond it.

The true teacher loves. That is why he teaches.

Now, in view of what I have said earlier, it is not reasonable to expect all spiritual teachers to be perfect. The teaching experience is part of the training and education of the teacher himself who learns as he teaches. But there is a clear difference between a false teacher who basically seeks to exploit his pupils and exalt himself and a genuine one who may not be operating from the lofty heights of full enlightenment but who is doing his job and fulfilling his *dharma*[5] at the level at which he is supposed to be doing it. So your teacher need not be the Buddha incarnate to be a true teacher and the right one for you.

Who your teacher is depends on who you are. Some of the great ones appear to have had no teacher and it is often said nowadays that teachers are not necessary or even an obstacle for spiritual reali-sation. That may be so but I don't think there's much doubt that you do need a teacher to bring you to the point where you do not need a teacher. Your real teacher is your own soul but as long as you are not fully attuned to your soul you will require an outer representative of God to help you reach that point. This representative need not always appear in the obvious form of a guru or wise counsellor. Sometimes it may be a friend or acquaintance, a passing stranger or even a tree or flower. The true teacher of all is God and He can appear in many guises.

Chapter 13

The Purification of the Lower Self

April 23rd 1979

The Master told me that the main reason I had come to Earth was to learn humility. He said that an evolved person should never feel superior to anyone else on account of his evolution. The Master Jesus and all the Masters of old had preached humility and demonstrated it too. They knew that they were as nothing and that all they were came from the Creator. Without humility, he said, you can reach a certain point on the path but then, if you do not acquire it, you will go no further. He went on to say that I should also strive to become less critical. Look for the good in people and the good will come out. Focus on their faults and you will magnify them and your own as well. He told me to meditate deeply on this. He then said that Michael had great dignity and pride, and though he sometimes hid his shyness beneath childishness, he nevertheless was an advanced soul. I should not allow myself to be disturbed by the childishness but look upon it as an opportunity for me to learn humility. Did I not see, he asked me, that when you learn humility a great burden is taken from you? Think on this, he concluded, and left after giving me his peace and blessings as usual.

Later on during that same meditation, after the Master had departed, one of his helpers came and spoke through Michael. This happened occasionally and for one of two reasons or so I was informed. It might be that the Master had urgent business elsewhere and could not finish what he wished to say but it might also be that the strain of supporting the presence of the Master had become too much for Michael yet he was still able to endure the less powerful vibration of the guide. May I remind the reader yet again that this was no ordinary mediumship and that it put severe pressure on Michael, particularly on his emotional nature which was stirred up and made hyper-sensitive by the experience. Here's what the guide said.

"Your Master had said that you should have more mind control and stability. At present your moods veer from high to low and you are at the mercy of your thoughts. You must keep on an even keel and remain balanced at all times. When antagonistic thoughts or negative emotions arise you should breathe in, palms outstretched, imagining God's purifying rays entering your mind. As you exhale imagine all the bad influences departing. Do this ten times and strive to subdue the mind." The guide then told me that I have a tendency to want to help people who have nothing to do with me but crush people close to me because of a fear of possession. "This must cease" he said.

I will comment on these talks a little further on. At this point I would just like to say that I include the Masters' usually unflattering remarks about me (after all they were teaching me and therefore showing me my faults) not in any sense of self-flagellation or false humility but because I think they are more widely applicable. All human beings have similar faults because these are the faults of a self-conscious creature that is still limited to its self-consciousness. We may have our particular points of weakness but these are not unique and usually are shared to some degree with everyone. To think that my faults are peculiar or even unique to me would be a form of egotism, would it not?

April 25th 1979

The Master said that Michael and I were now entering a stage of intense purification. We might possibly become ill though not severely and would experience a degree of mental anguish as well. We should not be concerned by this but ignore it as much as

possible and have faith that all would be well and was proceeding as intended by the Masters. We were fortunate to be told this. Others would have to go through similar experiences without the consolation of guidance and the reassurance that what was taking place was part of a natural process. We should at this time be careful with our diet and also occasionally fast. Meditation was highly important for us at the moment and I should improve my concentration. At present I was too much like a bouncing ball, up and down all the time. I must have maturity.

April 26th 1979

I was told to meditate for at least twenty minutes each morning and evening and, if possible, at noon as well. During this time I should try to link up with the Masters and should attempt to maintain that link throughout the day while working in the market. Everyone in life must work, the Master said, and I had to do my daily work which I should attend to and do well even if it was not my true task. I said that I still often felt separate from Michael to which the reply was that the Masters had decided that we were suited so who was I to quibble? I was highly favoured and should not forget it. To be with someone with whom one had everything in common is of little spiritual value. He told me to have humility and be more mature and also not to expect too much too soon adding that "You will have heard it said that you have to give in order to receive. This is the truth. So give."

This was a bit of a dressing down. Sometimes the Masters would answer a question of mine by telling me what they thought I needed to know rather than answering it directly. If the question was prompted by something else they would address the something else. Here is a case in point. To my (not very) veiled complaint about the difficulties I was having in getting along with Michael they told me to look to myself. Their initial response might seem almost autocratic and it certainly was not open to discussion but it was correct. The

Masters were not authoritarian in the slightest but nor were they falsely democratic. They were the teachers and I was the pupil. They knew that there was an element in me that wanted the results of spirituality without making the necessary efforts and sacrifices, and they had to deal with that. They regarded that tendency as part of my immaturity which, of course, it was, and, although they were infinitely tolerant and patient, they would not condone or in any way reinforce capitulation to weaknesses. The subtext to my question was that I wanted the Masters to be on my side against Michael, to confirm that, yes, I was right and his worldliness and occasional exhibitionism were hard to get on with. They were having none of that. I had to get over my self-preoccupation and that was all there was to it. One of their themes, if I can call it that, was that I should not take the fact of their coming to me for granted. Not, certainly not, because they wanted gratitude or devotion from me, but because they wanted me to value and make full use of what was happening to me. For my sake not theirs. Unlike some inner plane beings that make contact with incarnate humanity in order to gain psychic energy, the Masters needed nothing from me. They only came to give.

Purification has always been regarded as an essential preliminary part of the spiritual path. In the past some traditions have encouraged an overly ascetic approach in an attempt to uproot worldly tendencies and attachment to sensual appetites. One has only to think of the mortifications of medieval Christian mystics as well as the extraordinary lengths some Hindu sannyasis have gone to in their efforts to dominate their lower nature. I once met a man in India who, so his disciples (for naturally he had such) claimed, had remained standing up for twenty years although he did have a horizontal bar he leant on occasionally. I presume he slept on that too. He was very friendly but he was not enlightened. The Buddha himself tried the approach of extreme austerity for six years, starving himself in an attempt to subdue the senses and find inner peace but he eventually realised that this practice lead nowhere and so abandoned it much to the disgust of his fellow ascetics, pridefully entrenched in their superior spirituality. But he who was to become the Buddha saw that, in order to win enlightenment, the mind must be able to function properly and, for that to happen, the body must be cared for not tortured or neglected. So the extremes of asceticism are not the way but, as the Buddha found and taught, the Middle Way is, and the Middle Way does require purification. Purification from what exactly though?

In order to become aware of the soul, thought, emotions and the physical body must all be cleansed of impurities and become almost transparent with no independent life of their own. Otherwise the spiritual light may shine but it will not be perceived anymore than the sun can be seen properly through a grubby window on a cloudy day. Everyone on the planet has or has acquired wrong ways of thinking. Everyone pollutes their emotional nature with anger, desire, fear and the like. Almost everyone puts a lot of the wrong sort of stuff into their body. Now it is true that if vegetarianism led to enlightenment then sheep would be wise but a body clogged with meat and foods of a similar low vibration will not help its occupant to be sensitive to the higher vibrations of the soul. I would not say that vegetarianism is essential for spirituality but I would say it is preferable and not only from the moral point of view. Whether one is a vegetarian or not, moderation in one's diet is certainly important as "food lust" will only increase attachment to and identification with the body. As the Master intimated, fasts have their place at certain times to cleanse the body of impurities built up over many years, and they are also a valuable spiritual discipline. I did fast on a few occasions though never for more than three or four days at a time. Fasting definitely has a purifying effect and also increases one's sensitivity to the world beyond though it should not be thought of as a way of entering the kingdom of heaven uninvited on that account. Having said all this, one must also point out that any undue focus on the physical side of things will only distract you from what really matters which is what Jesus meant when he said that what comes out of your mouth is of far greater importance than what goes into it.

A pure mind is more important than a pure body and to that end the refinement of the emotions, the development of non-responsiveness to anger and fear and the purging of our habitual self-centred ways of thinking are all vital. The ways of doing this are many and well known and include such things as service to others, detached self-observation, meditation and concentration on a higher power by focussing on a chosen deity, saint or spiritual image. I think the most important of them, though, are perfectly summed up in traditional Christian terminology as poverty, chastity and obedience.

In the context of the medieval monasticism in which these rules were first formulated, they were interpreted literally but that's not how we need look at them nowadays. The spiritual path is above all an inner path and we should regard these ancient rules of the spiritual road as rules to be followed more on the level of inner attitude than outer observance, even if outer observance may sometimes be necessary too. It would be just as much of an error to deny that. Poverty is non-attachment to material things and a willingness to let go of whatever you might possess when and if required. It is being able to do with no more than you need. Chastity is inner purity, possibly but by no means inevitably manifesting as celibacy, a state which, if enforced, might for many people simply lead to repression and an over-preoccupation with sex. Nor should chastity be restricted to sex. It may be extended to cover the whole field of desire. Obedience does not mean obedience to one's spiritual superior as in the monastery but to the voice of your own soul. Naturally that means being able to distinguish what comes from the soul and what comes from one of the many layers of the personal self, and until the ability to discriminate between the two is sufficiently developed you may indeed need to listen to an outer authority, though no true spiritual authority will ever demand obedience nowadays.

So we need to cleanse our physical, emotional and mental selves.

What we must cleanse them from, what we must make ourselves non-responsive to, are (again expressed in traditional Christian terminology) the world, the flesh and the devil. What do these mean? The flesh is easy to understand. It is the pull of desires associated with the body over and above what is necessary for its proper functioning as a vehicle for the soul. The world is this world. It is its praise and its blame. It is public opinion and consensus, whether political, social, cultural or even spiritual. It is worldly wisdom or anything that is not seen by the true light of God. All these we must be impervious to. The world is also the rewards and goals of worldliness, the desire to succeed in or by admired by this world, the desire for money, fame or power. What is the devil? It is the fallen consciousness, the self-willed ego. It is that in us which refuses to love or forgive or submit. It is pride, the worst of the seven deadly sins and the one that caused Lucifer to tumble down from his high estate.

The task of spiritual purification is an ongoing process that lasts for as long as you are on the path, since no one can truly be said to be pure in whom a trace of ego remains. A point I would like to make here, though, is that not all the work of purification of the lower self is necessarily done by the aspirant himself. The Masters pointed out to me that in addition to my efforts, which were obviously necessary, they worked from above to make me more sensitive to spiritual impression, and that this could lead to stress and strain in the lower vehicles. **You might possibly become ill .... and could experience a degree of mental anguish as well**. I have no knowledge of what took place but imagine it could be envisaged as a controlled release of light into the aura, carefully managed so as to inspire but not overwhelm. If this sounds vague to the analytical mind, thinking of it symbolically might make it clearer to the intuition. As a matter of fact, I did not become ill though I did find myself feeling run down and tired, but that is a common experience as anyone seriously embarked on the spiritual path will tell you. The work required takes an enormous amount of effort and energy, even if you appear to be doing nothing more strenuous than sitting in a chair with your eyes closed.

The Masters told me that it is standard practice for anyone at a certain stage on the path to be helped by teachers on the inner planes, whether they are aware of it or not. Let this be a consolation to all those who are struggling and feel alone. You are not alone. You are surrounded by the love and support of beings on the higher planes who will always hear you if you call to them even if you do not always hear their response.

I like the idea of the ego being an intolerable weight that we only become aware of as such when it is removed. This is what the Master meant by his remark that **when you learn humility a great burden is taken from you.** It is most strange but we cling to something for dear life that is actually the cause of all our suffering and sorrow. We even seek ways to preserve it whilst ostensibly trying to get rid of it. I was told that **the main reason I had come to Earth was to learn humility** which led me to reflect on what humility might be. It seems obvious at first. Humility is conquering pride and superiority. It is not putting yourself above others, even not thinking of yourself at all. All that is true enough but there is more. Humility as lack of self-regard is a quality that we must strive to acquire at all stages of the spiritual path but, in the final analysis, a humble self is still a self and true humility is only possible when there is no self at all. **The Master Jesus and all the Masters of old .... knew they were as nothing and that all they were came from the Creator.** They really knew this, not as a theory or an ideal but as a living fact and we must know it too. We really are as nothing. There is no self, there is only God and recognition of that is humility. In that sense humility is the very last lesson to be learned but that does not mean we are not obliged to attempt to confront pride and self-concern at any and every point on the spiritual path.

Every candidate for initiation knows this as a matter of theory and logic but the ego's sense of self-preservation is strong and it is highly skilled at imitation and concealment. Just as the devil is supposed to be able to pose as an angel of light so the ego can mask itself and hide behind various smokescreens of its own creation. That is why unflinching self-knowledge is required. It is a temptation for an evolved person to feel superior to others who do not have his insight or who may still be pursuing worldly ends. It is a temptation often succumbed to but that is to ascribe to oneself something to which one has no right. Is your insight really yours? Do you possess wisdom? A strong personality might find it easy to attract others who will then admire and look up to that person. But where does that strength and ability to impress come from? We know from the effect of their lives that there can have been few individuals with as powerful a presence as Jesus or the Buddha but **the Master Jesus and all the Masters of old …. knew they were as nothing and that all they were came from the Creator.** Anything we have, we have been given and what has been given can be taken away. This is surely cause for humility.

It is worth considering why we do not have humility in the first place or rather why we do have pride and superiority. Looking into myself I think that part of the answer is fear. The ego is born in separation and where there is separation there is fear. There is fear of the other with whom one is now in some kind of competition but there is also fear of death. The ego's prime need is to maintain itself but it only has this need because at some level it realises its own non-existence. Consequently it is engaged in a constant battle to preserve itself and one way it can do this is to give itself more and more importance. A sense of superiority strengthens the ego and might even seem to prove its own substance, particularly if it can find ways to justify that supposed superiority. But this is all based on illusion. Ultimately the ego knows it is not real. It is afraid of death and will do anything it can to avoid that encounter and be forced to face its own nothingness. However we are more than the ego and only if we identify with it will we share its fears and concerns. If we abandon it, if we perceive its non-reality, then we are released from its suffocating constrictions into the freedom of unlimited life.

The ego arises when the soul, incarnate in the dualistic world of matter, identifies with thought and memory and creates a separate identity for itself. Thus it is the sense of separateness that gives rise to the ego. But separateness is an illusion. Your soul is an individualisation of the Creator. Other people's souls are equally individualisations of the Creator. But God is one. This is a basic truth of every spiritual tradition without exception. Therefore our souls are one (not the same but one) and there is no separation. Therefore there is no separate self, no ego.

When I say that fear is the reason behind pride I am not saying that it is the only reason (love of power, for instance, can also be a strong factor) but it is a fundamental one and I would go on to say that a proud person is actually a weak person because he is insecure. Even on the psychological level it is well known that a feeling of superiority quite often masks one of inferiority. By the same token a humble person can be regarded as a strong person because he alone is secure in who he is and does not feel the need to compare himself with others. One could equally well approach this subject from a different angle and say that the true cause of pride is lack of love. Love is the manifestation on the level of feeling of the awareness of non-separation. Love and humility are therefore two aspects of the same thing which is why it is that only a humble person truly loves. Nobody, not even the Masters, loves the ego but the humble person is not bound by his own ego and is consequently able to see beyond the ego of others. He is able to see God in others and that is why he loves.

Chapter 14

Pride and a Spiritual Scouring

May 1st 1979

The Master said that they were gratified with my progress. He said that I would receive grace but there would continue to be hard work and learning. I asked about Susan and he said there was no cause for concern there. Michael spoke against her not from possessiveness but awareness of the dangers of getting sidetracked from the spiritual path. However the Masters were confident of my resolve to remain on it. I then asked how best to deal with Michael's bouts of upset and near hysteria and he said that these moods were sent by the Masters and contained lessons for both of us. I could stop them by not reacting to them and sending thoughts of love to Michael which he would receive and be calmed by. He told me that in order to accomplish our task there must be unity between Michael and myself. I needed to understand that the world is a far from perfect place and I must learn to deal with imbalance and negativity, sometimes in extreme form, without being affected by them myself. That is why they sent me these lessons. He concluded by sending me love and blessings.

Susan was a friend with whom I had had a semi-romantic relationship before meeting Michael. I was still in touch with her occasionally much to Michael's disapproval hence my question to the Master. His attitude that there was no cause for concern was quite different to Michael's who very definitely thought there was and that I should not continue my correspondence with her. It is one of many examples of the clear difference there could sometimes be between Michael and the Masters.

Like most mediums Michael could be subject to fits of emotional volatility and this was hard for me to deal with in the early days of our association. I soon found out that the Masters spared me nothing on account of my youth. It was in at the deep end and I had to learn to manage Michael's emotional excesses (which usually manifested as sudden losses of temper and shouting) and my reactions to them which was not easy in either case. However I realised that this intense way of training obliged me to deal with the issues it raised. I couldn't just ignore or avoid them. They would force themselves on me to the extent that I was left with no option but to learn the lessons they brought or else suffer the consequences. I have to say this could be both distressing and exhausting but the Master's words that **the world is a far from perfect place and I must learn to deal with imbalance and negativity without being affected by them myself** explained the situation and helped me to see past its outer aspects to the purpose behind them. Even so, understanding what was going on when the Master was present explaining it to me was quite different to being in the heat of battle when Michael would be shouting at me and I had to maintain both detachment from his intemperate behaviour *and* the unity with him at an inner level that the Masters required. Hate the sin, love the sinner indeed. After these outbursts Michael would often be left with very little recollection of them which would either indicate that he needed psychiatric help or confirm the Masters' words that they were behind the process and using him as their medium. Michael himself told me this was the case though admitted that it could only work because he had these tendencies anyway.

Lest I give the wrong impression, I should stress that Michael's normal nature was very sweet, kind and loving. In no sense could he be called an intellectual but his spiritual instincts were highly developed and his heart was true, and this seems to be what the Masters look for in those they work with in this world. They are not concerned with those who may be regarded as great in the world's eyes but look for a pure heart open to spiritual truth. These were the sort of people Jesus came to and little appears to have changed in the intervening 2,000 years. Michael was genuinely not concerned with making spiritual progress on a personal level or if he was it was very much a secondary issue for him. He principally just wanted to love and serve the Masters.

A further important point I need to make here is that Michael's outbursts never came out of nothing. It would always be some deviation from correct spiritual behaviour on my part that would instigate them. A critical remark, the hint of a superior attitude, impatience, intolerance, those were the sort of things that would prompt a reaction from him. It may be that the reaction was out of proportion to what caused it but this was the way my own short-comings were brought home to me. It was a sort of feedback, extreme but effective and operating in such a manner that I could not ignore it.

May 5th 1979

The Master said that I had made good progress in some respects but there was one large hindrance to my opening up fully and that was my pride. He told me that the irritation and fear I feel both stem from pride, which is a grave fault on my part. I speak to people as though I knew better, even to him sometimes. If I am to help anyone I must make them feel an equal and make them feel important not myself. He told me that I must constantly be on the watch for pride and conquer it by frequent prayer and meditation. Otherwise my progress will take much, much longer. He then went on to say that I do not have the love of a truly spiritual person. He pointed out Michael as an example and said that his love was boundless. He thought of others whereas I thought only of myself and the reason I had been born on earth was to overcome this. "Think of others and have love. Do not judge or be superior."

Well, if you accept instruction from higher beings you have to be prepared for straight talking. As the reader may well imagine I listened to this and felt very small. I had been spoken to in a forthright manner before by them but never quite like this and even now, thirty years later, I can vividly recall the flush of shame that crept over me as the talk went on. When the Master said that I sometimes even talked to him as though I knew better I wanted to interrupt and protest but didn't dare and I suppose the fact I wanted to do so rather proved his point. The funny thing is he was certainly stern but he was not unkind and, though I felt humbled, I did not feel humiliated. I knew what he said was true enough. I felt it was somewhat of a one-sided appraisal of my character but had the wit to appreciate that its purpose was to bring my faults home to me in such a way that there was no room for denial or excuses. I loved the Masters and wanted to do the best I could for them so I listened to them whatever they said, knowing, despite what he said, that they really did know better than me, and not just in terms of general spirituality but in personal ones too; that is, they knew me better than I knew myself.

We all admit to certain of our faults but we still tend to justify or excuse them in an attempt to diminish their importance. We even think that the fact we admit to them means we don't really have them, not seriously anyway. "Oh yes, I'm rather a critical person" we say with a smile. As we know it, it doesn't really matter, does it? That's the idea at any rate. But, of course, it does matter and our little confessions are frequently just ploys on the part of the ego to avoid dealing with the faults confessed, attempts to deflect any criticisms that might arise from them, to minimise them really. I knew I had these faults but I obviously didn't know it well enough to do something about it. Now I had no excuse not to address them.

The Master said **that the irritation and fear I feel both stem from pride**. This may seem to contradict what I wrote earlier about pride being derived from fear but in fact it's all part of the same movement of ego. Fear, pride, superiority and so on all come from the sense of separation. That is the core of all negative qualities. I felt irritated with people who did not measure up to my idea of what was right because I felt superior to them and I felt that because I did not have a true feeling of unity with them. It is all right to think that there are elder and younger brothers and sisters in the human race as long as you do truly feel that we are all brothers and sisters and you feel *that* first. That is to say, it is perfectly correct to recognise hierarchy as long as you also recognise unity and you see that as the primary relationship between souls with hierarchy as the secondary one. That is because unity relates to our essential being whilst the hierarchical aspect only relates to realised being. I felt fear because any sense of superiority is constantly being threatened. The feeling of superiority is a sort of self-protection but always perceived to be under attack because known to be based on unreality.

May 6th 1979

One of the guides came and spoke to me. He told me I should not criticise Michael but unite with him and that we should work together. I could certainly tell him things I thought were wrong but I should do so in a spirit of love not from irritation or superiority. I had much to teach him but I could do so best by example, not by nagging. My annoyance at his faults was magnified by "the Blacks" and I should ignore them. He then told me to keep occupied and this would stop me from thinking too much which I had a tendency to do, as a result getting muddled. Spiritual truth was simple, he said, but it was easy to get lost in philosophical speculations which led nowhere. I should learn to use my hands in a practical manner and be more down to earth. This would help me to concentrate on what was important and not to be led astray by too much thought which would merely waste my time and energy.

May 7th 1979

The Master said that at last I was putting my back into spiritual work and overcoming apathy. He told me that I should learn to accept things without resistance. All that took place did so by their will. The modern way was to question and rebel and, though this might be good to a certain extent, it was often carried too far. It took wisdom to know when to question and when to accept and I must learn that wisdom. He said that Michael had much strain on him at the moment and might shortly be ill. This would be a test for me and I should look after him unselfishly. He praised my determination to follow their instructions and said I should continue to do so with a glad heart. "Work hard and know that all is well" he concluded.

May 11th 1979

The Master said that he was pleased to see I was giving strength and support to Michael and I should continue to do so. I was here to learn, he said, and Michael is the person with whom I should tread the path at the present time. I had chosen this and it was also their wish. I could learn from his capacity for love and he could learn from my spiritual understanding which was greater than his though I should not feel superior on that account as all came from the Creator. He too told me that I should use my hands more saying that there is much untapped power in them.

May 12th 1979

The Master's message was that I should occupy myself during the day and not think so much. He said I dream and moon about too much and live too much in the mental. I must be more practical and learn to live on the earth plane. Again he said that I should work using my hands. Simple tasks were enough but I should use them regularly. This was the best way for me to conquer my karmic weakness which was lack of humility. The Masters would think for me and I should follow them and not bother myself with a lot of theory. He was pleased by what he called my great love for Michael as he said that we would be together for quite a while on Earth. My black moods are caused by the evil forces attacking me so I must keep myself busy allowing myself no time to brood.

These talks bring to mind the famous saying that the devil finds work for idle hands. It seems to be based on some sort of fact. During this period I was experiencing a bit of a reaction to the initial excitement of finding the spiritual path as the reality of it being mostly about hard work and renunciation, or rather the reality of what those things actually entailed, was brought home to me. Giving up the ego seems rather a splendid thing until you have to do it. Then there were the problems, due to our very different temperaments, in my relationship with Michael that I have already discussed and which I had not anticipated. These two factors affected my emotional state at the time and it appears that this chink in my armour was exploited and magnified by what the guide called "**the Blacks**", an unfortunate phrase nowadays but here used in its traditional sense as referring to the dark powers.

I am very well aware that the idea that **black moods are caused by the evil forces attacking** will seem ludicrous to the modern mentality. I've already said this on more than one occasion but, as the Masters thought it important enough to repeat, so will I. The very notion of 'dark forces' will provoke mirth and astonishment that anyone in this day and age could believe in such superstitious nonsense. All I can say is that every religion speaks of them as a reality not a mere personification of selfish impulses, and anybody today with real experience of the spiritual world has a similar understanding. Is it surprising that a culture that denies the existence of non-material planes has no knowledge of non-material beings? Or that a belief system that sees everything in relative terms regards the existence of evil beings as a primitive fiction? You can certainly react to the idea of evil forces superstitiously, seeing them under every stone and ascribing to them a power that they do not possess, but you can also react intelligently and take steps to deny them influence within the field of your own psyche. We cannot blame these forces for our personal failings as they can only enter where the door is open but we can be aware of their existence and make sure that the door remains closed. You might say that if you are unaware of them they cannot harm you but unfortunately that is not the case. They can influence you adversely whether you are aware of them or not but if you understand the way they work, by taking advantage of your weaknesses, you can protect yourself against them. In my case the tendency I had to succumb to annoyance and irritation created a dark spot in my consciousness that gave them a point of entry and they could then exaggerate that darkness, creating the potential, if I identified with the exaggerated state, for a spiral of negativity that could be prolonged indefinitely.

So the Masters' advice was to be aware of the machinations of these "**Blacks**" and then ignore them. Pay them no mind, give them no energy, don't fight them, don't respond to them in any way. I was informed that even thinking too much would give them an opportunity to distract me from the essential and take me into the labyrinthine ways of **philosophical speculation that led nowhere**. That statement may surprise many people accustomed to see reason as the highest faculty of the human being but it has been known for many hundreds of years in all the mystical traditions of the world. Thought can never perceive truth. Even if it builds an elaborate system based on genuine intuitive insight, that is not truth and will only distract one from the purity and simplicity of direct perception. This is why the Masters, in line with spiritual instructors throughout the ages, recommended that I should keep myself occupied in practical ways, part of which involved using my hands more. So many people today have not developed the ability to use their hands creatively. Indeed we often don't do much more with them than tap on a keyboard. Unless we are musical or artistic we are not encouraged to use our hands in school very much, particularly in the later stages, and thereafter we rarely have time or opportunity to work with them, especially those of us who are stuck for most of the day in an office, increasingly the majority. But there is power in the hands, creative power, healing power, even the power to bless, that is waiting to be released but can only be so if it is called forth. I cannot claim suddenly to have become a wood carver or ceramic pot maker or illuminator of manuscripts, but I did take up tapestry work which certainly had a therapeutic value in that it worked the fingers and absorbed the mind, **allowing me no time to brood.** So, if the devil has work for idle hands, then maybe occupied hands help keep the devil at bay or, if not the devil, the restless dance of the mind which frequently amounts to the same thing.

The Masters did not disdain the mind. Their attitude, which is the traditional spiritual attitude, is that it is a good servant but a bad master. Thought is actually regarded by them as a material process and, as long as we remain centred in it, we limit ourselves to the material world. We remain material beings. With spiritual potential certainly but not spiritual and with no chance of being so without a radical transformation of consciousness. Thought is a builder of form and that it all it is. It cannot perceive, only clothe perception, and if given undue importance, will actually prevent perception.

This brings me to possibly the most controversial thing that the Masters had so far said to me, controversial for the 21st century mind anyway. I don't think it would have been seen in that way in other times and climes. It is this. **The Masters would think for me and I should follow them.** Isn't this just what every authoritarian cult leader says as he mercilessly exploits his sheep-like flock, who then happily walk with glazed eyes and fixed smiles over metaphorical cliffs? Well, yes it probably is, but it needs to be understood in context. First of all, the Masters never told me what to think or what I should believe. They left that entirely up to me. Their only concern was with practical spiritual instruction and the point they were making here was that I thought too much and, as they went on to say, **bothered myself with a lot of theory,** tying myself up in mental knots. Truth is here and now (that's become a hackneyed catchphrase unfortunately, but it is so), and thinking, which is in time, causes one to lose the essence of the moment. But there is a further point. What cult leaders do is take elements of genuine spiritual teaching and distort these, interpreting them on the level of their own power-crazed egos. Surrender to the guru is a genuine spiritual teaching, an effective way to release the disciple from bondage to his lower self, but it requires two equally essential things. It requires intelligence on the part of the disciple, he cannot just passively relinquish responsibility and hope for the best, and it requires absolute integrity on the part of the guru. In fact, ideally it requires the guru to have transcended the state of ego identification completely. With these two requirements in place all will be well. When the Master said that **the Masters would think for me and I should follow them** he was not asking for blind acceptance of their will on my part but an intelligent understanding of the necessity to abandon self-will and trust the guru.

The balance between personal responsibility and following a spiritual teacher is a delicate one. Spiritual teachers do not exist for their pupils to become dependent on them but so that these pupils may outgrow the need for them. Their only purpose is to enable their students to find the Master within, their own higher self, their own connection to God. They are initiators but initiate means to begin and the role of the teacher is to start off the disciple's growth, to bring it to the point where the inner connection is sufficiently strong that they may retire. **"Guru is a bridge, not a prop"**, says the Master in *"Towards The Mysteries"* to a man whose guru has died and who feels bereft without her, and he then goes on to say that **"the guru must come from within, not from without"**. So I had to follow the Masters as an act of self-surrender and trust but I also had to be totally responsible for myself and not depend or rely on them in any way. If I had they would have soon withdrawn.

Chapter 15

Eclipse and Death

In the talk on May 12th the Master stated that Michael and I **would be together for quite a while on Earth.** This turned out to be correct as we lived together for twenty one years until his death in 1999. By that time the Masters, as they had informed me would be the case, were no longer talking to me to the degree they had been but I felt myself often to be aware of them on an intuitive level. Inevitably this method of communication is much more open to distortion by the recipient's mind and he is then karmically responsible for anything he might bring through and pass on. But it is the preferred means of communication partly because it demands less energy on the part of the Masters but principally because their goal is to bring us up to spiritual levels and this is where that contact takes place. For it to be effective it demands that the contactee is reasonably conscious on intuitive levels and also that his mind is sufficiently pure and free of conditioning to translate the communication without excessive deformation or alteration. It can only be translated on the mental plane (i.e. in words) in the language and ideological framework of the recipient but, within these limitations, it can be a faithful representation of the original impression. I have no doubt that many more of us than might be thought are, in varying degrees, impressed in this way without being conscious of the source of the impression.

The Masters had continued to speak to me through the mediumship of Michael until shortly before his death but on a much reduced basis. In fact, over the last five years of his life it was probably only about eight times a year that they came, on which occasions they would not do much more than lovingly greet me, point to a few matters they thought needed attention and assure me of their continued presence. **"We are closer to you than your own**

hands and feet" they would say. In one sense I missed the earlier frequency of their visits but I was now much more able to enter into their presence by imagining myself to be there. They had always assured me that this was an effective way of approaching them and I found it to be so. When a monk practises the presence of God, he is doing a similar thing. What we call it doesn't so much matter. Whether we think of it as God, Jesus, the Masters, or even our own soul, it is the spiritual presence that imagination conjures up that is important. The use of the word imagination may confuse. What we are doing is not imagining something that is not there but opening our mind up to receive something that is already there. With practice one can enter into an inner stillness and do this at any time one wishes. It simply requires faith, humility and an undistracted mind and you can learn to attune your mind to the easily recognisable vibration of the Master. You enter into the holy place by envisioning the holy presence.

This is not the final state, in which there is no need to envisage any presence because there is no sense of separation, but it is a step on the way to that final state. On our journey from savage to sage, if I may so express it, we move from a body consciousness to a mind consciousness to a soul consciousness to a God consciousness in which all distinctions are transcended, the subject is seen to be the same as the object and there is no longer any you or me, there is only God. But we cannot attain to that ultimate condition without experiencing all the states that lead up to it, and, for most of us at present, the next step is to start to become aware of the spiritual world. This we can do through the practice of meditation, prayer and the use of the creative imagination as outlined above.

In the twenty one years we spent together Michael and I lived in a variety of places. Curiously enough, and with no deliberate intent on our part, they were always either up in the hills or down on the coast, both locations supposedly conducive to spiritual practice. The last place we lived together was in Eastbourne on the Sussex coast. Our flat was on the outskirts of the town in the little village of

Meads at the foot of the downs by Beachy Head, very close, as I found out during our time there, to where the occultist and composer Cyril Scott had lived at the end of his life. He is perhaps best known today for his trilogy of books written anonymously in, I think, the 1930s, which purportedly describe encounters he had with a Master living in physical embodiment. He writes from the Theosophical point of view and I have to say that a lot in these books, including the depiction of this Master, who mostly seems to be a mouthpiece for Cyril Scott's own views, smacks to me of fiction but maybe it was fiction based on some kind of fact. At any rate, it was an interesting coincidence to find that he had lived nearby.

We had bought this flat in a rather odd way. For the previous eight years we had been living in France near le Mont St-Michel in Normandy but we had decided to move back to England as Michael, who did not feel he had that much longer to live, thought he would like to end his days where he had been happy as a child. His parents had separated when he was very young and his mother had sent him to boarding school at the extremely early age of four. Nowadays we would regard this as most uncaring, and even then it was unusual to send a child away to school that early, but Michael appears to have been fortunate in that he loved his school and, as the youngest child there, was rather spoilt. It was a small prep school and the headmaster was a kindly man who genuinely seems to have cared for his pupils. So Michael had good memories of Eastbourne and we decided to go on a two day property hunting mission during the Christmas holidays when I was due to return to England to visit my family. Our budget was small but there were enough two bedroom flats that we could afford and we went round about ten in our allotted time. It was all a bit of a rush but we found one near the centre of town that we thought was suitable and put in an offer that was accepted.

Back in France a month or so later, just before we were due to exchange contracts, we received a letter from the estate agent telling us that the vendor had withdrawn from the deal. Presumably he had received a better offer. This put us in something of a quandary as we had sold our house in France and were due to move out in March, barely six weeks away. There didn't seem to be much else to do other than to put in an offer on one of the other flats we had seen. The trouble was we had seen so many in a relatively short space of time and couldn't really remember which was which! We did however recall that we had liked the Meads property but felt it might be a little out of the way. It had seemed a long drive in the agent's car to get there and we didn't have a car. Then I remembered something. The sitting room in that flat had had a green carpet and orange walls. This had struck me at the time of viewing since, twice by accident and twice by design, every single property that Michael and I had owned since living together had had a green carpet and orange walls in the sitting room. There was no doubt, even though we could not remember much more about it than that detail - this was the one! And so it proved. The flat was still on the market. Our offer was accepted and we moved in a couple of months later. From every point of view this flat was preferable to the one we had originally made an offer on. The flat itself was lighter and more spacious, and the situation was just a few hundred yards from the downs and the sea, and, although not in the town, the town was easily accessible by bus or a half hour walk.

In case the reader wonders, we would never have dreamed of asking the Masters' advice on a matter like this or anything to do with affairs on the material plane. They would not have told us if we had. However they were more than capable of guiding us in a manner such as the one described above. The flat we had made our first offer on was near the centre of town which, not having our own transport, we had thought might be an advantage but it was not nearly as good a place for us to live as the one we ended up buying which was definitely in a much more harmonious environment. The reason the Masters would not have told us directly but were willing to guide us is because that way the responsibility is ours. We make the decision not them. It's certainly all too easy for spiritually inclined people to start looking for signs everywhere and imagining them where they are not but sometimes signs are given and it's foolish to ignore them. In my experience one may be given a sign indicating the path one should follow but only after one was made an effort to determine that path oneself.

It was in Meads that Michael and I witnessed the solar eclipse of 11th August 1999. The eclipse was not total at that location but about 90% which was impressive enough. As we watched the moon begin its inexorable progression over the sun in a fortunately cloudless sky, the atmosphere stilled. The sky turned a dark, vaguely ominous shade of blue and the birds stopped singing which, as they were mostly seagulls, and it takes a lot to keep them quiet, was very striking. Then the moon rolled away again and the sense of eeriness passed. From start to finish the whole process did not last more than a few minutes but it was such a dramatic reminder of the fact that we live in a universe of almost inconceivably powerful forces that we stayed silent for some time afterwards.

Over the previous year I had made a study of both astronomy and astrology and felt fortunate that this unusual event had occurred at a time when I would be most interested in it. My astrological researches had proved to me beyond reasonable doubt that a person's horoscope accurately reflects their character though I remained to be convinced that astrology's predictive powers were quite so great. Sometimes one could point to certain configurations after a particular event and see them as potential indicators of what had occurred but mostly, as far as I could see, vagueness was the order of the day where prediction was concerned, though I should say that that may well be more down to our ability to interpret than a fundamental flaw in astrology itself. On the other hand, the connections between individual horoscopes, what is called synastry, I did find gave up their secrets more readily. For instance, Michael had the sun in Scorpio and the moon in Virgo and I had exactly the same but in reverse with only a degree or two's difference in each case, a classic example of a good match and a positioning I found too exact for coincidence.

Given my interest in astrology at that time, I was intrigued to see what effect, if any, the eclipse might have and, as it turns out, I soon did though not in a way I would have chosen. Traditionally eclipses were regarded as harbingers of doom and, for Michael at least, that is just what this one was as two days after the eclipse he had a heart attack. I arrived home on the afternoon of the 13th August to find him lying on his bed obviously in severe pain. I called an ambulance and he was taken to hospital where the diagnosis of a cardiac arrest was confirmed. Over the next week or so I visited him every day and he seemed to be getting better. Always good natured and stoical (I never heard him complain once during the entire twenty one years I knew him), he took the whole thing lightly and was getting on very well with the other patients in the ward as well as the nurses. On the afternoon of the 23rd I went to see him as usual and was told by the doctor that he would be able to leave hospital and go home the next day. I had brought him some peaches and jokingly said I might have saved myself the trouble as he would be home tomorrow. He laughed and said he would keep them anyway. Then I said goodbye and left.

That evening at around 8.30 the telephone rang. It was the hospital to say that Michael had suffered another heart attack and was not at all well and I should come straightaway. I don't know if this is the usual way hospitals announce such things, to break one in gradually perhaps, but I realised immediately from the tone of the speaker's voice that he was dead. When I got to the hospital I could see by the nurses' faces that that was indeed the case. They took me to see him and I held his hand and kissed him on the forehead. It may seem a strange thing but we had loved each other in the way the Masters had predicted at the start. My emotions were very mixed. On the one hand I knew that he was not dead, that he had, as the doctor had correctly said, left the hospital and gone home. On the other, he was gone and on a personal level I was deeply sad.

Death is an extraordinary and humbling thing to experience.

Obviously I can't yet speak of it from the inside, where it is surely the most significant moment of a person's life, but from the outside it brings one face to face with eternal verities more than anything else. It strips away the façade we all hide behind and leaves us naked. There is an awful truth in it but there is an awful beauty too. To me it demonstrates that we are spiritual beings. It is so clear that the body is not the person. The body is still there but the person is gone. Someone whose mind has been soured (I think that's the correct word) by the materialistic outlook will not see things that way but such a person is the most deluded of human beings and, from the point of view of true things, the most ignorant. Perhaps I should not be so forthright but I think it needs to be said. The hour presses and we must wake up. The human race really cannot afford to spend any more time denying its true purpose on this planet. Life here is one thing and one thing only, a school for the raising of consciousness. We are incarnate in matter not to fall into the illusions of duality and waste our time in worldly pursuits to satisfy the ego but to spiritualise matter and raise it up into light which we do first and foremost by transforming ourselves, by raising ourselves up into light.

After leaving Michael the nurse took me to the ward to collect his few personal effects. I was both pleased and touched to see that he had eaten the peaches as the stones were there on his bedside table. Then I went home and prayed. I tried to contact the Masters inwardly but received no sense whatsoever of succeeding in that aim. That was all right. The experience of death for anyone is a kind of initiation and initiations have always to be gone through alone. In succeeding days I was occasionally conscious of a presence, not comforting or supporting but simply there. At first, though, and for quite a while there was nothing but that very nothing I found oddly strengthening. When you come down to nothing you know exactly where you are.

May I say something here for anyone who finds themselves in a similar situation which means virtually all of us at one time or another. Do not let your faith be shaken by the experience of death, however it happens. There is always comfort or, as I would rather put it, understanding to be had if you will allow yourself to be open to it. Mourning is right and proper but excessive self-indulgent lamentation will isolate you as the emotional disturbance it creates will debar your consciousness from receiving impressions from higher vibrations just as agitated water cannot properly reflect the sunlight. Seek to withdraw into stillness and silence and you will find peace and understanding, perhaps only fleetingly at first but it is there for you to access if you will. There is always a purpose to death. Try to understand and embrace that purpose and learn to move on. Don't cling to the past. Don't try to bring the dead person back. Know that you will meet again in some way for where there is love there cannot be separation. Death is the shattering of form for the release of life to a higher state. Without death life would be a living death after a while so try to see it as the blessing and liberation it truly is.

Of course to think in this way is hard in the aftermath of a bereavement but frankly what's the alternative? Such reflections soon brought me to the point where I could be glad for Michael that he was set free from his old carcass to rejoin the Masters he loved so well and whom he had served so faithfully, and also, for myself, be intrigued at the possibility of a new chapter opening up. It occurred to me that we had been together for three seven years cycles and that seemed a satisfyingly appropriate period of time for something to grow, mature and reach completion. Following on from that train of thought I decided to look at the astrological factors that were present at the time of Michael's death and saw that transitting Mars was almost exactly conjunct his natal sun then as well as (since they were on practically the same spot) my natal moon. More interestingly, transiting Saturn was precisely opposite my natal Saturn to the degree. The last time that had happened was twenty nine years previously when my grandfather had died. But most significant of all was the fact that Michael's Jupiter was on 17 Leo 38. The solar eclipse of 11th August, two days before his first heart attack, was on

18 Leo 21, less than a degree off Michael's Jupiter. It is true that the Sun is normally considered the main ruler of the heart but Jupiter also has secondary rulership over, as a standard textbook on the subject has it, "heart diseases and ailments". The eclipse had been true to its reputation.

Chapter 16

The Light is Always There

After that leap into the future, prompted by the Master's remark that Michael and I **would be together for quite a while on Earth,** let me return to the main thread in my narrative. In 1979 I had no idea how long Michael and I would be associated. Truth to tell, I was not thinking about the future at all. I only knew that this was what I had to do now and the future could take care of itself. I remember my mother's distress when I went to live with Michael in Bath. He waited for me at the railway station near my house on a cold, snowy New Year's Day morning for over two hours while my mother had one last attempt to persuade me not to go, the main thrust of her argument being, perfectly rationally, that this might seem like a good idea now but it would have consequences which I could not currently foresee in ten or twenty years time. I was throwing away my life, she said. From her perspective she was quite right and I really did feel sorry for my parents for what I was doing to them. I had no desire to be a selfish or ungrateful son but I knew that I had to do what I was doing. What it led to did not matter. The fact that it was right to do now was all that was relevant. Besides, if it truly was right to do now then it would be right from a future perspective too. All the same, I would probably have been surprised if I had been told that Michael and I would be living together for twenty one years.

The next date I have a record for of a talk taking place is in June. I don't know if there had been a break in the talks or if I had just not made notes (I didn't always) but it's possible that the Masters did not visit for a month, observing how I was practising their previous teachings before giving more. It appears to be a rule in the spiritual world that if one uses what one is given then one is given more. If one makes insufficient use of what has been offered, the teaching will cease until such time as it may serve a constructive purpose again. The Masters are eminently practical and have no desire to waste time or energy.

June 11th 1979

The Master told me that Michael was going through a lot of strain at the moment due to the pressures of being used in this fashion. I must understand this and be tolerant of his reactions. He was pleased that my knowledge was now manifesting itself on the Earth plane but said that their impressions to me were sometimes coloured by wishful thinking on my part. I must be true to my conscience, he said, but make sure that it was my conscience I was being true to. He sent his love to both of us and told me that I must accept responsibility if I wanted to progress. Knowledge and power were only given to those who wished to pass them on to others.

June 12th 1979

The Master said that he and the other higher intelligences were still down in our atmosphere influencing me. He said that I was in the process of opening up like a lotus blossom but should not give in to weakness or inertia as those would delay the flowering. He emphasised that I must have humility. This was my most important lesson. He reminded me of the truth "taught by the great Master" that he who would be first would be last but he who would be last would be first. I should regard all people as manifestations of the Divine and not feel superior because I might have more knowledge. I could learn humility, selfless love and practical accomplishments from Michael. I might indeed have greater knowledge than him but knowledge without humility was "like a fruit without juice, dry and without the ability to nourish your brother". Finally I was told that I must come to terms with the Earth plane even though it was distasteful to me. I was born into

the world and must live in the world even if it was not my home.

There are different kinds of mediumship but as far as I, no specialist in this field, understand the matter, they can be boiled down to two principal types. One, possibly more common, in which the medium's personality remains in the body and the communicator must work through the medium's mind, accepting that the message will be coloured by the conditioning and limitations of that mind. If there are a group of people present then their minds can also have a telepathic influence on the message. In this case the message will usually reflect the consciousness and conceptual framework of the medium or channeler and the voice that speaks will be his or hers, though possibly slightly altered. With the other type the medium is taken completely out of the body, the voice will be different and the communication has the potential to be of a purer sort. At least it will reflect its source, whatever that may be, more accurately. I was assured by the Masters that Michael had no influence at all on what was said through him, either on a conscious or an unconscious level. The nature and quality of the talks, even the vocabulary used, confirmed that to me beyond a doubt, and, to back this up, I might say that very often at the beginning and end of talks a language I did not recognise was spoken. As well as English, Michael spoke fluent French and Urdu (learnt during his time in India during the 2nd World War) but it was neither of those. It was not a European language, most of which I would have been able to recognise to some degree. It did not even sound Indian or Oriental to me though I can't say for sure. The Masters usually sounded the OM at the commencement of a talk either to announce themselves or to 'tune up' the atmosphere, as I have described on the occasion of their first revealing themselves to me, but I don't think it was Sanskrit that was spoken as I would have recognised elements at least of that.

As I have said, it is rare for the Masters to use this second type of mediumship. For the medium the vibrations of such an elevated being are extremely difficult to handle, this in addition to the pressures of being taken out of the body whose vehicles are then used by another. Hence what the Master called Michael's reactions which were of the nature of emotional outbursts and loss of temper, usually over and done with as suddenly as they came on. The reader might say that surely a spiritual person should be beyond such uncontrolled behaviour but that is to fail to grasp the stresses and strains of this kind of mediumship. Those of us who have not experienced it are perhaps not best qualified to pass judgement on it. As a matter of interest, exactly the same kind of reactions are described by Swami Omananda in her books on the Boy who was used by the Masters in the same way as Michael though much more extensively. It is said in her books, and also told to me by the Masters, that only an individual of great inner purity could be used in this way. Michael's work as a medium was not on the same level as the Boy's but it was of a similar nature and he suffered similar strains.

The foreign language spoken at times during the talks indicated that more than one person was involved in bringing them through. The Masters had their assistants who may have functioned on lower planes and so could help effect the transition down through the levels of being. In the spiritual world there are many planes of consciousness as indicated by the Master's statement that he was **still down in our atmosphere.** Some schools of occultism tabulate these and tell us that there are seven main ones with various divisions within each plane. This is interesting and helps to give us some idea of the structure and geography of the greater world beyond this small part of it but I think it would be an error to take these schemas too literally. I sometimes imagine followers of this or that esoteric school entering into the post-mortem state happily thinking they know just what to expect, but then becoming quite shocked to find how different it is to their preconceived notions of how it should be. The reality is certain to be far subtler and grander than is comprehensible to our three dimensional modes of thinking. However you don't have to take any description of the higher worlds literally to recognise that the basic idea of the spiritual planes corresponding to degrees of consciousness, and there being separation between different levels, meaning that one can only ascend to a level that corresponds to one's own inner state, is a good one. And just as we cannot reach higher levels without purifying and refining our own state of being so the Masters cannot descend too easily into the murk and density of the lower levels. This is where the helpers can help. By the way, that the Masters do so descend is a definite sacrifice on their part but sacrifice is their nature which is part of the reason they are Masters.

Assuming the genuineness of the source, the whole problem of spiritual communication can be summed up in these words. **Their impressions to me were sometimes coloured by wishful thinking on my part. I must be true to my conscience but make sure that it was my conscience I was being true to.** I say 'assuming the genuineness of the source' but, of course, we can't always assume that it is what it says it is and, even if we can, we still have to recognise that communication comes from many different levels and only very seldom from the level of the Masters; that is, from someone who has transcended duality and really knows what he is talking about. A look at the general pot pourri that is channelling should be enough to convince anyone of that.

Setting aside the question of source for the moment, the point here is that when dealing with any communication we may receive, whether it be in the form of a channelled message or a spiritual impression, we must try to make sure that our reception of it is as pure as possible and that we do not distort it by wishful thinking, prejudice or a belief system that requires all things to be adjusted to fit it. How do we do this? We have to start by self-observation which is the only way to acquire self-knowledge. We have to look at ourselves with unflinching honesty but without judgement or condemnation. We have to be clear about our true motives and desires and then abandon those that have personal agendas which we can do by humbly commending ourselves to a higher power to which we vow submission and service. Then we have to recognise that we cannot always escape our conditioning but we can at least try to be aware of it and be limited by it as little as possible.

If you are on the spiritual path you need constantly to question your interpretation of reality, not for the sake of change but to make sure that you do not close your mind. Without running after novelty for its own sake, you need to be open to the new. Many people have been seekers for a while and then found a philosophy of life that suits them. It may be a mystical or esoteric philosophy and it may seemingly contain the highest truth but it is still just words and ideas and if you are not willing to move beyond it then you will remain stuck on the mental level. Your interpretation of spiritual impression will be restricted to what you already know and are comfortable with. "Behold! I make all things new" says the Lord. Creation is recreated afresh at every instant, eternally changeless but constantly renewed. The spiritual powers are continually seeking to bring us further up. We need to make sure that our minds and hearts are open to what they have to say and that we do not block out or limit their messages through the filter of our preconceptions and conditioning or a desire for the familiar and secure.

When the Master told me to **be true to my conscience but make sure that it was my conscience I was being true to** he was pointing out the difference between the voice of the soul (which, broadly speaking, is what the conscience is) and the mind. The soul perceives truth because it is one with truth. It is not separate from truth. The perception of the mind is limited by the ego but we need to see this ego as much more than simple self-centredness. The ego is what we as separate individuals are. It is our hopes and fears, it is our background and opinions. It is everything we think. The soul does not think, the soul knows. Our conscience, correctly understood, is not the product of our religious or cultural upbringing or some moral code that we have adopted, all of which are, generally speaking, part of the ego. Rather it is a deep knowingness that was not developed over a period of time or in response to any external factors or personal predilections but is innate and was fully formed from the beginning.

We need to learn to listen to our conscience because the more we do, the louder its voice will be. The modern world and modern educational methods aim to train the mind and the mind only as a result of which fewer and fewer people are able to discern the inner voice. It is not a mistake to train the mind, of course, but it is a grave mistake to restrict education to that. As long as we are confined to our current materialistic mindset, and I include much conventional exoteric religion as part of that, the possibility of encouraging children to explore silence, stillness and inwardness seems rather remote. But I think it is of critical importance, especially given the frankly barbarous nature of much contemporary popular culture to which most children are exposed, an almost wholly negative influence in my view. Naturally this cannot be done by forcing children into meditation classes at 12 o'clock on Mondays, Wednesdays and Fridays but opportunity, encouragement and the right environment need to be given, though, to be properly effective, this really needs to be done within the context of a more enlightened worldview, one that takes into account the existence of spiritual realms and acknowledges not only the reality but the primacy of the soul. This is why, I would suppose, books such as the Narnia tales of C.S. Lewis and Tolkien's *The Lord of the Rings* are so popular with imaginative children. They provide a little of the spiritual succour to the sensitive child that the modern world denies.

Occasionally the Masters would permit themselves a small poetic touch. When they said that **knowledge without humility was "like a fruit without juice, dry and without the ability to nourish your brother"** what they were saying was that in the spiritual field if you have knowledge without humility (or love which amounts to the same thing) your knowledge, great as it might be, is of no use to anyone. It does not carry the spiritual vibration so cannot feed the soul. Knowledge, tainted by the presence of ego, does not transmit truth, not essential truth anyway. Its operative influence will be restricted to the mental level so it may communicate information but will not convey inspiration and so will have no spiritually fecun-dating effect. The difference between a real spiritual teacher and the rest is precisely the difference between the spiritual and the mental. To paraphrase St Paul's famous words, you might have great knowledge and power but if you lack love these things are of small account.

To **regard all people as manifestations of the Divine** gives us the essence of spiritual teaching. We truly are all manifestations of the Divine though I freely admit this is not always easy to see. But that is because our perception is muddied by mind and the sense of separation. Because we see through the veil of ego we cannot see past the egos of others unless we are fortunate enough to meet an individual who has transcended ego in which case the divine nature shines through. This is why we are often able to love babies and small children in a way we find difficult with older people. Our ego is not challenged by their (as yet undeveloped) ego so it is easier to see them as manifestations of the Divine or the nearest we can get to that in our current spiritual state. However all people are incarna-tions of God just as much as was Jesus Christ. Indeed this was the mistake of the early church, that they restricted divinity to the prophet who exemplified it. I am in no sense trying to diminish the importance of Jesus. In the same talk the Master described him as **the great Master** and their attitude to him was always that he was the Master of all the Masters. But Christ himself taught (echoing Psalm 82) that we are all sons and daughters of the Most High, that we are gods in the making, and it was only the later distortion of his teaching that denied divine status to all humanity and told us that we had to be saved and could only be so by believing what we were told to believe by the organisation that had usurped his name.

A small proviso though. We may all be manifestations of the Divine but, as long as we exist in the relative world, that is to a greater or lesser degree. I may be as much God as Jesus but he has realised considerably more of his divine nature than me. To put it mildly! And I may be a manifestation of the Divine but I cannot know myself as such until I have transcended identification with my lower self, with the "me", so in that sense "I" am not a manifestation of the Divine but the Divine is manifested through my being. No human personality ever realised God. As it is said, no man has seen God and lived. God is only realised when the human personality is not because, although all human beings are manifestations of the divine, that does not mean that either "you" or "I" are. In fact, it is the "you" and "I" that hinder that manifestation.

It is the case that many spiritually sensitive people find it hard to come to terms with the material world. This is a realm of darkness and confusion for anyone who has some memory of the higher planes. At the same time, it is equally true that there are a substantial number of people who seek to flee the responsibilities of life in this world by turning to some kind of mystical or magical teaching, hoping to escape to higher worlds to compensate for their inability or reluctance to get to grips with his one. Let us be clear that spirituality should never be used as an excuse to avoid the lessons of the physical plane. The spiritual path is not an escape from life but a fuller embracing of it and no one with any kind of imbalance within themselves will get far on it. In fact the energies released by contacting spiritual states will only exaggerate and bring out any imbalances. There is a big difference between rejecting the world because it is wrong and rejecting the world because you cannot face its challenges. If we are born into this world, we have to deal with it correctly and that is not done by running away from it. The Masters told me **that I must come to terms with the earth plane even though it was distasteful to me. I was born into the world and must live in the world even if it was not my home.** That is to say, if you are here it is because you are meant to be here so be here. As always Jesus put it best when he told us to be in the world but not of it which, like so many of his sayings, can be looked at in more than one way. The spiritual aspirant should certainly not be of the world but nor should he try to avoid the fact that he is in it.

June 17th 1979

The Master blessed me and said I was sticking to my true beliefs so progress would be made quickly. He told me to continue teaching Michael but not go too far or too rapidly. I now had authority and power given from the Masters but I must use them sparingly. Michael was the brother they had chosen to look after me in the world and I was responsible for his spiritual progression. I must work hard and not become downhearted. Then all would be well. Inevitably doubts would arise but these must be ignored. I was like the seed growing in the darkness and struggling towards the light. The light was always there even if I could not see it. I asked him if what I had said to Michael was correct and he said that I knew it was and did not need to ask him. I would feel what to say to Michael and should have confidence in myself. Having confidence was not the same as lacking humility. The teachers of old were confident in what they said because they knew it did not come from themselves but from God. I asked how could one tell that what one said came from God and not oneself. After all a lot of people claimed that what they said came from God. He replied that illusion and self-deception are indeed rife in this world but if you are true to yourself you will know. The key is love. I then asked about Michael's homosexuality and he said that homosexuality was unimportant. In their eyes it was the same as heterosexuality but that love must be pure. They had no fear of Michael's love for me degenerating as it was completely spiritual.

There's quite a lot to comment on here. First of all I want to make a point connected with the innocuous instruction to **work hard,** surely an uncontroversial remark? Well, not necessarily, not in all quarters anyway. I've already touched on this but would like to expand on it a bit here. There are some teachers of non-duality (or a modern, trivialised version of it called by some neo-advaita), regurgitators of the teachings of enlightened souls but far from enlightened themselves, who preach that you cannot reach truth in time only in the present moment so nothing you can do, no effort you can make (all of which is of the ego) is of any use. You must simply be, here and now and then you will know truth. They are not wrong but they are not right either and their inability to offer a more nuanced understanding shows that they are simply repeating a party line which they have partially understood but by no means internally realised. In effect these people have made a concept of non-duality and are imitating that concept; quite possibly after a mystical experience of some kind but the experience has passed and they have simply turned the memory of it into a thought based system, forgetting that mind can imitate no-mind but it can never be no-mind.

To avoid confusion on this matter let us be quite clear. There is a spiritual path and effort and hard work are essential on that path if one is to get anywhere. The path has stages and you move forwards on it in time even if, ultimately, realisation can only take place out of time, in the moment. However to reach a condition of readiness for that moment requires a maturing process and that in turn implies time. The fruit can only fall from the tree when it is ripe. If you try and pull it off before then it will be inedible. It is perfectly true that the relative can never realise the absolute but, in our present state, we are relative beings and no amount of pretending that we are not (which is basically what these teachers are doing and what they are recommending their followers to do) can alter that fact.

The notion that you don't have to struggle or search because you are already enlightened and all you have to do is realise that fact is both true and untrue and consequently one of the most easily misunderstood and misapplied of teachings. "You" are not enlightened and, what is more, never will be no matter what "you" realise. Enlightenment is when you are not, and while it is certainly correct to say that you cannot go beyond the mind through the efforts of the mind nor can you through the non-efforts of the mind. The mind must be cleansed of illusion, its perception purified, its discrimination sharpened, its sensitivity to spiritual truth increased before it can be gone beyond and that takes time and effort. Then and only then can the transformation of earthly caterpillar to spiritual butterfly take place. This transformation is not something the individual can effect by his own personal efforts but, by ridding himself of desires and attachments, he can bring himself to the point where it can, through the grace of God, be effected.

May I repeat this point because it is such an important one. There is a path that leads from the relative to the absolute even if the final stages of that path can only be taken by transcending it. But you won't get to those final stages if you don't go through the earlier ones and that does require a lot of dedicated hard work. Work to purify and refine the psyche, work to deal with the unresolved, and often unacknowledged, psychological and emotional blockages and problems, even wounds, we all have to one degree or another. You cannot transcend the self until you have fully purified the self. That is the nub of the matter. And you will not purify the self as long as your motive for doing so is the quest for enlightenment. The Masters never spoke to me of enlightenment. The spiritual path is not about enlightenment or the pursuit of a higher state of consciousness and, quite frankly, if that is your motive then you are a beginner. As I have said before, it is love of God not desire for heaven that is the mark of a spiritual person. Take that non-literally if you like but make sure you are not doing so to justify some shortcoming within yourself.

The teachings of non-duality are the highest teachings in that they point to the absolute. However in one sense they are also the simplest teachings, (it is, after all, very easy to say, "All is one, there is no self. You are pure consciousness"), and therein can lie a problem. Intellectual comprehension can far outstrip true awareness and make the unripe ego imagine itself to be much nearer the goal than it is with the consequence that it no longer believes it need practise time-honoured spiritual disciplines. From the perspective of the modern Westerner, advaita (to give non-duality its Indian name, that being the form in which it is most often encountered) can also appeal as seemingly more intellectually rigorous than conventional religion or even esotericism and, best of all for some, it can appear to be a philosophy that has dispensed with or gone beyond the need for a God. However that is to limit reality to the absolute and comprehension of reality must encompass both the absolute and the relative to the neglect of neither. A correct understanding of non-duality denies neither the individual nor God (known and acknowledged in the context of traditional advaita as Isvara) though it sees ultimate reality as beyond both as they are conventionally understood. It is not that the enlightened soul loses individuality but that he is no longer limited to individuality which is not destroyed but transcended. It is not that he becomes God but that he realises the fundamental identity of his being with God's being and ceases to be confined in any way by identification with form.

I know that some people will disagree with this and say that I have not understood non-duality but I am not disputing that all life is one. What I am saying is that consciousness needs a vessel in which to manifest even if it is not identified with that vessel. I am saying that God, the Supreme Spirit, did not create us and send us out into the manifested worlds for lifetimes of experience merely for us at the end of it all to vanish into absolute formlessness as though we had never been. As life we are one, as manifested individuals we are this and not that, and it is this distinctiveness which adds to the overall richness of life.

After that little digression it's time to go back to the Master's talk and his words that **I now had authority and power given from the Masters.** I had no illusions about what this meant. It was in relation to Michael only and does not imply that the mantle of the Masters was on my shoulders in any other sense. And I may have been teaching Michael but I was not his teacher or if I was then we were both each other's teacher. The Masters did say that I was responsible for his spiritual progression but their words on other occasions made clear that I taught him best when I let it happen through me and did not try and force the issue with my conscious mind. It was not that I taught him but they taught him using me as their medium to do so. If I tried to be the teacher, I actually interfered with the process.

We can extend this to apply to any spiritual teacher. If the teacher sees himself as a teacher then he is not a teacher. The teachings come through him not from him. I remember reading that Krishnamurti had no idea what he was going to say when he sat down to give one of his public talks and this is the right approach. **The teachers of old were confident in what they said because they knew it did not come from themselves but from God.** Of course, a normal teacher or speaker will give a poor performance if he is not fully prepared and pretty much knows in advance what he is going to say but spiritual teaching is not about passing on knowledge, not primarily in any case. If any individual is sufficiently open to the divine power and reasonably empty of self then that individual can be used as a conduit for spiritual truth. What comes through will naturally be determined by the state of consciousness of the person concerned but his job is not to try to be a lantern himself but an open window through which spiritual light can shine into the world.

When the Masters told me I should let the spirit speak through me (which is what they meant by saying **I would feel what to say to Michael)** I wanted to know how I could tell that it really was the spirit and not just myself. Their answer was simple. Just be true to yourself. That is to say, be honest with yourself. I'm sure we are all familiar with examples of individuals claiming that God is speaking through them but there is a world of difference between letting the spirit speak through you and bombastically claiming that what you say comes from God. If you humbly open your heart to the truth then the truth will speak through you, though only to the degree that you are able to receive it, which means to the degree that you are sensitive to the spiritual plane. The more in tune with the source you are, the more accurately you will be able to reflect the source and the more confident you will be that it truly is the source you are reflecting. This confidence will not manifest as an arrogant conviction that you are a mouthpiece for the divine, but as an unshakeable faith in the message coupled with a complete disregard for the messenger.

Now obviously the situation is not always quite as black and white as I may have made it appear from the above. Given that the need is great and the Masters must work with what is available there are many examples of those who might have had some kind of limited connection to the source but who have allowed that contact to inflate their ego. Consequently they may at one time have transmitted true teachings at the level they were supposed to be doing that but will have subsequently lost their inner connection because of an appropriation by the self to what lies beyond self. Those who confuse the medium (themselves) with the message (spiritual truth) will pay the price even though they may not be aware of this for some time.

During the course of this talk the Master said that **inevitably doubts would arise but these must be ignored.** However advanced you are on the spiritual path you are going to have to wrestle with doubt. Whatever your understanding, whatever experiences of the soul you may have had, there will be times when all of that seems a long way off and you will wonder if it was really true or just stories and imagination. This may be more likely in the contemporary Western world in which the prevailing culture denies the existence of a transcendent reality, but even if you live in a traditional culture in which a sense of the sacred has not been lost there will probably come a time when everything just dries up. You look within and there is nothing. You seek succour without and there is none to be had. Doubt comes to all on the path and, in an extreme form, may sometimes last for years, years when the light is lost and darkness appears to be all there is. Doubt can be a natural reaction to initial excitement once the novelty of spiritual discovery has worn off but it can also be a test that throws us back on ourselves. There are times when the doors of heaven seem to be wide open and there are others when they are tightly shut. These are the times when we can consolidate and put into practice what we have been given, when we assimilate what we have learnt. They are times when we are tested as to the sincerity of our spiritual motives and the worthiness of our heart.

The quote from *The Imitation of Christ* I mentioned earlier is very apposite here. "You are not making progress if you receive God's grace but you are making progress if you bear the withdrawal of grace with patience, humility and resignation". The withdrawal of grace may cause us to doubt it was ever really present but if we stay true to our inner vision without losing faith we will be rewarded. Spiritual darkness is separation from God but we need that separation in order to grow if we are to become fully individual as well as fully universal in consciousness. **I was like the seed growing in the darkness and struggling towards the light** said the Master. **The light was always there even if I could not see it.** His metaphor may not have been the most original but it was appropriate. We are seeds of God, little godlings, growing up towards the light in the nourishing soil of matter. The darkness of matter may at times oppress us but it also serves to protect us from the blaze of too much light before we are capable of withstanding it.

As already related, Michael was homosexual, celibate when I met him but not always so. As a young man I was at first a little apprehensive as to whether that may have been part of his reason for making my acquaintance hence my question. The reader is entitled to point out that the answer to this question came through Michael himself so might have been influenced by him but, as I have been at pains to make clear throughout this book, in the form of communication used, unlike channelling, there was no input from the medium. Michael's mind was simply not a part of the process.

The Masters' attitude as to whether a person was homosexual or not was that it **was unimportant. In their eyes it was the same as heterosexuality.** This was in 1979 when such an attitude was not nearly as common as now. However they went on to say that **love must be pure.** What did they mean by that? It was not a comment based on any moral values they might have had (they had no moral values, as such) but an observation that, to be in tune with the reality of the spiritual world, love should be without attachment or desire. It should be a reflection of the soul without any input from the ego. So they were saying that whether a person is homosexual or heterosexual by nature is unimportant. What does matter is how they act on that. I refer the reader back to chapter 8 for a fuller discussion of the subject and what the Masters said on a subsequent occasion. Here I wish mainly to add that, unlike certain tantric gurus, the Masters regarded the principal purpose of sex, insofar as its physical expression was concerned, to be the procreation of children and, as homosexual sex could not function in that regard, it was a misdirection of energy with probable karmic consequences. That is the explanation for their use of the word '**degenerating**' when they spoke of Michael's love for me and the fact that they had no fear of it going that way. So when they said, in the context of my question about Michael's homosexuality, that **in their eyes it was the same as heterosexuality** that does not mean they were saying that homosexual acts were the same as heterosexual ones from the point of view of divine truth.

Having said that, I should go on to point out that by the Masters' standards, which very definitely are those of divine truth, much heterosexual sex is also a misdirection of energy with probable karmic consequences. For them, as I say, sex exists primarily for the procreation of children. They would not deny that it can also, indeed should also, be an expression of love and that, if engaged in selflessly, it has the potential to take its participants out of themselves to a higher union, but child making is the principal purpose of the physical act. Now, in practical terms that does not mean that every sexual act should result in a child but you should at least be willing to have a child with your partner. You should feel that degree of unity. This probably discounts a large proportion of sexual activity.

That the purpose of sex is for the procreation of children is a deeply unfashionable view nowadays which many people will automatically dismiss (even though I would contend that deep down we all know it to be true), but to understand this view you have to understand something of the Masters' attitude to the body. For them **the body is a frame** meaning that its function is as a support for the soul in the material world and that it has no intrinsic value in itself. This is not a body denying attitude. For them the body is wholly natural but wholly subservient to the soul. The body is not an enemy but neither is it a master. Nor should it be a point of focus. It is the servant of the soul and, as such, should be looked after, cared for, its needs properly met but no more than that or it will seek to acquire a more primary role with the result that any spiritual connection will be diminished, if not lost, and the person locked in the lower consciousness of identification with form. The body is the temple of the soul. A temple is important and can be beautiful too but it only exists to house the divine light within. It has no purpose other than that and no true reality apart from that. Without that light it is a hollow shell.

Sex and what its place is in the spiritual life has always been one of the thorniest questions for those intent on leading that life. The celibacy advocated in the past may have represented an ideal but tended to imply a duality between soul and body and thus cause a split in the psyche. Moreover, even as an ideal, it is not for everyone at every stage of the path. There may certainly be times when celibacy is right, either for a period or a whole lifetime, but sex is a natural function and the legitimate needs of the body should not be denied or they will only torment the mind and take on even greater prominence than if they had been satisfied and one had simply moved on. Needless to say, the current over-emphasis on sex is even more misguided and that is the case for everyone not just spiritual seekers. It is misguided because it is ignorant and it is ignorant because it ignores the reality of what a human being is, restricting that to lower or outer levels only. I must insist that this is not a puritanical attitude, though many will undoubtedly choose to see it as such, but one that is simply based on what is true.

So what is the right approach for the spiritual seeker? First of all,

I would say, it depends on the individual. We must all follow our intuition as to what is right. There may be times when a celibate life is correct for us but there may also be times when our life lessons take a more external form and a family life with the responsibilities of children is the focus of our endeavours. Though, even then, the watchword should be moderation. Sex may be a natural function but identification with form, of which the physical body is the most obvious aspect, must eventually be transcended. So you do not suppress but you need not necessarily express either. Sex is not a 'sin' but it can easily be a diversion and the truth of the matter is that the spiritual person should not need completion by anything outside him or herself. You might think that this statement is rather extreme and should only apply to a realised person not an ordinary aspirant, but realisation will only come when you are realised which is to say that you are not changed by realisation so much as the change must come in you before you show yourself to be ready for it.

At one time I asked the Masters if one could lead a normal married life and still follow the higher stages of the spiritual path. I knew what had been said in the past which was, generally speaking, no and I knew what was said nowadays which is, generally speaking, yes. I wanted to know what someone who actually knew what he was talking about might say. There is a mystery to the whole subject of sex which, in its occult sense, we are still far from understanding despite what we may think. Tantra may hint at it as, in different ways, may alchemical lore and some of the Arthurian stories, specifically the Grail legends[6], but these have so often been distorted to suit individual agendas, with what is meant symbolically interpreted literally, that they are no longer, if they ever were, of much practical value.

I speak from memory here as I don't have a record of what the Master said but he basically took a very practical approach. He told me that sex consumes energy which, if so consumed, cannot go into spiritual realisation. Sexual energy and spiritual energy are two forms of the same thing. He said that one could lead a married life and pursue the path, but it would be that much harder as there was so much to distract one and divert one's energies and one's time. You only have a limited amount of energy at your disposal. You have to decide how you wish to expend this energy. Treading the spiritual path requires a great deal of energy so if you wish to do that you have to reduce the energy spent elsewhere. At the same time he added that the trials and responsibilities of a relationship and children can provide an excellent arena in which to learn many lessons that could not be learnt so easily or at all if one was on one's own.

He made two further points which might be of interest. Recognising that we live in a world in which sexual desire is constantly over-stimulated, he gave a technique for helping to sublimate it. Seemingly based on the Indian theory of chakras (the seven centres of force in the human body that go from the base of the spine to the top of the head), the technique involved focusing on the lowest chakra and drawing the energy from there upwards. Excess sexual desire will cause the chakra at the base of the spine to emit a dull red light. One should try to imagine that chakra as a vortex of energy spinning faster and faster and, as it does so, throwing off impure energy and changing to a pure white colour. Visualisation of a Master or spiritual ideal will greatly help with this as it summons the elevated vibration associated with such a figure. You must draw the energy up to the heart centre, which is positioned more centrally than the physical heart, transforming it there into the pink rose of selfless love which you may then imagine as opening up and shining the light hidden at its core out into the world. You could at that stage, if you so wished, continue to draw the energy further up still to the third eye positioned in the middle of the forehead from whence it can be projected out in a stream of golden light. The success of the operation depends on the strength of your ability to visualise plus the sincerity of your desire to achieve success. The literal truth of the description is not important. I am not saying it is not literally true but what matters is the engagement of the imagination at a deep level. This will bring results.

The second point made by the Master was that sexual energy is an aspect of creative energy and so the lower form (forgive the terminology but it does relate to physical expression) can be channelled into the higher. The urge to procreate is natural but the urge to create should be equally so, yet that is sometimes neglected in our contemporary culture. The effects of sexual over-stimulation can be countered by engaging in creative activity and the Masters were strong advocates of this as a means of bringing the sexual urge back to its correct place in the overall scheme of things. That is not where it is at the moment and our vaunted sexual freedom is frequently just a form of sexual slavery, slavery to the body and its reproductive urges which are natural as reproductive urges, unnatural and potentially spiritually disastrous when stoked up by the pursuit of pleasure. Again, please don't write this off as a puritanical attitude just because it might have points in common with one. Spontaneous enjoyment is not at all at odds with spiritual development but the search for pleasure, what the Masters call effortful as opposed to effortless desire, reduces the human being to its manifested vehicles and cuts the person off from the higher aspects of his nature. Denial of the existence of these higher aspects does not change their reality.

On another occasion when I spoke of these matters to the Masters they took a more absolutist stance. This was typical of them. They would not always give the same answer to the same question. There is no contradiction involved here. It is simply a matter of different levels of understanding. What is the case at one level may not be at another or, at least, may be viewed in a different light with a different scale of priorities. What they said was this. **This activity (i.e. sex) will retard you**[7]. That's quite a categorical statement so let me open it up a little. There are times when sex is a normal part of one's life expression. There are others when it will hinder progress and, generally, the further on you are on the path, the more aware you are of the soul, the less you should need sex. That doesn't neces-sarily mean you won't have it but if you do you won't be attached to it. Only you can decide what is right for you based on your own inner responses.

The reader may feel a bit short changed here as though we had set out on a journey to somewhere interesting but ended up going nowhere. But there is no easy answer or, at least, there is no single answer that applies equally to everybody under all circumstances. I think everyone must follow their karmic destiny bearing in mind the following facts. The body is a part of the whole human being. The body is the servant of the indwelling soul. We should not be ruled by desire. It is not wrong to enjoy God's gifts. Attachment is always wrong. Love is always right but only divine love has true under-standing.

Can we sum things up by saying that we are not the body but we are in the body? Or should that be we are in the body but we are not the body?

Chapter 17

What Are Spiritual Experiences For?

Not all my jottings down of the Masters' words have dates to them. There are some isolated sentences that I extracted from talks for which I kept no fuller record. One such is the following statement given in response to a question about meditation. **Do not seek to experience anything in meditation. That is not the true purpose of it.** This is worth looking at in a little more detail.

When I first began to meditate, my aim was to experience for myself states I had read about in the writings of mystics throughout the ages, but which I also intuitively knew existed. In those early days of discovery, this seemed to me to be what the spiritual life was all about, a progression to higher and higher states of consciousness, attainable merely by striving to attain them. Not long after I started meditation, I did indeed experience such states in which consciousness seemed to expand beyond the restricting confines of the mind and the 'I' dissolved (or appeared to dissolve) into a radiant sea of bliss. During those times I felt bathed in love and at one with the whole of life, potentially able to access the fount of all knowledge. Inevitably such experiences did not last long but I interpreted them as precursors of a more permanent condition that I hoped I would soon be able to access at will.

Just like me, those starting a spiritual practice frequently experience higher states of consciousness. They assume they have entered samadhi or become one with God, or however else they may express it, and that they are shortly destined to attain enlightenment. Some even set themselves up as teachers on the basis of their experiences regarding these as confirmation from above of their fitness to guide others. They think one or two experiences of ego transcendence means they have transcended the ego altogether, or are about to, and that, because they have touched the hem of Christ's garment, they will soon be donning his robes on a full time basis. The reality is more mundane. These experiences are usually more indicative of a soul beginning the path than one nearing its end.

The novice needs encouragement to begin his journey, some of which will necessarily be spent in the wilderness. He needs to find out for himself that there is a reality beyond his everyday consciousness, that what he has been told about really is true and not just the delusion of unbalanced minds so he is given these experiences by God's good grace (or by his teachers on the inner planes which is more or less the same thing). He has not earned them other than by opening himself up to the possibility of having them. So they do not reflect his attainment so much as his aspiration.

The key word here is experience. Any experience is outside oneself. Experience presupposes an experiencer and that is why I said that the 'I' appears to dissolve. In truth it does no such thing. Its borders may temporarily melt away but its core remains and, once the experience has passed, it can even be inflated if we react to the experience in the wrong way which, alas, it is very easy to do, especially if we are unprepared and lack the guidance of a wise counsellor to keep us grounded. It is all too common for a seeker to regard as his personal possession a transpersonal state that he has experienced, and to think that because he has experienced it, he has become it. To be sure, that is what he is in his essence but at this stage he has been granted but a taste and is still very much on the outside looking in. This is why it is said that the first lesson on the path is humility and the last lesson is humility too.

Many people have spiritual experiences of one sort or another. These may come through a spiritual practice or from contemplating the world of nature or at a time of crisis or just arise unbidden out of the blue. The problems start when we interpret them through the still unpurified mind/ego or when we think that such episodes mark us out as someone special. We may assume we know the truth when all we have done is seen the light shining through a door that is slightly ajar, a door that is still not properly open let alone one that we have passed through. Furthermore our ignorance of the hierarchical nature of spiritual states means we tend to regard anything beyond ordinary consciousness as cosmic consciousness.

What we experience in no way indicates what we are, what is known in Sufism as our spiritual station. What we are prepared to renounce, including outer happiness and inner joy, is a much better indication of our spiritual maturity. Think. If spiritual experiences were what mattered there would be no need to incarnate but we come to Earth to learn the lessons of Earth and that we will have no incentive to do if we are bathed in bliss. It is said that it is only through separation that we eventually reach completion and it could equally well be said that only by being cut off from God can we ever truly come to know God in the fullest sense. We are like the prodigal son who had to leave home in order fully to appreciate it.

If you are serious about the spiritual path, do not seek spiritual experiences. If they come, welcome them. When they go, let them without trying to hold on to them. Do not regard them as saying anything about you personally and do not expect in this world to reach a permanent state of bliss. Love God rather than his gifts and accept what He sends regardless of what that may be. Sometimes it's the nastiest tasting medicine that does the most good, and often it is the greatest among us who experience the most inner suffering, not because there is any virtue in suffering *per se* but because the giving up of self is the hardest thing anyone can ever do and only the most advanced are truly able to do it. Suffering is the solvent that dissolves the ego which is presumably what Jesus meant when he said that anyone who followed him would be required to take up the cross.

I am not implying that there is anything wrong with spiritual experiences or that they should be shunned or even regarded as other than wholly good if and when they come to us. They are genuine indications of our true nature and therefore should be welcomed joyfully. But they should not be sought. And if they do come it is important that we react to them correctly which is to say with reticence and humility. This, frankly, can be hard and it may be that sometimes they are sent to us precisely to provoke a certain reaction, to bring out whatever spiritual egotism may be lying dormant within us since only when something comes out into expression can it be properly eradicated.

There is nothing to be ashamed of if we do react to a spiritual experience with attachment or egotism. It would be better not to, of course, but this is probably the standard human reaction and we all react like standard (that is to say, fallen) humans until we learn not to. The Masters themselves have made mistakes similar to the ones we make now which is partly why they have such compassion for us. The only difference is they made their mistakes in the past whereas we are making ours currently. They have overcome whatever it was in them that caused them to go astray and so will we once we learn to seek the good for the sake of the good and not for what it may bring us.

What then should our approach be to spiritual experiences? How should we best use them? What matters most with a spiritual experience is what you do with it and what you should do with it is seek to align yourself with the reality of which it is an expression. That means don't seek to repeat it but seek to become like it. Look upon it as a message calling you home and so grasp the truth that it is first and foremost a summons to work. For the spiritual virtues do not come as a result of spiritual experiences. Rather that of which a spiritual experience is only a reflection will come when you have acquired the virtues.

And so, returning to the Master's words at the beginning of this brief discussion, what is the purpose of meditation if it is not to gain spiritual experience? It should now be clear that the primary purpose of meditation is to deepen our contact with the soul and allow its influence to permeate our mind so that gradually we may become it. However on this path motive is all and the reason we meditate matters as much as the fact that we do. By going into the silence we can uncover our true self but unless we do so out of love of God rather than desire for heaven or some other personal goal we will just be constructing a metaphysical Tower of Babel and so will not succeed in this laudable aim no matter what we might experience.

Chapter 18

"The World is in Need."

June 20th 1979

The Master, who came from a very far away plane, told me that I had asked to come back to the world to serve them but before I could do so I must learn my lessons. There remained flaws in my character caused by lack of acceptance and I must learn to be humble before I could begin my work. He told me to practise self-forgetfulness and than went on to say that I worry too much about the faults of others which were not my concern. I should just look to my own. "Your task is to correct your own faults. By correcting those you help others to heal their own wounds. By neglecting them you help neither yourself nor others." He went on to say. "The world is in need and there is much teaching to be done but you cannot commence your service to us until you have overcome the lower self."

I forget now why I wrote that the Master had come from a far away plane but I assume he said that himself. They would occasionally tell me such things. It was one of the few personal details, if you can call it that, they did tell me. I have mentioned that none of the Masters were physically incarnate but there are many spheres in the spiritual universe and some of them were further removed from our world than others. This may have had something to do with seniority or it may have related to function since, although the Masters are members of one body, they fulfil different roles within that body.

Here's a little story which you may interpret literally or allegorically as you think best. Imagine that you come into this world with a designated work to do. You, a pure unsullied spark of divine fire from the spiritual realm, are given a part of the material world in the form of a human being with the task of transforming that base metal into polished gold. It is your task to sculpt this rough and imperfect form into something grand and noble eventually bringing it to the point where the divine light may shine unimpeded through it, thus helping in the eventual upliftment and transformation of the material universe. But, enclosed in the limitations of matter, you make the mistake of confusing this earthbound human being for yourself and that leads to all sorts of further confusions. One of these is that it becomes easier to see the imperfections in the other human beings than in the one you inhabit. These imperfections may well be present but it is not your task or even possible for you to do anything about them, except insofar as you can provide an example to those others of what they should do. Your task is first and foremost to work with what you have been given and what you and only you can change. To do this effectively you must seek to re-establish contact with your true and original nature, that spark of divine fire.

In the Sermon on the Mount Jesus told his followers not to be concerned with the mote in the eye of their brothers but to look to the beam in their own. Here the Master tells me exactly the same thing when he says that **I worry too much about the faults of others which were not my concern. I should just look to my own.** I recognised the perfect justice of this remark and that I had to do something about it especially as, being born under the sign of Virgo, a critical tendency might be said to be one of my 'natural' failings – not that I am blaming my 'stars' for my own shortcomings since I don't doubt these can only bring out what is already there. At the same time, I also understood that, when they tell us not to worry about the faults of others, neither Jesus nor the Masters intended that to mean we should not help others by pointing out weaknesses that might prevent them moving forwards on the path. The reason we do this though is critical, as is the way we do it. Do we do it because we are upset or irritated by the other's faults? Do they make us angry or fearful? This was my case because I was reacting to them on a personal level. The Master told me to point out the flaws in another person only if those flaws caused no reaction within me at all and to do it in such a way that I was completely unattached to the response, not worrying whether I was accepted or rejected. Many times they would say to me that **all you have to do is sow the seed.** And once they made this comment. **Say what you have to say once and once only and then change the subject. For instance, would you like a cup of tea?** Yes, they really did say that.

There is an idea that one person who achieves raises up the entire planet and makes it that bit easier for others to achieve afterwards. Might this be part of what the Master meant when he said, referring to my faults, that **by correcting those you help others to heal their own wounds?** You could take this simply to mean that example teaches better than words, but I think we can go further than that obvious explanation and affirm that one human being transcending ego has a leavening effect throughout human consciousness. The Ascension of Christ had this effect on a grand scale and likewise, following his attainment of enlightenment, many of the Buddha's disciples were enabled to make a spiritual breakthrough. In the same way, I would maintain that each person who passes through the gateway to eternal life makes it simpler for those who follow after to tread the same path, and it is reference to this truth that we can detect behind the Master's words about healing others through healing yourself.

The Master also drew attention to my **lack of acceptance.** Acceptance in the sense he used the word here means lack of resistance. Conversely **lack of acceptance** means resistance. As long as we are acting from self we are resisting because self dams the flow of life. Modern man has developed a strong intellect and a strong sense of self. He (and increasingly she) defines himself in these terms and cannot let go. But the river of life flows and we must flow with it, letting it take us where it will and not fighting it. To act from ego is to fight. To accept is to surrender ego. Let go and let God.

The world is in need. You might say that this has always been the case. However at other times the Masters spoke of the particularly distressed spiritual state of our world today and said that never has spirit been so obscured. Though they first told me this thirty years ago there is no reason to think that things are any better today. On the contrary, as we have largely carried on the way we were going then, things are almost certainly worse. You might quite reasonably point to improvements in many fields but I would submit that in terms of what really matters, an intelligent understanding that life has a spiritual basis, we are further away from where we should be than ever.

It has become commonplace to say that we live today in a world in crisis. I think everyone recognises that on some level, though many of us either ignore or deny it. We talk about environmental destruction, climate change, problems to do with capitalism, globalism, the depletion of energy resources and so on and so on. We lament a decline in standards, a lack of meaning in our lives and an absence of vision. The list is long but the cause behind everything on it can be stated very briefly. The crisis of the world, acknowledged or not, is a spiritual crisis.

Would we despoil and pillage the Earth if we saw it as part of ourselves? Would we permit poverty and hunger to exist side by side with enormous, unjustifiable and pointless wealth if we truly saw humanity as one? Would we drug ourselves with an endless succession of material objects if we knew that by the nature of our being these could never satisfy us? Would we accept certain forms of art and entertainment if we knew that they really could corrupt our souls and lead us deeper and deeper into illusion?

Over the last few centuries we have become accustomed to a view of the world in which life, or human life at least, is more or less uninterrupted progress. The achievements of science in the outer world are too numerous and too obvious to mention and I won't do so other than to say that technological advances have given us more comfort and power than a medieval monarch, for all his supreme temporal authority, could ever have imagined possible. Since the

18th century rationalist Enlightenment, as it is called and as in certain respects it was, we have liberated ourselves from much superstition and ignorance, and brought justice, fairness and equality to ever larger sections of oppressed humanity. Advances in medicine and sanitation have lead to higher standards of health and improved longevity. Externally, things have got better and better. Or so it seems.

There is another view of the world though and, according to this, our outer lives may have improved but our inner lives have suffered correspondingly. In fact they have become enormously impoverished as a result. The modern worldview might be described as almost entirely horizontal in its outlook. It recognises no transcendent dimension to life and limits the human being to that part of it that can be perceived by the mind and senses. The traditional worldview was one largely based on a vertical perception of reality and it would say that modern man not only denies his spiritual source but, in so doing, actually denies his humanity and that is the cause of his sickness. No doubt you could say that there are flaws and advantages to both points of view, but the loss of God outweighs by an incalculable amount the benefits that technology has brought, many of which are quite possibly only benefits from the point of view of material man anyway. Truly, what does it benefit a man if he gains the whole world but loses his soul? But that exchange is precisely the way the modern era is heading. This is the goal, unstated and probably unrealised, of the modernist dream.

Some people regard the horizontal focus of the last few centuries as a necessary balance to the traditional vertical outlook which they say had become too one dimensional, too formal and needed to be adjusted. The adjustment would inevitably involve a period of reaction, over-emphasis and neglect of the virtues of the previous approach in order to develop new virtues which will eventually take us on to "a higher turn of the spiral" once spiritual values are rediscovered. Others though see it as a complete aberration which can only lead humanity to its downfall. Of course, they say, it has its good side. Nothing can be all bad and it would never have had any appeal if it did not bring certain benefits and correct flaws and limitations inherent in the old approach, either due to its own nature or else to corruption caused by human nature. But its advantages and benefits are insignificant compared to the loss it has engendered. They point to the ancient belief, existing in many traditional cultures, in cycles of ever decreasing spirituality that go from a prehistoric golden age to the present time of spiritual darkness, but material prosperity that dulls us to the reality of what we have forfeited. They regard our increasing dependence on machines as separating us more and more from our true source, and say that by viewing ourselves as machines, which is basically what materialist science does, we are in effect becoming machines. We are losing our souls. But then they go on to say that even many of the revived forms of spirituality around nowadays, far from being signs of recovery, are actually part of the downward spiral, being but shallow and superficial counterfeits whose principal purpose or, at any rate, effect is to sidetrack those who react to the prevailing materialism and lead them away from the serious business of saving their souls into psychic labyrinths and self-indulgence. They hold no brief for the idea of a glorious New Age just around the corner, popular in such circles, claiming that, spiritually speaking, humanity is not evolving but degenerating with personal development being the stated or unstated real goal of many of those drawn to the spiritual rather than true holiness. Traditional teachings tend to back up this idea of degeneration, with the Mosaic religions all talking of an "end time" when God is ignored and the forces of Mammon run riot, and Eastern religions, in particular the ancient Vedic religion of India, positing a descent into the dark age of the Kali Yuga with, to be sure, a Satya Yuga or new Golden Age to follow but only after a wiping clean of the slate as is also predicted in the Christian book of Revelation.

You have then these three attitudes to the present day. One, the world is as science sees it and what it sees is all there is to see.

Human knowledge will increase and technology will eventually either banish inequality and suffering or else we will destroy ourselves. Two, we certainly do live in materialistic times now but we can look forward to an era when science and religion are no longer adversaries but reconciled, each with its own sphere of expertise. The horizontal and vertical axes will co-exist in perfect harmony and this will be the Aquarian Age of peace and love. Three, there is no inevitable evolution but life in this world is actually entropic and humanity is plunging downwards as prophesied by most of the mainstream religions. There will be no spiritual renaissance but an apocalyptic conclusion with the commencement of a new cycle to follow though the bulk of humanity will not be here to enjoy it.

Obviously I dismiss the first of these possible scenarios, in its materialistic aspect at least, but which of the following two are the more probable I cannot say. You might think that the first is more logical as well as being more in tune with current ideas on reincarnation, implying, as they are taken to do, a more or less continuous progression. It certainly has a pleasing fairness and reasonableness to it that will appeal to the modern sensibility and, for what it's worth, seems to be supported by a certain amount of channelled information. The second approach has the backing of tradition but appears to regard most of humanity as unworthy, which may seem rather a high-handed and elitist attitude but what if these times are a testing ground when the sheep are sorted out from the goats? That's not to say that the 'goats' are consigned to a cosmic dustbin, but there might be a separation of various groups of souls with some of the less spiritually aware and more spiritually obtuse being sent to different world systems, where they would be given the opportunity to have experiences more in keeping with their inner state. If this world is being prepared for a new cycle, such a winnowing would presumably be an essential requirement.

I have no more knowledge than anyone else as to what the future might hold. but one thing I do believe and that is what the Master said. **The world is in need.** We are approaching a time of decision, a time when humanity will not be allowed to carry on the way it has been going, when it simply must awaken from its spiritual slumber. The question is will we awaken on our own or will we be forced to awaken by circumstances beyond our control?

The talks became a little more infrequent at this stage and over the course of the next couple of weeks the Masters visited only once, and that for just a few brief moments. Possibly they felt I was finally beginning to absorb some of their teaching.

June 25th 1979
The Master came briefly and told me to love, have faith and accept. Spiritual progress comes through service and sacrifice he said. Have humility and be mature.

The Masters were constantly telling me to be mature. I don't know if I was particularly immature for a twenty three year old. No more than most, I would say. The meaning I took it to have was that I should get on with the task in hand without lapsing into wishful thinking or self-preoccupation. Spiritual seekers can be very self-preoccupied. Maturity, true maturity, is self-forgetfulness.

They were also constantly enjoining me to have faith. Faith is not the same as belief and it is certainly not the same as credulity. Credulity is lack of discernment, belief is opinion but faith is an act of the spiritual imagination. It is an intuitive awareness of things unseen. It is an openness to the transcendent, a listening to the voice of the heart and a readiness to accept what lies beyond the everyday, without necessarily understanding it or even having solid evidence for it. There is evidence enough if one knows where and how to look, but it is written in the book of nature and inscribed on the human heart in a form that cannot readily be interpreted by the analytical mind.

Faith, properly understood, does not mean faith in a particular form of truth such as Catholicism or Islam. That is belief though, of course, it can also include elements of faith. But faith in the higher sense is confidence in that which lies beyond form, and without faith of this kind there can be no spiritual growth as indicated by St Augustine's famous statement *credo ut intelligam* - I believe so that I may understand. You must be open to truth in order to know truth. The seed lying in the darkness of the earth would never grow if, on some level, it was not aware of the bright light of day above. Strange as it may seem, it is a form of faith that enables that seed to become a flower.

Faith does not mean never having doubts but it does mean trusting the heart so that you are never overwhelmed by doubts. Doubt comes from the mind and is inevitable. It is also healthy to a degree in that it shakes the tree of intellectual certitude and clears the way for a higher understanding. Never lose faith but never allow the mind to consolidate itself so much that its form becomes fixed and no longer open to change and growth.

Spiritual progress comes through service and sacrifice. This is something we need to remember always but it sounds very unglamorous, doesn't it? Compared to the magic and power that attracts the occultist and the peace and bliss the mystic seeks, the notion that **spiritual progress comes through service and sacrifice** might not seem very enticing. But it's true and how could it be otherwise, given that the individual soul must renounce all it holds dear to find what truly matters, must let go of all that is not God in order to find God? With their emphasis on humility, surrender and self-abnegation the Masters could often sound much more like wise abbots of a Christian monastery than those contemporary spiritual teachers who teach wisdom and enlightenment as the goal rather than the fruits of the path. There is a difference and it is one worth thinking about.

July 4th 1979
The Master said that there must be a balance between Michael and myself and that we must work together. He told me that I should carry out my earthly duties without resenting having to do them or

thinking that they got in the way of spiritual progress which was sometimes made through doing menial tasks and keeping busy. For instance, he said, scrubbing the floor engenders humility. I should keep myself occupied and not become too introspective. At this stage I should not go inwards but outwards and look to others, thinking of others not myself. Too much introspection would lead to stagnation. Have love in abundance, he concluded.

The Kingdom of Heaven is within but sometimes we have to look without as well and remember that the first commandment is to love God but the second is to love your neighbour who is also God, though in His manifested and limited aspect rather than His absolute and transcendent one. Awareness depends on inner realisation but you cannot neglect the outer with the excuse that truth is found within. Ultimately the inner and the outer are one and you will not reach true understanding if you do not fully realise that, in the classic Buddhist teaching, *Samsara* is *Nirvana*. My besetting sin, common in those of a mystical disposition, was to underrate the outer in relation to the inner, to see it as somehow inferior. This was not necessarily wholly mistaken as, hierarchically, the inner is the superior or pre-eminent principle, and it was assuredly better than the opposite point of view. But it was incomplete as the outer is the inner in its relative mode. Otherwise put, the two together make up reality. In a certain sense, Michael and I represented inner and outer polarities in the context of our relationship and that is why I was told there had to be a balance between us. I could give the spiritual impulse but he could ground it. Without Michael my spiritual awareness would probably have remained vague and nebulous, an idea in search of the proper form to give it expression. He could earth it and help it to develop and grow. Without me he might have continued to seek spiritual understanding in exterior teachings rather than turn inwards to see it as it is.

Reverting to the practical, the plain fact is that the performance of menial tasks can be very conducive to spiritual progress if undertaken in the right spirit. Simple, repetitive, physical work that occupies mind and body (I am not talking about working in a factory or, the modern equivalent, tapping at a computer keyboard both of which, without too much exaggeration, can justly be described as soul destroying) will prevent the self-absorption that comes from too much introspection and help to **engender humility**. Traditionally monks, both in the East and the West, have always known this to be so. I wonder how many souls, well advanced along the path, might be discovered leading apparently unproductive lives of quiet simplicity, far removed from the fame and fortune that attracts and ensnares most of us? It is a fallacy to think that the most enlightened are always those who might appear to be so.

July 6th 1979

As usual the Master made his appearance after sounding the OM. He gave his love and blessings and then told me that I should think of them throughout the day and act according to instructions. "Think of us as a circle of entities above you and consign all your troubles and problems to us. You will then find relief. Do not analyse everything endlessly but accept. At the moment you cannot see the wood for the trees so you cannot know that all is as it should be. Have faith and know that all will be well. Learn to roll with the flow and do not resist, letting us guide you"

Before they spoke the Masters usually sounded the OM in the same way they had done when they made their first appearance to me. This had the effect of both purifying and intensifying the atmosphere and put me on my toes, psychologically speaking, ready for their talk. They may have had another purpose for this connected to the process of mediumship, preparing the vessel as it were, tuning it to the correct pitch for their entry. I seem to remember they did explain something along those lines to me once but, at this remove from the events and without notes, I cannot be more specific. I also recall asking them about the meaning of the OM and they told me it was a sacred word embodying the basic tone of the universe as much as any sound could in our world. To them it was indeed a universal sound, originating in India but not just Indian.

I should think of them throughout the day. Always 'them', never 'me'. The Masters were a brotherhood who may have had specific roles within that brotherhood but who thought of themselves as a unity. We talk a lot about group consciousness nowadays. This was the real thing. You might think of it as a higher version of tribal consciousness but without any exclusiveness on the one hand or merging or diminishment of individuality on the other. In the spiritual realm groups exist of many kinds and on many levels. Membership of a group in no way precludes oneness with those in other groups any more than it does the oneness of each member of that group with God which is a wholly individual and private thing. One of the difficulties people have with certain spiritual concepts is that they think of them in opposing terms, if this is true then that is not, but spiritual reality is all inclusive and encompasses many complementary truths as parts of its whole.

Think of us as a circle of entities above you and consign all your troubles and problems to us. You will then find relief.

A few times when I was living in Bath during this period I visited the nearby city of Wells. The 13th century cathedral there is one of the most beautiful ecclesiastical buildings in all England. Its western front, about 100 feet high and 150 feet wide, was decorated with over five hundred life-size sculptured figures of saints, prophets, angels, kings and queens with Christ in glory at the apex. Not all the figures have survived and those that do have lost their original paint and gilding but the façade is still a magnificent sight. The cathedral's medieval stained glass, especially the fine Tree of Jesse depicting Christ's descent, is equally striking but what appealed to me as much as either of these was the chapter house where the cathedral's administrators would have gathered to discuss issues relevant to church life. This is a large octagonal chamber with a central column suggesting the Tree of Life whose stone "branches" arch up to the ceiling in an almost organic way from whence they spread out in fan vaulting more delicate than you would think possible to achieve with stone. Around the edge of the chapter house there are seats set in niches where each member of the clergy would have had his place. I imagined the Masters sitting in meditation and council in a heavenly version of a place such as this, a place filled with light that they would draw from the holy source above and then project downwards to the world below. Such was the **circle of entities** to which I **could consign all my troubles and problems.** Visualising the Masters in a specific setting like this helped me to establish contact with them, which had not been easy at first, but when I succeeded in doing so I did find relief from care and worry. Things were put in perspective. What applied to me then applies to you now. You have only to make the link in your heart and imagination and your spiritual guides, and you do have such, will relieve you of any burdens you may have. You must really hand them over, you must let go, but if you do and hold nothing back then your load will be lightened.

It goes against the grain for us modern people not to analyse. That's our culture. That's what we are educated to do. How can we understand something if we don't puzzle it out? As a person born and brought up in the modern age, that was my attitude. I had to think about everything and try and work out its meaning. And there is nothing wrong with this up to a point. We cannot just act thoughtlessly or foolishly and we should always endeavour to understand. But we do it, as the Master said, **endlessly.** Thought, analysis, can take us so far but there is a point beyond which it cannot go and if we continue turning things round in our head that's where we will remain, in our head, in thought. Such is not the Masters' way. Theirs is the way of faith and acceptance, two words which tend to strike horror in the modern mentality implying, as they do to that way of thinking, a terrible giving up of freedom and self determination. But what is freedom? Is it the ability to do what we want or does it depend on the understanding to do what is right? Is it the freedom of self or the freedom from self that is the greater? The fact is that the mind cannot know truth. The self cannot go beyond self. It has to let go. Thinking with the mind in the head can never take us beyond the mental level, beyond thoughts about truth to truth itself. The Masters will guide us but we have to let them, which means we must have complete faith in them and accept their guidance without hesitation or reserve.

I know this advice might seem to justify all sorts of foolishness and abuse. There are countless stories of individuals abandoning common sense and surrendering their intellect and will to domination by unscrupulous cult leaders or religious figures of dubious integrity. This is obviously not what I am recommending at all. Going beyond thought does not mean being stupid. Before you put your faith in a spiritual guide make quite sure that guide is bona fide and genuine. Exercise discrimination. Test the spirits. God gave us a mind so use it. But once you have tested the spirits and found them to be true then is the time to accept their instruction and guidance wholeheartedly, and to do so without subjecting it to endless analysis. Which doesn't mean you can't think. Just don't think too much.

At the moment you cannot see the wood for the trees. It was true. I certainly could not do that. We never can. Caught up in our own problems and difficulties it is very hard to **know that all is as it should be.** We can often seem to be making no progress at all but the state of being spiritually becalmed does not mean that God has abandoned you. It could mean precisely the opposite. You are being tested in order to become more spiritually self-reliant. Growth is taking place but in secret. I felt that after a flying start my so called inner life had rather dried up. This was absolutely as it should be since it is easy for the neophyte to become addicted to spiritual pleasure. I was too inexperienced to know this and I was not told it directly because I had to find it out for myself if I was to know it properly.

It might seem strange that despite having the great gift of the

Masters' instruction I doubted that all was proceeding as it should, but the process of spiritual development can be very unsettling psychologically. Your emotions and thoughts are brought out and stirred up and sometimes ground you believed to be solid starts to shift. I had experienced many highs and lows over the last few months and still not found the essential point of balance – see earlier talks. Moreover the contrast between the stimulus afforded by the Masters' visits and my meditations on the one hand and the mundane life I lived in the course of my work in the antiques market and in day to day relationships with other people on the other was something I was far from having learned to manage properly. I mention this not to immodestly draw attention to my own failings but to reassure anyone reading these lines who might be experiencing something similar that they need have no cause for concern. Such experiences are typical. One just has to learn not to react to the ups and downs of the spiritual path but to treat them with complete detachment. The best way to get through any hard times or confusion is to **have faith** and **learn to roll with the flow.**

And speaking of rolling with the flow, I have met people who are disappointed to find that Masters could use clichés like that. Certainly in my experience they do tend to express themselves with economy, dignity and without resorting to stale truisms that have lost their meaning through over use but if a well-worn phrase is the best way of saying something then why not use it?

When the Masters told me that I could not **see the wood for the trees** I have to assume that meant they could. This raises the interesting question as to what their understanding of time might be. There is no doubt that they would have transcended the normal limitations of time, since awareness of time, by which I mean what's called psychological time, is the result of the modifications of the mind, and a good definition of a Master would be one who has transcended the mind. But could they foresee the future? Was it something that they could plainly know or could they just see a range of possibilities, any one of which might come to pass depending on choices made by individuals involved? That would just be a human skill raised to a higher level. My feeling is that as they had transcended a time bound existence they could indeed see into the future. How far or how clearly I have no idea and I'm only basing my belief that they had this ability from impressions I got from things they said and hints they let drop. But I see no inherent contradiction between the existence of free will (which, by the way, certainly does exist – it's the reason for our existence) and knowledge of what will be. Knowledge of the future does not impel those moving towards that future to act in any particular way. The familiar image of time as a river can be helpful here. Those at the level of the river can see only a limited point on it, the present. The higher you go above the river, the further up or downstream you can see until there is a certain level (the level of divine omniscience?) at which the entire river from source to sea can be seen.

One day I should really write down a list of questions I should have asked the Masters but didn't. This question of time would certainly be one of them. The reason I did not ask about many things on which I would have loved to have had the benefit of their wisdom was that I did not want to abuse the gift of their presence. They had come to teach me not to satisfy my curiosity. What mattered was what mattered. I did not want to waste their time or treat them as my personal oracle. I don't suppose they would have answered those questions anyway. I can just imagine being politely but firmly told that I would understand these things in due course but they were not important now. Which I suppose is true.

The July 6th talk actually carried on a little more after the point at which I left it. A few nights before, Michael and I had, most unusually for us, been to the theatre. Anyone who knows Bath will know the Theatre Royal, a lovely little playhouse which dates back to the 18th century when Bath was a fashionable spa town. We had shared a box with some fellow dealers from the antiques market among whom were a couple called Peter's mother and Peter's father or, at least, that's what we called them. They had just had a baby, unsurprisingly named Peter, and, as can be the way with new parents, they immediately lost their own identities. Henceforth they were to be defined solely by virtue of their relationship to their offspring. During the interval Peter's father laughingly said that now he and his wife only existed as extensions of their child they were more twin souls than ever. The phrase must have stuck in Michael's mind because as we went home he mused whether we too might be twin souls. I realised later that he only used the phrase loosely and meant that we were connected in some way but at the time I was horrified. Despite my celibacy I still had a very romantic nature and the ideal of a perfect love had huge appeal for me. I had recently discovered Wagner's Tristan and Isolde and also become familiar with the occult doctrine of twin souls which states that all souls are created in pairs, one male, one female, and, although these may be separated for the purposes of their spiritual evolution, they eventually join up again either in this world or, more probably, the next there to experience the bliss of union. This idea appealed to something deep within me as I suppose it does in most of us. I don't doubt that it is based on a truth as it reflects the divine duality of spirit and matter emerging from the unmanifested void prior to manifestation but it has absolutely nothing to do with spirituality. You will never find completion in anything external, even your own twin soul. Completion can only be found in union with God. Obviously I had not absorbed this doctrine anywhere near fully enough because the notion of Michael being my twin soul, fond of him as I was, was deeply upsetting to me.

I had completely over-reacted to what was most likely a throwaway remark, certainly not meant in the way I took it, and that is why on the Master's next visit I questioned him about it, obviously fishing for a denial of Michael's theory.

The Master said that what Michael had meant by twin souls was that we were linked up for a time to accomplish certain work. Not any more than this. We should love and work together as a unit for

only then would we accomplish our purpose. Our destinies ran along the same lines for the present time and it was their will and also the will of our own higher selves that we should be together for this period. "Put aside childish thoughts." he said "Obey the impressions we fill you with and be true to your self."

A gentle reprimand for my silly, self-indulgent fears. To the Masters, self concern of any sort is childish. An innocent remark by Michael had brought out an attachment I had and made me realise the profound difference between heavenly paradise and spiritual enlightenment.

Chapter 19

Thoughts on India

It was at about this time that Michael and I first discussed going on a holiday to India. Like many people I had long had a fascination with that country, liberally fuelled in my case by stories my grandfather had told me of his time there during the Second World War; stories that were probably on the tall side since some of them concerned encounters with tigers and crocodiles, but which nonetheless made their mark on an impressionable young mind. Also, when I was about five I had collected cards of Indian birds and animals. These came with, and smelt strongly of, tea from Darjeeling and they fired my imagination in a way I could not explain. Even the word 'India' touched off something inside with a sense of beauty and mystery. I know I am far from alone in having this reaction but when I was small the idea of India triggered an emotion in me that was deeply stirring.

One of my fondest childhood memories is of my grandfather taking me to an Indian restaurant at about the age of 11 or 12 (there weren't so many in the mid sixties) where I had my first taste of spicy food. I also had one, maybe two, glasses of wine and finished my evening happily curled up on the floor of the passenger seat of my grandfather's car. Despite (or maybe because of) being a doctor he had quite liberal views on the subject of children and alcohol. My brother and I had been allowed to put our fingers in his glass of whiskey pretty much as soon as we could walk. Notwithstanding my mild state of intoxication, I still remember the décor of the restaurant with pictures of Shiva, Parvati and Vishnu gazing down from the walls; gods very different from the Greek and Norse ones I was used to from stories and picture books and conveying a much greater aura of divine mystique. Hearing the sound of a sitar for the first time also made an indelible impression on me. It all seemed strange and, yes, exotic, but it was oddly familiar too.

So I had had an interest in India from an early age and when Michael suggested a holiday there I was enthusiastic. It was not that I wanted to go to India to find a guru or that I expected to encounter a living spirituality that matched up to my ideals. I was not so innocent as to believe that existed there in our day anymore than in the West. It was more the country itself that intrigued me. There is no doubt that India embodies something quite profound for the whole of humanity. I've never known how to define it and the difficulty of definition is probably part of its allure. Calling it a sense of the spiritual is too easy. It is that but it is more for a sense of the spiritual exists or has existed in many places. The Indian version is of a particular and quite unique sort. It embraces the One in the Many and the Many in the One and sees both as part of an endless dance of give and take, now merging and blending, now hiding, now revealing each other. The sense of the Infinite is more potently felt in India than anywhere else. The grace, beauty and magical power of Maya, who both adorns and veils the ineffable divine mystery, is more keenly intuited and ardently worshipped. All this marks out and gives India its special quality.

Michael knew the north of India better than the south so that's where we decided to go. He spoke Urdu well, having learnt it during his time in India during the twilight years of the British Raj, and he taught me a few words and phrases before we left. Some languages one takes to readily enough whilst others are a bit of a struggle. I found that Urdu came to me without much effort, and, although I never became anywhere near fluent (not helped by the fact that English is so widely spoken on the sub-continent), I learnt a reasonable amount in a short time and I am not especially a natural linguist. But Urdu and its close cousin Hindi both seemed to 'fit' with relative ease so I was linguistically prepared for our trip. We booked our flight to New Delhi for late August. I remember that a return ticket cost £400 in those days which is more or less what it cost twenty or more years later, so much had long distance air travel taken off during that time.

When I told my parents of our plans they expressed surprise. Did I not remember that as a child my skin had been highly sensitive to the sun? I had managed to get sunburnt in Scotland on a couple of occasions and only a few years before had gone hitchhiking through France wearing a pair of washing up gloves with the fingers cut off, so prone were the backs of my hands to react to ultra violet rays with a bright red rash. I had soon discarded the ridiculous things (who would have ever given me a lift like that?) but instead had to walk around with my hands clasped behind my back like a minor royal which probably looked almost as silly.

I remembered all this and I did have some concerns about the heat but not enough to worry me unduly. I had asked the Masters if they were in favour of us going to India and their reply was that they had put the idea into our heads as they wished me to absorb the atmosphere of that country. They even said it would be easier for them to communicate with us in India as the psychic atmosphere (my expression, I don't recollect their exact words but this was the meaning) was less dense there. Is that because they had an Indian connection or was it that centuries of meditation had rendered the atmosphere purer or that there was less rampant materialism there at that time? It could be any or all of these, I couldn't say. Modern India is as materialistic as the West but then there were still the vestiges of a traditional spirituality which influenced the mindset of most people who dwelt there in some way or another.

We intended to be away for a month. We had a rough itinerary in mind but had not booked anywhere in advance. Our plan was to go to Delhi, stay there for a few days and then move on to wherever seemed best at the time. Calcutta, Varanasi, Agra, Bodh-Gaya were all discussed as possibilities. Perhaps a trip up to Kathmandu or Ladakh as well.

Everything was prepared, not that there was much to prepare. You didn't need a visa in those days and we had not bothered with any vaccinations. I did buy a hat on Michael's advice and am very glad I did. A hat is an essential piece of equipment for the pale-skinned Westerner in India and one that was neglected by many people then to their distinct disadvantage. I think travellers are more sensible now. Michael had a thing about hats anyway. In all the years I knew him he never went out without wearing one. He said this was how he had been brought up and it's true that virtually no-one in the 1930s and 1940s, of whatever class, left the house bareheaded. Still, the fashion went out, along with many other things, in the '60s but for Michael it remained obligatory, whatever the weather, to cover his head when he went out. It seems very peculiar in retrospect but it is how things were and nobody questioned it. I wonder how many things we do nowadays that nobody questions will seem peculiar to future generations. I would hope many things.

So there we were, all set to go when just a few days beforehand we found out that we would not be able to close our stand in the market for an entire month as we had assumed would be possible. If we could not man it ourselves then we had to find somebody else who could otherwise we would have to give it up. Although it didn't make much money, it was our livelihood and we needed to retain it in order to carry on with our particular way of life. Always reluctant to ask the Masters for their help in mundane matters (that's not what they were there for), we didn't on this occasion but, with only a day or so to go before our departure, somebody who had heard of our predicament volunteered to look after the stand and didn't even want to be paid as long as we took care of the rent and allowed him to sell his own stuff. I didn't wish to be superstitious but I thought a prayer of gratitude to the powers that be was appropriate on this occasion.

Chapter 20

"Love Disperses All Darkness."

I am running a bit ahead of myself here. It was around mid July when we first conceived the idea of a trip to India but the Masters made more visits between then and our departure in September and they carried on with their by now familiar teaching. They were no longer coming quite as often as they had in the early days but their visits were still regular and meant an enormous amount to me. I did not rely on them but I was always tremendously helped by them. I say the teachings were familiar and so they might have been as regards content but good spiritual teachers do not just teach by means of words. Their very presence was an inspiration as they embodied the teaching they gave. They were the teaching. And if the teachings were now familiar that does not mean that they were any less vital. Do we not often think we know something when really we just know about it?

July 16th1979
I was told that I must forget myself. My fears of losing what I felt inside were groundless. Nothing good, nothing true can ever be lost. "You must learn to think of others and do so in truth. Do not just think about thinking of others. Now is not the time for you to teach orally. You should try to set an example but nothing more is required from you at present. You still resist too much. Your feelings and intuitions are right in the main but you are not yet in a position to begin your mission of teaching in this life. Do not lay down the law to others but be patient and learn what you must. If you wish to pass on the law, you must be one with the law."

I apologise if some of these excerpts of the Masters' talks (and they are excerpts, I did not record everything) seem a little patchy. I hope they don't give a wrong impression of the Masters' fluency of expression. I did write them down immediately after the talk had finished, but I usually only noted what you might call edited highlights though included verbatim quotations whenever I could remember them, which was quite often, such was the impact of these teachers.

Actually I must correct myself. It was not quite straightaway after the conclusion of the talk that I wrote it down. As soon as the Master departed I would go over to Michael to be ready to catch him if he fell. Usually during meditation we would sit in chairs opposite each other about four feet apart. (I sometimes meditated by myself cross-legged but never managed the lotus position and Michael said if he got into it he would never be able to get out again). We sat up, our spine straight, feet slightly crossed over each other and hands folded in our laps. When Michael went into trance his body would seem to become even more erect and it would project a powerful presence. I usually kept my eyes shut when the Master spoke, the better to concentrate on what was said, but sometimes I watched the process and was able to observe a tautening and apparent lifting up of Michael's body when the Master entered. His head also lifted and went back a bit and his hands would extend slightly with the palms upraised. His eyes remained closed. The OM announced the Master's arrival though it was frequently preceded by words spoken (through Michael, of course) in an unknown (to me) language. When they left, always after giving love and blessings in a way that felt like a genuine benediction rather than a perfunctory formulaic farewell, they sounded the OM again and that would be my cue to go over to Michael. The Masters had told me that he would need attention after coming out of trance though had not said much more than that he would require love and support, leaving it to me to deal with the situation as best I could. I soon learnt that Michael did need support, physical support in fact, when returning to this world as if I were not there to provide that he would topple over. He never actually fell off his chair but he came close on occasion and would certainly have done so without someone there. He would usually ask for a glass of water and need some moments of peace and quiet before returning to a normal state. He was not good at describing how he felt but did tell me that, although he had little recollection of what took place when he was in trance, he felt surrounded by love and protection and the contrast between that and re-entering his body and this world was painful. That's why it took him some time to adjust.

While Michael was recovering from his trance I would write down the Master's words. I wrote them down as fast as I could so I could get it done while it was still fresh in my mind. Then I would put the notebook away and think about what was said. After which it was more or less time for bed. Our custom was to meditate at around 9 o'clock in the evening and when the Masters came they would do so shortly before we would normally have finished the meditation some forty minutes later. The talks would generally last for about quarter of an hour, though could be shorter and on certain occasions, when Michael was particularly robust, lasted for half an hour or more.

One of the reasons we adopted this way of doing things was that it meant I went to bed with the Master's words still ringing clearly in my mind. We lived in a one bedroom flat and Michael had the one bedroom while I slept in the sitting room which was also where we meditated. So when I went to sleep I did so in a room which still bore the almost tangible imprint of the Master's presence. This was a great aid to putting myself in the right frame of mind before going to sleep. It is widely assumed by occultists and mystics of all stripes that when aspiring disciples sleep they are taken for instruction to the Master's ashram (spiritual retreat) on the higher planes or else serve in some capacity such as their helpers did. This was confirmed by my guides. There may not be any registration of this by the physical brain but that does not mean that our nocturnal experiences and encounters are without purpose and bear no fruit. I would certainly not say that our dreams are records of genuine experiences on the inner planes. The vast majority of them obviously are not and are adequately explained by scientific theories of the brain's activity during sleep. But some, particularly vivid, possibly do originate at a deeper level although even these I would guess to have more symbolic than literal meaning which is not to deny that there might be a class of dreams that are actual memories of real events.

I mentioned that the talks could be longer if Michael was strong. In this context strong does not just mean physically so and the Masters made it abundantly clear that arguments and resistance on my part during the day would tire Michael so making it harder for them to use him at night. As the ego basically is resistance, letting go of that can be a tall order. But the Masters had established a kind of psychic rapport between Michael and myself so that, if I acted in accordance with their instructions, there would be harmony between us but, if I fell away from proper spiritual behaviour, that would destabilise our relationship which would, in turn, tire Michael and cause him to become emotionally volatile, leading to arguments and the inevitable vicious circle which only I could break by what basically amounted to contrition and repentance. This was presumably a delicate operation for the Masters and their helpers, only possible with someone mediumistically inclined, and it demanded a fair amount of vigilance and self awareness on my part in order that I might avoid sliding into automatic modes of behaviour. The method might sound threatening or even manipulative if you didn't understand the motivation behind it but it definitely speeded up the learning process. I knew about it, accepted it and recognised its efficacy. It was rather like having a personal spiritual weathercock. It is said that the universe acts as a mirror reflecting ourselves back to ourselves. This was something similar only more immediate and more unmistakeable. Instant feedback, you might say.

Let me add that this process did not mean I had to do what Michael told me. That wasn't what was intended at all. It was more a case of me not forcing my will onto him. In the Master's words, I had to learn to **not lay down the law to others but be patient and learn what you must.**

The Masters did tell me that my role in later life was to act as a spiritual teacher. There is nothing remarkable in this. They did not say it in such a way as to make me think of myself as anyone special. There are many people who fulfil similar roles, some in the public eye, some not, some clearly functioning as spiritual teachers, others not necessarily appearing in that light or recognisable as such by outer trappings. I stress this because I want to make clear that it does not mean I was given backing for any kind of exalted mission. Yes, they did speak of a mission but no doubt we all have one that it is our task to fulfil the best we can. And what is a teacher anyway? It is only someone who is passing on what he or she has been given. Just a link in a chain. True, the link must be strong (able to bear the weight of the teaching and pass it on correctly) but it is always the teaching that counts not the teacher. That said, there are good and bad teachers and my gratitude to my teachers is not something I could adequately express in words. So I am not trying to minimise a teacher's role but merely put it in perspective as far as I personally am concerned.

When the Master said that **my fears of losing what I felt inside were groundless** he was going to the heart of something that had been of deep concern to me. We live during a time in which practically all contact with the spiritual reality behind the material world has been lost and what there is on offer is frequently a parody or distortion of the truth. The veil is thicker than it has ever been. That's a fact. My fear was that my grip on spiritual things was tenuous and might loosen to the point where I would lose touch with them. I had some connection but it was neither strong nor stable enough. But isn't that a common problem for all of us on the path? We may have fleeting moments of insight when everything seems clear and illuminated but these moments pass and we wonder if they were real. We try to hold on to them but that just means we live in the past and have the memory of them but not the reality. Alternatively, we are still aware of them deep inside us but the din of the world overwhelms these fragile shoots of truth. The demands of everyday life, the disbelief or even hostility of those around us, the apparently unassailable logic of worldly wisdom all combine to shake our confidence in what we know at a fundamental level of our being but may doubt with the surface mind. As everybody who treads the path in a serious sense finds out, the world is the enemy of truth and conspires against it. So the Master's reassurance that **my fears of losing what I felt inside were groundless** was very welcome. And when he added that **nothing good, nothing true can ever be lost**, I felt (I can still remember this many years later) as if a great weight had been lifted from me and I knew suddenly and absolutely that all the awfulness of the world, all its suffering, all its darkness, all its ignorance, meant next to nothing and was no more than a little dust that had settled on some gold. Don't misunderstand me here. I am not saying that these things don't matter but I am saying that they will pass and that ultimately truth alone remains.

If you wish to pass on the law you must be one with the law. This is not the case in the everyday world, is it? A teacher need only know the law or rules of whatever it might be he teaches in order to pass that on. The sole requirement is a mental grasp of it. In the spiritual world, however, that is only the first step. In the spiritual world to pass on the law properly, you must be the law. Strictly speaking, this is an absolute but, in the context of our far from perfect world, as long as you have gone a certain way down the road to spiritual knowledge and are aware of your limitations, you can still serve as a teacher in some capacity. At that time, though, I did not even qualify on those limited grounds. I might have had a reasonably good knowledge of spiritual things but I was still very far from having internalised them. This is why I was told quite categorically that **now is not the time for you to teach orally. You should try to set an example but nothing more is required from you at present.**

The next time the Master came was one of those occasions when he came with high explosives.

July 20th 1979

The Master told me that it was time to stop thinking that I knew better than Michael. They had sent him to me and they spoke to me through him not just when he was in trance but throughout the day. Was I so proud that I rejected a sound teaching because it did not come in an attractive package? Did I not have sufficient understanding to be able to sift out the basic truths in what Michael told me from the unimportant limitations of his personality? It was time for me to submit and let go fully. I must give up my opinions, theories and preconceived ideas. I had to be crushed in order to learn humility and I must accept this. "Stop arguing" he said "Stop thinking you and only you are right and make sure that you do this in thought as well as word and deed. Forget all your high-faluting spiritual fancies and get down to ordinary mundane existence. Listen to our brother. Forget yourself."

As the reader will plainly see this was a chastening talk. There were occasions when the Masters seemed to step up a gear and jolt me out of any self-satisfaction I might have been feeling or any slipping into automatic pilot. They had many times made clear that they inspired Michael during the day to say things to me they felt I needed to hear but I had always had difficulty in accepting this. At least, I did accept it theoretically but was rarely able to perceive it when it happened or, to put it more truthfully, was just unwilling to perceive it. When they told me to listen to Michael (to whom they never referred by name but always called either our or your brother) this was part of the instruction to submit and let go, an instruction which to a proud person who thought he had a lot more spiritual understanding than Michael was very galling. That was the point, of course. As they said, **I had to be crushed in order to learn humility.** That was fine, almost romantic, in theory but very painful in practice.

The Masters did not reject theoretical knowledge. What they discouraged was entanglement in thought. When they spoke of **high-faluting spiritual fancies** (their exact words) they were not saying that an understanding of the inner worlds was without value. They were saying that if it gets in the way of the essential, the essential being love of God and self-forgetfulness, it becomes just another one of the many diversions on the spiritual path. In those days I wanted to learn all I could about spirituality but I was often in danger of distracting myself with ideas. This is not at all unusual for beginners who think that the more they know, the further on they are. But really the truth is very simple and you do not need to have an extensive grasp of Vedanta, Tibetan Buddhism, Zen, Western occultism or whatever it might be to know it. In fact, it is more than possible that such a grasp might obscure it. The spiritual path is littered with those whose knowledge of it gets in the way of them treading it properly.

After this talk I felt pretty wretched. More than that, I was actually a little bit frightened. I felt I was letting the Masters down and that if I did not pull myself together they might abandon me as a lost cause. That was a horrible thought but a mistaken one. The Masters do not abandon their disciples, though they might withdraw for a time if the appropriate response is not forthcoming. This was a tactic on their part (which is not to say that the words and the sense of urgency behind them were not real), and it was a necessary tactic as they saw I was not responding sufficiently to gentler instructions. When the love of God does not propel one on to righteousness sometimes the fear of God must be brought to bear. I don't suppose that idea will sit well with everyone especially if you think that it is never right to frighten people. That may be so but fear is a powerful instigator to action. I would say that everything depends on motive which is not the same as claiming that the end justifies the means. An end might justify some means but not any means and while the Masters may have used fear, they always acted out of love. Of course, they were not really even using fear. That was only my reaction. They might have alarmed me but they never threatened or bullied. They simply stated the facts in an uncompromising manner that left no room for argument or evasion. You could say that on this occasion they were manifesting God's rigour rather than His mercy. You can't have one without the other.

The forthright tone of the talks continued with the next one which came a week later, a week in which I had been left alone to "stew in my own juices" and reflect on what had been said. I had been warned that accepting the Masters as teachers would involve a radical stirring up of my psyche, and was far from being the glamorous adventure sometimes portrayed in spiritual literature by those who have little real experience of that of which they talk. On this path you are turned inside out, your dark corners exposed. You are required eventually to give everything to the quest and hold nothing back. I have no wish to discourage anyone from setting out on the spiritual journey, but don't think that you can embark on it without being prepared to sacrifice all you hold dear in this world and the next one too, for that matter, by which I mean that, if you really wish to know God, you must give up your desire for spiritual rewards as well as material ones. The sacrifices demanded by the path are real and cannot be avoided. Don't believe those spiritual teachers who say they can or who claim that you can tread the path without suffering. Suffering is not sent by God. It comes from our attachment to the ego but we are all attached to the ego or we would not need the path which has as its specific purpose the breaking of that attachment.

The spiritual path, the real spiritual path, is not the pleasant stroll through sweet scented sunlit meadows it is sometimes portrayed as being. At least, not very often. More often it is an uphill climb along infrequently trodden narrow tracks strewn with sharp stones. How could it be otherwise if it were to mean anything? And, if it were not, do you not think many more of us than have would have reached the goal?

To balance any impression of doom and gloom I may have given here I should add that there is joy on the path too. It is not all hard slog and suffering. There certainly can be that but there is also God's grace that supports and comforts us when we have made the sincere decision to make our way back to Him. And, in the light of what is gained at the end of the journey, any sacrifices made along the way are seen as next to nothing. Here I just wish to challenge the notion propagated in books of the "get spiritual quick" variety that stripping away the ego is a relatively easy affair that will happen when we decide that we want it to happen. To give up the ego is the hardest thing anyone will ever do. That is the cause of spiritual suffering.

July 28th 1979

The Master spoke and said I was still too swollen-headed and thought too much of my own glory. In order to cultivate humility I should think of myself as the lowest of the low. He said I did not pray enough. Did I think myself above prayer? He said that even the greatest saints prayed and that, while meditation was necessary for me, I needed to have the humbling experience of prayer also. I should guard against arrogance and superiority all the time, even in what he called my playtime. He then spoke of our trip to India saying that I would learn a lot there. I should prepare myself by reading about the places and people of India and while there should keep my eyes open and my mouth shut. This country was important to me and I would understand why in time.

Then the Master departed and a "companion in spirit" talked to me, encouraging and comforting me. She talked of the love, beauty and music of the higher worlds where she was and where, after fulfilling my duty in this world, I would one day return. She said that all hardships now would be amply compensated for and that if I could see the whole picture they would not appear to be so hard anyway. "Your difficulties are mostly caused by fear and resistance" she said. She then warned me to be wary of evil in all its myriad forms. "Love your brother" she said "and remain with him. Love disperses all darkness".

Later on the Master returned and told me to act on what was said to me. He said that I did not try as hard as I could and that I often rested content with understanding what was said to me and did not put it into practice. Try harder and think always of others, he said. He told me that anything I prayed for with humility and sincerity I would receive. Then he said that Michael was doing a great deal for me, much of which I was unaware of. He repeated that they spoke to me by overshadowing Michael and I should listen and obey. "Do not be distracted by your brother's manner" he said adding that Michael, like everyone, had his part to play and I should not confuse what he really was with the role he played. "Do not judge the soul by the mask it wears in the world" he concluded.

I have spoken of Michael's outer manner being one I often had difficulty with as it could tend towards the frivolous and the worldly. That was his persona, in part, as I have said, a defence mechanism against the world but to a certain extent it was also who he was or at least what his personality was. The Master's instruction was that I should have the intelligence to see past this to what lay behind but perhaps, because I was too identified with my own part, I could not see that the part somebody else was playing was just that, just a part. In time, where Michael was concerned, I learned to do this, and realised that he had his mask but he was not particularly identified with it. It was an aspect of him in this life but it was an exterior aspect and one he was not bound by. In a perfect world, of course, there would be no mask or the mask would wholly reflect what lay behind it. It is also true that, generally speaking, the more spiritually aware the soul, the thinner the mask. However, as must be apparent, this is a fallen and most imperfect world and as long as it is, and human beings have lessons to learn and karma to work out, there will be these masks.

It is often said that we are all actors in this world with our particular parts to play but it is a rare actor who does not make the mistake of identifying with his part – and identifying others with theirs. That is, if I may say so, a basic metaphysical error and one that often turns comedy into tragedy but we learn from tragedy and our experience of it brings us that bit closer to who we really are. By suffering the consequences of faulty identification we slowly learn what our true nature is. We shed our disguises and finally assume our real identity.

The theory of actors and parts helps us to avoid judging by appearance but, like many theories, it is open to misinterpretation. Certainly one should not identify the actor with the part or, as the Master said, should **not judge the soul by the mask it wears in the world**. But that does not mean that we are not responsible for any wrongdoing we may do or that, to take it to grotesque extremes (as I have heard it taken to), a man such as Hitler was only fulfilling his destiny. The person who behaves wrongly is, at the very least, identifying with his part and therefore, by definition, limiting himself to it. In effect, he is becoming it. The fact that we might be playing a part in this world cannot be used as an excuse to absolve us from the consequences of our actions. What it means is that behind the personality, which can sin, is the soul which is pure. But if we are identified with the lower self then we must bear all the consequences that come from the actions of that self. We may have a specific role to play but we must be detached from that role and centred in the higher self. If you are identified with your part, you attract its karma. If not, that is much less likely though still possible. Jesus' words in the Sermon on the Mount sum up the situation. "For offenses must come, but woe to that man by whom the offense comes."

The Master told me to pray. Can I tell you a secret that a lot of the gurus and partisans of non-duality don't know? A secret beyond non-duality. It is duality! I'm not trying to be clever here but there are people in these days of easy access to esoteric teachings who are stuck in a concept of non-duality. They think they know the truth but they are becalmed in mental waters and sometimes the only way for them to move on is to move back. Back to an "I and Thou" position in which they see themselves (as indeed they are) as a created being, a servant of the Almighty. Only then can they acquire the true humility which will break down self, a self which can quite easily adopt a non-dualistic mental position and so thwart the dawning of real rather than theoretical non-dualistic comprehension. I was, not dismissive of prayer, no, not that, but I believed it to be a somewhat inferior version of meditation, appropriate for those who grasp of spirituality was restricted to the religious level but not necessary for those whose goal was mystical enlightenment. I was very much mistaken. Prayer is an integral part of the spiritual path. It purifies the heart and mind and brings one closer to God as nothing else can. You might say, and with some justification, that when everything is traced back to its source there is no creature, no creation and no Creator but until then there most assuredly is, and, in point of fact, there is even then as long as the creature exists in creation and retains any aspect of its createdness. The Master said **that even the greatest saints prayed** and, while some might point to the Buddha as one who did not pray, I have to say that we don't really know what the Buddha did or did not do, especially before he attained Buddhahood. And does not the idea of the Bodhisattva, which is an essential, almost defining, part of Mahayana Buddhism, imply prayer of some sort?

The Master also told me **that anything I prayed for with humility and sincerity I would receive.** You can be sure that by this he did not mean things of a material nature. There are some so called spiritual groups who have the extraordinary notion that it is somehow proper to pray for material reward. This is such a miscom-prehension of what prayer actually is as to be almost wilfully perverse. There is certainly nothing remiss in wanting a reasonable standard of living, and I have no doubt that the Masters make sure their disciples have all that is necessary (within the bounds of karma) to enable them to tread the path in the way they are meant to - though that may not be much. But to seek to employ prayer for personal advantage seems, if I can say so without sounding melodramatic, perilously close to black magic. Prayer has one purpose and one purpose only, to create or restore the link between the incarnate soul and God. Pray for light, pray for guidance, pray for strength but know that what you are really doing is forging this link. We are forgetful creatures. Prayer is remembrance.

The keywords in the Master's statement are, of course, humility and sincerity. These betoken the ego-less state that indicates ripeness to receive. We may pray as much as we like but only if we pray with "a broken and contrite heart"[8] will our prayer be heard. Or rather only then will it be possible for us to receive an answer to our prayer. This is the point. It is not that God does not hear our prayers. It is that we cannot hear the answer. I appreciate that this might sound like an excuse for the inefficacy of prayer. Nevertheless it is the truth. If we wish our prayers to be answered, we must ask them in the right spirit. Naturally the right spirit will determine what we do and what we do not pray for in the first place.

When I first discovered the spiritual path, after having been introduced to it by Michael, the discovery had two initial effects on me. On the plus side, it opened up life to a previously unimagined degree and, by giving meaning to existence, made me feel as though a hundred Christmases had come at once. (On that note may I add that our desire for meaning and our sense of its lack surely serve to prove that it exists. If life had no meaning, we would not notice its absence. We feel hungry because there is food and we have a stomach. We have a need for meaning because there is God and we have a soul). Unfortunately it also made me feel superior to those who were not yet aware of the spiritual dimension to life. I did not feel this in a particularly nasty or disdainful way but I did think that I now knew more than most and that knowledge made me a more 'advanced' person. Why do I admit to this unpleasant reaction? Because it's fairly typical, even if it's often disguised. We tend to appropriate knowledge to ourselves and imagine that because it is 'higher' that makes us 'higher'. The Master's pointed remark that **I was still too swollen-headed and thought too much of my own glory** showed that I was a long way off from overcoming this all too human tendency.

To learn humility, as I was many times told, was my principal lesson in life. This is actually the most important lesson for any candidate for spiritual initiation since what it really demands is the overcoming of ego, the full recognition that there is no separate self. In conventional religious terms humility is taken to mean something like a lack of self-importance, thinking of others before oneself, and the Master's advice **that in order to cultivate humility I should think of myself as the lowest of the low** belongs to this order of things. It is certainly excellent advice for someone like me who used his spiritual understanding to bolster his ego. For that matter, it is excellent advice for anyone who wants to make progress on the path. But there is a stage beyond that. The lowest of the low might be humble but he still has an ego. I recognised a hard core of selfness within me that, try as I might, I could do nothing about. It suffocated me but it was me. Occasionally, for very brief periods, it might melt but it would soon be back again and, as in the well known catch 22 situation, trying to get rid of it only strengthened it. On various occasions I asked the Masters what I could do about this and I include here a record of one conversation we had. I have no date for it but know that it took place a few years after the present stage in the narrative, when the Masters were no longer such regular visitors as once they had been and the talks were more in the nature of conversations than discourses by them. Alas, I did not record many of these at that period in my life but this is one I did note down. The lessons I needed to learn were still the same. In a sense the lessons always are the same from the beginning to the end of the path. They just present themselves in different ways as the tests become subtler and examine our responses at deeper and deeper levels.

"How do I learn humility?" I asked.

"You learn by accepting" he replied.

"Accepting everything? Even accepting what is wrong?"

"You learn by accepting what you experience and not resisting it. What you experience is what you are meant to experience. We do not say that you accept what is counter to truth. We are not talking about outer acceptance. We say there must be inward non-resistance to what you experience. How else can there be peace?"

"I do try to do this but often seem to fall short. What more do I need to do?"

"You need to let go and surrender. Hold nothing back. Give all to God. Let go of all attachments. As long as the ego has attachments, you will be attached to the ego."

"How does one get rid of attachments?"

"Be aware of them. Consider what attachments or desires are. They indicate incompleteness. You can never be complete as long as you are separate and you will always be separate as long as you have attachments."

As always the Master's answers were tailored as much to what I needed to know as what I had asked and I don't think his comments need a great deal of elaboration. The four main points of acceptance, surrender, non-resistance and non-attachment are time-honoured spiritual teachings, though I think he explains the purpose behind them in an interesting and succinct way. I knew I had not fully surrendered nor had I let go of my attachments. I wished to acquire humility but was holding on to that which blocked its acquisition.

There might be said to be two stages to acquiring humility. The first is thinking of oneself **as the lowest of the low.** This is a technique designed to crush the recalcitrant ego and is a basic part of any monastic training. But then to go beyond a humble self to no self-identification, further work is needed and this is what the Master's words above point to. If you consider his four points, they imply that there is no movement of the ego. If there is no movement of ego then there is no ego. It's as simple as that. So you remove the ego not by trying to remove it but merely by not reacting to it. By letting go, by not resisting, by dropping attachments. Occasional success will eventually become habit. It is not an easy task because the separate self is so deeply entrenched in our consciousness, but if one maintains watchfulness and really wishes to achieve it then it can be done. We have the example of the great saints and sages of humanity to bear witness to that possibility.

I must sound a note of caution though. It is rare that the desire for liberation really is greater than the desire of the ego to preserve itself. The ego can construct hundreds of spiritual paths, all small or not so small perversions of the true one, that delude it into thinking it is on the royal road to liberation when all the time it is subtly sustaining, even strengthening, itself. There are teachers only too happy to assist in this deception and it seems to be a law of life that if we have the potential to be the dupes of such teachers, we will find our way to them. Our experiences with them may leave us a little battered and bruised, even temporarily cynical, but we will eventually emerge the wiser, with a greater understanding of our self and a better grasp of the machinations of the ego. It is important to realise in these cases that, in the spiritual world, failure really does not matter. Success is built on failure so do not reproach yourself for your failures but acknowledge them and try again. Is there not a saying that only he who never tries never fails? The ego is the greatest enemy we will ever encounter. It is only to be expected that we will lose a few battles in the course of this war.

The war against the ego is the whole of the spiritual life but this is an enemy we cannot fight in the normal way because that only strengthens it. This is the well known dilemma also expressed by the paradoxical saying that if you seek realisation, you will not find it, if you seek God, you will not find Him. However the dilemma is only one for the ego because, at the same time, we are told "seek and ye shall find". The surface contradiction here is easily resolved by realising that it is what is in the heart that matters. Motive is all. Sincerity of purpose is the obligatory requirement for any spiritual aspirant. Armed with that you are well equipped to fight and win your battles.

It was strange to hear the Masters talk about 'playtime' but then they were not the sort of teachers who belonged to the all work and no play school. At the same time, they were clear that although one was allowed moments of relaxation (as they put it, **a reed that never bends is likely to snap**) that did not mean it was permissible to set aside one's spiritual endeavours then or indeed do anything that would conflict with treading the spiritual path. Not that, generally speaking, one wants to. It is the case that the more a person proceeds on this journey, the more worldly desires and pursuits drop away. It is not a question of denying oneself certain pleasures (though, in some cases, it may be so initially) but of no longer finding them pleasurable, of "putting away childish things."

Earlier when discussing the Masters I wrote that I had no experience of their female equivalents. I had completely forgotten this talk! However, reading through my notes brings the whole episode back with absolute clarity. I have no idea whether this companion in spirit (as she described herself) was a liberated being but she was obviously a very lofty soul. She emanated a loving gentleness that was profoundly affecting, and the balm of her presence had a consoling quality that caused me to feel an almost overwhelming sense of gratitude to her for taking the trouble to visit me. She had a feminine grace and purity that do not seem to be so highly prized nowadays but are just as much divine characteristics as will or intelligence. In addition to this, she transmitted a peace that made all troubles and fears just melt away. I remember the radiance of her peace very well. The Masters also brought peace but the peace she brought had a soothing quality all its own.

The question might be asked that, as this was coming through Michael, how did I know it was a female spirit? All I can say is that there could be no doubt. The soft voice, the gentle manner, the whole vibration of the person, all of these were clearly feminine. As always there was no trace of Michael and though this being spoke through a male body, the voice was feminine. The scent of lily of the valley she brought with her just confirmed all this. I never knew the Masters to be accompanied by such a heavenly perfume. Nowadays many people talk rather glibly about the goddess and the feminine aspect of divinity. Curiously this is happening at precisely the time when a true grasp of femininity appears to be being lost, leading one to suspect that there is a political as much as a theological imperative behind it. However there most definitely is a feminine aspect to divinity, most perfectly embodied by such figures of wisdom and merciful love as the goddess Isis and the Virgin Mary, and, in China, Kuan-Yin, and this is the closest I have ever come to experiencing it. It is probably not one many feminists would approve of though since one of its qualities is a perfect submission to divine will. I should add that it is the height of wisdom to submit to divine will since the only true freedom is freedom from self.

It is becoming increasingly apparent that certain aspects of modern feminism are actually antipathetic to true femininity because they seek to supplant the traditional feminine virtues, which are (largely, though by no means exclusively) to do with nurturing, intuitive wisdom and compassionate love, with those usually associated with the masculine. It is an old trick of the devil to sneak in falsehood under the coat-tails of truth, and he has successfully done so on this occasion by corrupting the idea of the feminine under the guise of the pursuit of an entirely legitimate and overdue fairness and equality, with which no-one could have the slightest argument. All human beings lose by this but perhaps the biggest losers are women themselves who are denied contact with their true nature. I sometimes think that if the balance between the sexes were right then everything would be and we would finally know true harmony, but that time still seems to be a long way off. The sexes are meant to be complementary but, in the name of equality, they are increasingly being lured into a competitiveness which can only bring about disequilibrium. The root causes of this are egotism, both male and female, and metaphysical ignorance.

It is fine and good to refuse to be bound by stereotypes (cultural conditioning) but we should not forget that there exist archetypes too, independent of human will and imaginings, and that a properly functioning society can only be one in which these are acknowledged (I don't mean slavishly enforced) rather than denied or ignored. For the individual as well, true fulfilment can only come from conforming to one's divine pattern. This is not a plea to return to past modes of behaviour which were also unbalanced but for human beings to learn to be guided by what is real rather than what is desired to be real. The current state of affairs is too far advanced for deviation from that course to be likely at any time soon but I write these words for anyone, male or female, who might be open to them.

My new visitor told me that **all hardships now would be amply compensated for.** Her reassuring words are something we should all store away for reference in times of trouble. No-one has yet lived a life in which they have not known periods of hardship and difficulty. Some have it a lot worse than others, of course, but no-one escapes sorrow and suffering completely. If we understood that these periods, whether long or short, would pass and with hindsight be seen as no more than transitory ripples on the surface of our existence, we would be able to endure them as they happened with a great deal more equanimity. You might say that only someone who has not suffered much in his life could make such a complacent statement, but it is not intended to make light of anyone's suffering. It is simply to put suffering in context. In the overall scheme of things is it so hard to believe that any hardships we might endure now will pale into near insignificance? The last thing this gracious soul was doing was denying the need for compassion. She was merely bringing me comfort and raising my eyes to the bigger picture. As she said, **if I could see the whole picture they (hardships) would not appear to be so hard anyway.**

I wish I could convey the impression she gave when she said that **love disperses all darkness**, a phrase so simple that one might pass over it almost without noticing. Not when spoken by a being such as her. She transmitted a love so pure and all enveloping as to make one think that this was a person who had become one with the source of love and breathed it as naturally as the rest of us do air. When the Masters spoke of love they made it clear that love was the basic fact of the universe. You can philosophise all you like but the supreme reality of life is love. This has rarely been better expressed than by St Paul in his first letter to the Corinthians in a passage so beautiful and so true that, despite it being so well known, I cannot resist quoting in full. I have put it in bold because if anything deserves to be highlighted, it does.

"If I speak in the tongues of men and of angels, but have not love, I am only a resounding gong or a clanging cymbal. If I have the gift of prophecy and can fathom all mysteries and all knowledge, and if I have a faith that can move mountains, but have not love, I am nothing. If I give all I possess to the poor and surrender my body to the flames but have not love, I gain nothing.

Love is patient, love is kind. It does not envy, it does not boast, it is not proud. It is not rude, it is not self-seeking, it is not easily angered, it keeps no record of wrongs. Love does not delight in evil but rejoices with the truth. It always protects, always trusts, always hopes, always perseveres.

Love never fails. But where there are prophecies, they will cease; where there are tongues, they will be stilled; where there is knowledge, it will pass away.

And now these three remain: faith, hope and love. But the greatest of these is love."

There you have it, a spiritual teaching than which there is none higher, but what exactly is this love of which St Paul speaks? In human terms we love this and we do not love that but, spiritually speaking, we just love. It is not so much that I love you, although I do, but there is a constant stream of love coming through me and directed to all. Thus I do not love something for what it is but because it is. This love is not blind, being aligned to truth it is perfectly able to see the slightest deviation from truth, but it is unconditional and does not require anything in return in order to complete it. It is absolutely complete in itself. We can let this love flow, which it will if we allow it to, or we can block it which we do every time we succumb to negative emotions such as fear, anger and dislike but also, and less obviously, apparently benign feelings which nevertheless have an opposite. Human love has an opposite. Spiritual love has no opposite because it is not based on any likes or dislikes of the personal self. It is not actually based on anything at all for it is just the reality of the universe and it lies at the heart of every atom. Essentially it is love that requires no object and gains its fulfilment simply from flowing out. That may be hard for us to imagine but it is nonetheless the core of our being, and we will know it as such when we let go of that which dams its flow, namely the sense of separateness. Love is the denial of separateness.

The Masters had told me that I did not have the love of a spiritual person and pointed to Michael as someone who did. It is true; Michael had a lot of love in him. This could even make him appear somewhat childlike on occasion, but then he was not the least bit concerned about how he appeared to other people. His behaviour sometimes reminded me of what I had read about Ramakrishna, a sort of innocence that did not seek wisdom or power or even enlightenment but simply wished to love and serve the Masters. I am not claiming for Michael the same spiritual status as Ramakrishna but he had a similarly unselfconscious and loving nature and did not over-complicate himself with excessive ratiocination which was doubtless why the Masters were able to use him as a medium. Perhaps, in his own small way, he was a genuine example of that much misunderstood concept, the holy fool.

Many spiritual people do not love, know they should love and try to love. That is understandable but it's the wrong approach. All you are likely to end up with is an imitation of love often seen in a certain type of person who wants to be spiritual and attempts to be so by affecting the warmth of love instead of lighting its fire. Do not think that adopting an external semblance of love will somehow ignite the heart. It won't.

So what do you do? Do not try to love. Rather do not stand in the way of love. Then you will love or rather you will not love. Love will flow through you. Every time you react to a situation negatively, you close your heart. It doesn't matter if you have been abused, unfairly traduced, mistreated or hurt. If that provokes a negative response of any kind in you, you close your heart. Open your heart and you will love. It is worth recalling here the profound words of the Buddha, which must surely have seemed completely revolutionary when he first spoke them. "Hatred does not cease through hatred. Hatred ceases through love". Note that he does not say that hatred ceases through not hating in return. That's not enough. Hatred ceases through love.

If you have to ask "How do I love?" you have not understood love. There is no why and how to love. It just is and it will arise when you forget yourself. That will not happen overnight. The bad habits and wrong ways of thinking picked up over lifetimes will take time to shift but replace bad habits with good ones and it will eventually happen. Forget self and it will happen.

Here's a small example of what I am talking about. The Masters were constantly telling me that I should love Michael but unfortunately you can't love someone just because you are told to. I was very fond of Michael but I also found his behaviour annoying on occasion. However, as I came to realise, these were the times I should have been most grateful to him as they gave me the opportunity to learn something I needed to. That was not to react when provoked. As was made very clear to me, these incidents happened for that precise reason. With the Masters' help and guidance I slowly (and it was slowly) learned to rise above my self-centred irritability and to replace it with an affection not dependent on circumstance. As a consequence of this, the situations that had annoyed me diminished in number and intensity. Needless to say this was only in the context of my relationship with Michael and simply meant that my lessons in this domain moved on to a new phase.

It is possible to construct from my experience something like a universal principle. Look upon difficult circumstances as opportunities. As much as possible you might even try to be grateful to the person who abuses or even persecutes you for giving you the chance to learn a lesson. Return bad with good and this will benefit both you and possibly your accuser too if they have not sunk too far into illusion. It gives them the best possible chance anyway. That does not mean it is necessary to meekly submit to wrongdoing (sometimes it might but at others it might be necessary to stand up against it), but you should not react to it in any measure inwardly. That is the absolutely crucial thing. Try to stand at all times in the light of love however difficult that might be. Then you will find that that light shines through you.

My female companion in spirit was not all sweetness and light. Actually she herself was, but she was wise as a serpent too and well understood the shadows cast by light shining in a dualistic world. **Be wary of evil in all its myriad forms,** she said. Evil, or, if you prefer, ignorance and illusion, does not always come plainly marked. The modern sensibility is uncomfortable with the idea that there might be powers of darkness deliberately attempting to subvert truth and lead us astray. In a certain sense it is right to be so. These beings have no real power. How could they possibly do so in a universe in which all beings, even they, are part of God's being? But they have denied God's being within themselves to such an extent[9] that they have cut themselves off from God, so the only way they can continue their existence in the form they wish is to absorb energy from human beings. Thus evil is essentially parasitic. The catch as far as they are concerned is that, due to their low vibration, the energy they absorb must be of a similar low state. Hence their need to get us to 'downgrade' pure energy by giving in to negative emotion which they can then tap. This is no doubt a strange concept for many people but although the fact of the existence of these beings might be a cause for wariness, it is not one for fear. Yes, they do exist and their purpose is to deceive us into non-spiritual behaviour but they can only do that if we let them. They have no power over us unless we give it to them. Having said that, while they are totally devoid of love, they are not without intelligence and can mask their deceit in a **myriad forms** so it behoves us to be alert. Yet all that this really this amounts to is that we must be alert to ourselves. If there is no impurity in us, then the devil and all his hordes may come (I am speaking figuratively here) but they will find nothing in us to latch on to. They will fall back defeated as did the demons of Mara from Gautama immediately prior to his enlightenment. So when I was told to **be wary of evil in all its myriad forms** what I was really being told was to look to myself.

The reader cannot fail to have noticed that the Masters told me many times to guard against evil. I have discussed it on a number of occasions in these pages as it really does appear to be the case that **the greater progress (you make) the more (you will) be assailed by evil in all its forms.** See the testing of the Buddha just mentioned as well as the temptation of Christ by Satan during his forty days in the wilderness and any number of examples in the lives of the saints. There might be said to be two aspects to this 'assailing'. It can be viewed as a testing, a probing to find out our weaknesses with the real aim of showing them to us so that we can address them. This is, as it were, its legitimate side. This is perhaps why it is allowed. However, from what the Masters told me, it also represents a deliberate attempt by the forces of darkness to undermine spiritual progress and divert souls from the truth since anyone who raises himself up out of duality reduces their power in the world. This power is only illusionary and could be removed by God in the proverbial twinkling of an eye but the illusion and the results coming from it are allowed to stand because of free will. So really to remove evil from the world we must remove it from our own hearts.

Evil may be the opposite of good in human terms but it is not the opposite of God. God has no opposite. Now that is not to say that evil is a part of God as is sometimes confusedly claimed. It is apart from God, possible because of God's gift of free will, a gift that is designed to make of men gods themselves but which also opens up the possibility that they can reject God, deny the oneness of life and fall into self will and separation. Ultimately, though, evil is nothing more than a temporary disturbance in the fabric of creation, unable to affect anything but its outermost fringes, those in which duality holds sway.

Chapter 21

A Trip to India

Countries have qualities. You might even say that, in a certain sense, countries have souls, if by soul one understands the intrinsic nature of a thing, that which defines it and sets it apart from all else. How these qualities arise and whether they change over time or with the influx of a new group of people are matters for debate, but the basic fact remains. Countries have qualities. Some would say that these come from the culture of the people living there, and that's surely true to an extent. Others would point to the climate and landscape, and these also play an indisputable part but there is something else and that is the 'vibration' of the country itself. This is an almost spiritual thing which does not arise from the physical make up of the country in question but from a deeper level, and it influences, perhaps even determines, both the topography of the country and the psychological make up of its people.

Not all countries are of equal significance as far as humanity is concerned and none is more significant than India. By virtue of its antiquity, its spiritual focus and its metaphysical understanding, it stands apart from all others. That is not to deny the achievements of other nations and peoples but India has something special. Once Michael and I had decided to go there, the Masters confirmed that this was indeed their wish in order for me to further my spiritual education. It could be argued that India as a political unity is only a recent creation but that's just a dispute about externals. India has existed for millennia. In my opinion civilisation has existed there for longer, possibly much longer, than is currently recognised, and though there are plenty of sacred places in many lands, India is a sacred land. Now, it can't be denied that, at the present time, its sacred qualities are much diminished but something of them remains which is why the Master said **that I would learn a lot there.**

I did prepare myself for the visit by reading up on Indian history and culture as well as learning the smattering of Urdu that Michael taught me. I also resolved to **keep my eyes open and my mouth shut,** slightly harsh words you might think but words that made it abundantly clear that I was there to learn. Actually, keeping your mouth shut has a long established mystical pedigree since it indicates silence, and silence is at the heart of mysticism. I have never taken a vow of silence as such but, as an experiment, I have remained without speaking for several days and know that it can be an effective spiritual exercise. Talk distracts and takes you away from yourself. It externalises you. Really to know yourself, you need to become silent. This is what meditation is all about, of course, and a vow of silence might be considered quite crude compared to meditation since the real silence is of thought not tongue. But it is still a kind of fasting, and fasting is not only a means of purification, it is also a way to get to know yourself by reducing external stimulation to a minimum. I did not take the Master's words to mean I should take a vow of silence whilst in India (that would have been a little extreme - it was meant to be a holiday) but I realised he was saying that during my time there I should observe and should do so silently, that is to say not just without spoken comment but also without judgement or comparison. It is possible that I am reading too much into a simple statement but by now I knew very well the way the Masters worked, and that even their simplest statements bore thinking about.

I see from my old passport that we went to India on 27th August. We flew to New Delhi, arriving at around 2 o'clock in the morning. Once through immigration we got a taxi for the drive from the airport to our hotel. As it had been dark when we arrived, and the airport was cut from the same nondescript international cloth as most other airports, I hadn't yet seen anything of the country. It was still dark as we drove to the city but it was warm so I rolled down the window, inhaled the night air and promptly burst out laughing.

The driver turned round to see what was going on and Michael gave me a quizzical look too so I had to explain my behaviour. As I had smelt the scents of the Indian night, the odour of the flowers and fragrant trees that lined the road from the airport, and felt the warmth of the perfumed Indian air, I was struck with a sense of such familiarity that all I could do was laugh. I knew this place and knew it well. Believers in reincarnation will not find that surprising and, as I was one, I didn't, but even so the intensity of the experience took intellectual belief to another level. I'm sure non-believers could come up with plenty of their own theories to explain it but they didn't have the experience, and, in this case, I am inclined to think that the most obvious explanation is the best one.

I am glad my introduction to India came through the nose rather than the eyes. Smells can bring back long forgotten memories better than anything else and that is what I believe happened here. It is true that the brain was only formed at the beginning of this current lifetime so could not have memories of previous lives. However it is perfectly possible that, under certain conditions, the physical brain can link up to the greater consciousness that lies behind it which does have memories of its more extreme past.

We stayed in a pleasant, old fashioned hotel with a touch of faded grandeur, as was common in those days before everything had been done up to cater for mass tourism, and there I had my first taste of *nimbu pani* which was to prove an invaluable restorative on many occasions in the hot days ahead. I found it amusing that Michael forbade me to drink any water in India which hadn't been boiled while being quite happy for us both to drink large quantities of *nimbu pani* which is made from lime juice, sugar and ....water. Well, perhaps he knew something I didn't. At any rate, unlike most Western travellers to those parts, neither of us was ill with stomach trouble during our stay.

We spent a few days in Delhi seeing the sights and then took the train to Calcutta. Michael wanted to show me where Ramakrishna had lived and I also wanted to visit a city long considered one of

India's cultural powerhouses as well as being interesting from a historical point of view, as one of the first places that the British established themselves. The reader may disapprove of colonialism but I think the broader view can accept that the British influence on India was not, on the whole, a negative one, and that both countries benefitted from the connection.

The Ramakrishna Mission had a large guest house in Calcutta and Michael knew some people there from a previous visit, so that was where we stayed. It was simple but comfortable and had the atmosphere of a spiritual centre without the tendency to take itself too seriously you sometimes find in such places. One of the first things I did in Calcutta was to buy myself a lungi, a plain green one which I still have today though the cloth is now paper thin. I could write a hymn of praise to the lungi. It struck me then, and remains my opinion still, that there is no garment more comfortable or attractive. There is a purity, simplicity and what you might almost call an integrity about it which makes it the most appropriate clothing for the spiritual devotee. I have worn lungis about the house ever since. Modern Western apparel reflects the modern Western mindset. Its tightness, over-elaborateness and lack of flow, and the way it emphasises the body in a physical sense whilst denying the dignity of the human form going very well with a materialistic approach to life. That, at any rate, is my opinion. I don't expect everyone to share it.

While we were in Calcutta Michael wanted to visit an old friend of his who was a nun in the Ramakrishna order. She was called Sister Kalyani and she worked as a nurse in a hospital run by the order. Her spiritual path consisted of service to others, particularly the sick and suffering, and on meeting her I was touched by her devotion to her patients and her quite obviously genuine altruism. There was a gentleness about her that had a real healing quality. One does not often meet true goodness in this world and when one does it is a thing to treasure. Sister Kalyani had the face of someone who had experienced her share of sorrow but her eyes and manner showed a saintly person and it was humbling to meet a woman who demonstrated so clearly spirituality on active service. It was humbling because I knew that, despite my dedication to the spiritual path, I could never do what she was doing as I lacked her selflessness. We all have different paths and what is right for one is not necessarily right for all but here was someone who acted as she did quite simply out of love for humanity. Of how many of the more overtly spiritual gurus and holy men could one say as much?

On the way back from the hospital to our guest house we were hailed by a passing rickshaw wallah who asked if we wanted a ride. Nothing odd about that except that in Calcutta in 1979 some rickshaws were still pulled by men and this was one of them. I was dubious but Michael was made of sterner stuff and we got on board. I have to say that this was one of the more uncomfortable rides I have taken. Physically speaking, it was not unpleasant but the feeling of being pulled by a fellow human being was decidedly unsettling for someone of my generation. However Michael, being of an earlier vintage, reasoned as follows. I wouldn't object to being served by a waiter in a restaurant and if this man was earning a living by doing this, who were we to be concerned? I could think of answers to that and I'm sure anyone reading about this incident nowadays could too but I have to say the rickshaw wallah himself seemed not to feel any affront to his dignity. He chatted away happily as he trotted along and naturally we gave him a large tip. Even so I felt as uneasy as I imagine most Westerners would in that situation.

I believe Calcutta was one of the last places that practice survived at the time and it may have gone from there now. But it had been common forty years earlier. After our ride Michael told me a story from his colonial past. He had been A.D.C. to the Viceroy of India for a period during the 2nd World War, just prior to Independence. The Viceroy was in Simla at his summer residence and expecting a visit from Mahatma Gandhi. Michael was sent to the railway station to meet him. A group of rickshaw pullers were waiting there, all desperate for a chance of taking the great man to Viceroy's Lodge but they were destined for disappointment because when Gandhi arrived he was so horrified at the thought of being pulled by a fellow man that he walked, and Michael had to walk with him. It seems that the Mahatma was an hour late for his appointment, much to the Viceroy's irritation!

The day after visiting Sister Kalyani, we went (in a taxi this time) to Dakshineswar, which is on the east bank of the Ganges about four miles from Calcutta. I don't suppose it had changed much since Ramakrishna's day, despite the many visitors. It was certainly an idyllic spot then, where you could imagine a saint might have lived and taught, though a part of me always wonders when visiting holy places like that whether some of the peaceful atmosphere we detect there comes from the expectations we bring to bear. Scepticism aside, the temples, orchards and groves of Dakshineswar, its situation on the banks of the river Ganges and the imprint of Ramakrishna's presence made it a very pleasant place.

There is a sort of innocence about Ramakrishna that gives him a special quality among modern saints and mystics. I can't share his enthusiasm for the bloodcurdling goddess Kali (not, by the way, the Kali of the Kali Yuga who was a male demon) whom he saw as Supreme Mother and Shakti or primal energy of the universe[10] but, along with Ramana Maharishi, he must count as the major revivifier of the sacred current in Hinduism over the last couple of centuries, and, as saints of any religion go, he is surely one of the more sympathetic. I am, however, reminded of a book by the aforementioned Cyril Scott (*The Initiate in the New World*) in which he quotes a Master as saying that Ramakrishna was near to the state of Adeptship but had not reached it yet. This seems to me plausible but who can say?

From Calcutta we flew to a little place called Bagdogra which was the nearest airport to Darjeeling, our next destination. The bus trip through the Himalayan foothills lasted a number of hours but I would have been quite happy if it had gone on for longer. It was rather bumpy but that was beside the point when the scenery was so glorious, and not only glorious because it constantly changed in aspect too as we climbed ever higher into a more temperate zone. As we passed little huts shrouded in luxuriant vegetation, with smoke curling from ramshackle roofs and small brown faces peeping at us from behind slightly opened doors, I had another sense of _déjà vu_. But then the mists came in and soon it began pouring with rain so I had to attend to more practical matters as the bus had no windows, or not what you would recognise as such. Just openings with a piece of tarpaulin at the top which had to be unwound and then, when it was, promptly blew back inside together with the rain. Never mind, the rain was quite pleasant after the heat of the plains (I don't suppose I'm the first Englishman to say that), and we arrived shortly afterwards. The clerk at the hotel desk told us with a smile that it had been raining for days so it seemed rather incongruous to see a large sign in the bathroom requesting us not to use much water as there was a severe shortage.

Darjeeling was one of those evocative sounding names that had set me dreaming as a boy and I loved the town when I got there. Although a lot of the time the mist and rain persisted, occasionally they would clear and then the views were magnificent. During a break in the weather we went up to Tiger Hill and saw the great Kanchenjunga. Aglow in the morning light it looked as though it could very well be the home of the gods, but then the Himalayan scenery in general speaks of the creative spirit to anyone the least bit inclined to supernatural belief. The elemental spirits of rock and snow, wind and lightning can also seem very present in the mountainous landscape, even nowadays when our plundering of the Earth has driven them far from us in most places. They were certainly taken for granted by the local people, more in tune with their surroundings than we, lulled into insensitivity by our artificial environment, can ever be. You might think a belief in elementals superstitious but their existence is attested to by all traditional cultures, both sophisticated and primitive, and it is only us moderns, cut off from our roots, who have lost sight of them. And superstitious or not, I've never met friendlier people than those in Darjeeling who, like mountain people everywhere, seemed to have an abundance of good humour, resilience and integrity.

We visited a tea plantation which took me back to my card collecting days, and a nearby Buddhist monastery which also triggered a sense of recognition. I am not claiming an earlier existence as a Buddhist monk but I believe from what they said that some of the Masters, or at least some of their helpers, might at one time have had that connection[11]. I knew that the Masters were sending us to places they deemed beneficial to my spiritual education and this felt like one of them. It was not so much the monastery itself. It was not very old and the statue of Maitreya it housed, though imposingly large, was adorned with a little too much of what looked like make up. Rather it was the tradition of which it was an embodiment, and the crinkled features of the friendly old monk who welcomed us in out of the rain and showed us round were those of someone who had thoroughly absorbed the best of that tradition.

I saw a tiger in Darjeeling. Unfortunately it was in a zoo. I know, and am sympathetic to, all the conservationist arguments to do with preservation and breeding but it's very hard to justify them when you see such a magnificent beast penned up in a cage, and feel its frustration as it paces backwards and forwards to no purpose. We should not ascribe human emotions to animals but neither should we deny that an animal that cannot live according to its nature will suffer. The splendour of this particular beast probably makes us more sympathetic to its plight than that of humbler creatures, which is no doubt unfair, but then there is something about the tiger that makes it almost the pure embodiment of an archetype of power, grace and savage beauty. Of course, it is also, along with the elephant, the animal that most epitomises India.

Our original intention had been to go on to Kathmandu but when we tried to book our bus tickets there we discovered that travel restrictions currently in force meant that you were required to go out of Darjeeling the same way you came in so we had to go back to

Bagdogra. No-one could explain what the point of this was but then I was getting used to Indian ways. So we abandoned our Kathmandu plans, returned to Calcutta and got a train to Varanasi.

Varanasi is not just one of the most ancient and holiest of Hindu cities, it is also the nearest large town to Sarnath, the deer park where the Buddha preached his first sermon. We stayed at a dak bungalow in the cantonment area which reminded Michael of his colonial days. For those unfamiliar with these terms, dak bungalows were simple but clean lodgings where travellers going along the main postal routes could stay and change their horses, and the cantonment area of a town was where the military was stationed. We had no horses and not much of a military nature remained when I was there, other than slightly more order in the surroundings than in the rest of the town, but a feeling of the past still hung over the place like gradually dispersing smoke. Our room was next door to that of some Tibetan Buddhist pilgrims, all monks, including a boy of about ten years old who asked me through gestures if I wanted to play football with him in the bungalow garden. Who could pass up such an invitation? I think the poor boy was being dragged round endless pilgrimage sites with the grown ups and was getting just a little bored as any small boy surely would. Over the next few days we had several matches and must have made an amusing sight, him in his purple robes and me in my new green lungi, both barefoot on the grass kicking a ball about, unable to communicate except through smiles.

At dawn on the day after our arrival we went down to the Ganges to watch the pilgrims salute the rising of the sun, a ritual hundreds or, more likely, thousands, of years old. As people do, we hired a boat and rowed along the banks of that venerable but filthy river observing the waterfront with its temples, palaces and funeral pyres. Hordes of people thronged the ghats, chanting, praying, pushing and shoving; many of them seemingly oblivious to anything but their religious duties. Some remained on the shore while others stood waist deep in the water with their hands raised and their faces lifted up to the rising sun. The combination of religious fervour and filth seemed incongruous. Both were very much in evidence but the former, as far as I could tell, was based more on age old tradition and custom than any real insight into the nature of things. But still the spectacle was extraordinary and invited one to feel in a small measure a part of one of humanity's oldest ceremonies.

After we disembarked we walked back up through the narrow streets. Extending my arms I could easily have touched the buildings on either side. Doorways led into small temples and Brahmin's houses and we were beckoned into one by a priest who showed us the outermost court but no more. For a small remuneration naturally but why not? Back in the street again, a garlanded white cow with the typical big hump on her back came down towards us at quite a pace. We carried on walking towards her before realising that she had no intention of stopping. It was her town and she knew her rights. There was not room enough for both of us and just in time we jumped aside into luckily available alcoves or she would have barged right into us. Well, again, why not? It was her town.

While we had been in India the Masters had spoken to me on a couple of occasions during meditation, chiefly with words of encouragement and advice to be open to everything I experienced on the trip. They had made no further comment than that not telling me what to see or think but leaving it up to me to do my learning for myself.

One night during our time in Varanasi they came after meditation and made the following remarks. These were in response to a slightly peevish question I had asked about why modern representatives of Indian spirituality seemed, for the most part, to be pale shadows of their illustrious forebears. As so often they did not answer my question directly but told me what they wanted me to hear.

Do not be a perfectionist. There is nothing perfect to be found anywhere in your world. Seek the true perfection within but do

**not expect it outwardly. If you do, all you will find will be disap-
pointment. It is your task to demonstrate the highest you can but
not to condemn others who do not live up to your ideals. So see
and uphold the truth but do not judge.**

Here was straightforward advice with a hint of rebuke for my intolerance. I must admit to being a typical child of Virgo with the perfectionist streak that went with that parentage. As a consequence I was
inclined to dismiss much that did not, as the Masters said, live up to
my ideals. Perhaps that was also due to the idealism of youth which
aspires to the best but can sometimes be a little too critical of what
falls short of that; and which is often more demanding of others than
of itself. Certainly I was too judgemental. In my defence what lay
behind this was a genuine dislike of seeing the false masquerading
as the true but it also formed part of my spiritual insecurity, which
arose from the fact that my inner knowledge was not deeply rooted
enough. Frequently when I complained to Michael that this or that
spiritual group or person was not what it purported to be he would
say, "Yes, I know but why worry about it? You know what is real."
But I did worry and my lack of confidence in what I knew made me
critical. It was as though by criticising others I was somehow
protecting myself.

There are two strands to the Master's statement that one should
see and uphold the truth but not judge which I can sum up by
saying that we should have discrimination but not discriminate.
Clear-sighted discrimination is essential for discerning the real from
the unreal. It comes from intuitive perception and once the real is
intuitively perceived that is what we should live by, not being
swayed by any worldly considerations or attitudes, even what passes
for the best of them. At the same time, we should not judge or
condemn others who do not see as we do. That would mean we may
have seen the truth but are not living it. Then again, if we should not
judge nor should we make the opposite mistake and close our eyes
to the truth, regarding everything as equally valid. That is the error,

common today, of relativism. There is truth and there are higher and lower truths. One could equally well invert the Master's words and say **do not judge but see and uphold the truth.**

Demonstrate the highest you can. Many times the Masters emphasised to me that the best teachers teach by example. Not in itself a revolutionary idea but they would go on to say that **you teach best by silence and the rays you give out** which I think is a relatively new concept even if it is clearly implied in many esoteric traditions. It tells us that there is an actual force which the true teacher in touch with his soul radiates that has the potential, if the recipient is open to receive it, to change that person or at least reach more deeply into his or her heart than words ever can. We may think of this as the force of the teacher's purified aura projecting the quality of his transformed consciousness. It is the manifesting of spiritual energy using the teacher as a conduit to the physical.

There is an image that goes some way towards demonstrating the reality behind the Masters' words. It is that of the Buddha sitting cross-legged in meditation. So powerful must have been the Enlightened One's presence that even his image has power. I am aware that this image did not come about until some centuries after the Buddha's passing, but I do not think it beyond the wit of the spiritual hierarchy to inspire artists of the period to create such an image (one based on reality, I might say) as a focal point through which spiritual energy could stream forth into the world. Images of Christ have a similar power though they transmit a somewhat different vibration. Naturally no image can hope to convey more than a fraction of the teacher's actual presence but they are adequate substitutes, by no means devoid of power.

The next day we went to Sarnath where the Buddha first taught the Dharma and set the Wheel of the Law in motion. It was here he came after attaining enlightenment, having resolved to share his discovery with others. His decision to make public his realisation (not inevitable, he could have simply retired to the forest) and teach others the way to attain it was almost as momentous as the enlightenment itself. It opened up to all something that hitherto had been kept the most closely guarded of secrets. Christ did exactly the same thing as far as the Western world was concerned. Both teachers pulled back the veil of existence to reveal the truth to anyone who cared to follow them and the reason they did so was because of their boundless love for suffering humanity. That is why these two saviours are the two most loved human beings of all the countless millions who have ever trodden this Earth.

In the Deer Park of Isipatana the Buddha found the five ascetics whom he had previously left after realising that their way of austerity was not going to lead him to enlightenment. The change in him must have been immediately apparent for straightaway they became his first disciples. He taught them the Middle Way of avoiding extremes, the Four Noble Truths concerning suffering, its cause (desire), its cure and its removal by following the Noble Eightfold Path consisting of Right Views, Right Motive, Right Speech, Right Conduct, Right Means of Livelihood, Right Effort, Right Mind Control and Right Meditation. It is notable that basically the whole of Buddhism is here already in the First Sermon. Shortly afterwards he preached the Second Sermon in which he showed the non-existence in absolute terms of the personal self.

The contrast between the deer park at Sarnath and the river front at Varanasi is striking and aptly illustrates the difference in the two religions they represent. The seriousness and calm order of early Buddhism stands in marked relief to the seeming outer chaos but inner visionary insight of the Hindu faith. It is a difference somewhat similar to that between Apollo and Dionysus of ancient Greece, and it is good that both approaches to the higher worlds exist reminding us that no one outer way has a monopoly on truth. The stupas and temples of Sarnath conveyed a deeply reverent atmosphere but what I responded to most were the lawns and trees of the park itself which spoke of the Buddha's presence there better than any of the buildings. I could imagine him standing in the park beneath one of the great shade trees, white birds softly singing as they flew hither and thither above him, and his disciples listening transfixed as he preached simply but eloquently of his discovery, any doubts as to his attainment simply swept away by the authority of his manner and the peace he emanated.

The main attraction of the Sarnath Archaeological Museum is the seven foot high Ashokan lion capital, now the national symbol of India, with its four back to back lions on a drum ornamented with a lion, elephant, horse and bull. Excavated in 1905, along with the column on which it originally stood until that was partially smashed by Muslim invaders, it is undoubtedly magnificent. But symbolic of India? Perhaps it is appropriate for the modern secular Indian state but the figure of the dancing Shiva surely sums up the essence of India far better as does, also in the Sarnath museum, the beautiful fifth century sculpture of the Buddha in which he meditates in the lotus position with his fingers delicately forming a *mudra* and a finely carved stone halo encircling his head. This sculpture embodies what Buddhism is all about and is worth a thousand sermons.

That evening after we had eaten our dinner, the only guests in a large dining room with five waiters for the two of us, we walked in the public gardens around the cantonment area. From one of the small houses surrounding the old parade ground we heard the sound of a sitar and went closer, the better to listen. Practically the whole side of the house was open to the warm night air and soon we were spotted and beckoned inside. The musicians (there was a tabla player too) then proceeded to give us a private concert which turned into just about the best musical event I have attended. Not simply because of the music, wonderful as it was, but that combined with the gentle Indian night, the scent of incense, the decorative rugs and cushions, the soft candlelight and the complete openness of the people made for an unforgettable experience.

Rightly or wrongly I took that as a gift from the Masters but, if it did come from them, it was more likely to be part of a test and here's why. The next day we left Varanasi to fly back to Delhi from where we were going on to Srinagar in Kashmir, which is where we had decided to go to after the trip to Kathmandu fell through. The journey involved spending a few hours overnight in Delhi airport between flights. At the little airport in Varanasi as we waited for our plane to Delhi, Michael began chatting to a couple of people in French. They were French and he spoke that language well, having lived in Normandy for a period in his childhood so who could possibly object? Unfortunately I could. I was still bathed in the afterglow of the atmosphere of the concert of the night before and the fact that Michael was chatting away about worldly things to a couple of people who obviously had no spiritual interests really irked me. That he seemed to be showing off his skill in French was also irritating. Quite ridiculous, I know. But I was still uplifted by what had been for me almost a spiritual experience in which I had felt myself transported back to classical India and took Michael's insensitivity (i.e. he didn't feel exactly the same about it as me) as a sort of betrayal. Once aboard the plane I couldn't contain myself and rounded on him, accusing him of showing off and having no real spiritual feeling. He exploded with anger and virtually shouted at me telling me that it was none of my business what he said to anyone. When we got to Delhi his anger got worse and, as we waited for the flight to Srinagar, he ranted and raged at me in an almost frightening way saying that he was going back to England and didn't care what happened to me. He appeared to be completely out of control. His eyes were virtually popping out of his head and he seemed to have no concern that people were staring at us in astonishment. I haven't known many more humiliating moments. Then all of a sudden it ceased. His rage departed and he lay down across some seats in the airport lounge and went to sleep. I stayed awake feeling miserable until it was time for our flight.

When we got to Srinagar everything was back to normal. I was very puzzled at the sudden change in his behaviour, both going into and coming out of the rage, but realised that my lack of emotional control had sparked it off. Neither of us, however, spoke further of the matter. Our plan had been to stay on a houseboat although we had nothing booked. But a taxi driver at the airport said he knew of a good one on Dal Lake and we thought that we might as well take a look at it. Naturally we assumed that the driver had some deal with the houseboat owner but, in the absence of anything else, it seemed worth investigating. As we drove out from the town to the lake we passed some decidedly dilapidated boats packed closely together on a rather dirty stretch of water and feared the worst but then the water got cleaner and the boats improved until we reached a beautiful lake with freshly painted wooden boats moored along its shores. The driver stopped at a quay where some long rowing boats were tied up and we got in one with the name Cheeky Charlie proudly displayed on the side. The taxi driver got in as well and we rowed to the houseboat he had spoken of. It was delightful. The owner was an elderly Muslim who was so pleased that Michael spoke Urdu that he practically insisted we stay with him. After seeing the boat we wanted to anyway but felt obliged to put on a mild show of resistance as part of the necessary bargaining process.

The boat had two decks, the lower of which had two double bedrooms, bathrooms and a living room area. The upper deck was a sun terrace open to the sky with a small central covered space, and that was where we ate. When we arrived there was a young German couple staying in the other room. They were very friendly but left after a day or two and for the rest of the week we stayed there we had the boat to ourselves. Made of cedar wood and about a hundred feet long by almost twenty wide, it was decorated with finely carved wooden Kashmiri furniture and the painted papier maché typical of the region. A small verandah at the front, down which stairs led into the water, was its means of entrance. We took our meals on the boat, all freshly prepared by the resident cook, working in another smaller boat moored up alongside, and all extremely good. Slightly less hot than elsewhere in India but full of subtle flavours and accompanied by excellent chapattis. A small earthenware pot of curds came with every meal and taken with the local honey was positively ambrosial. There wasn't a great deal to do there but that was fine after our previous weeks of travel. I read, sat in the sun on the deck and walked along the shore. The houseboat had its own small rowing boat and every morning I took this out to the middle of the lake and jumped in the cool clear water for a swim.

One morning we hired Cheeky Charlie to take us to Srinagar which was a couple of miles away. As we neared the town the clear waters of the river became increasingly foul. Pretty soon the boat had to push aside debris as it made its way along. Some you could identify, some you'd rather not. We disembarked and had a look around the not very spectacular town but then entered a shop which seemed more interesting than most. Inside we found the usual array of tourist stuff, though of better quality than that phrase might imply, and I bought a dressing gown and some papier maché odds and ends as presents. Then Michael spotted a Buddha figure which the shopkeeper told him was made of some special alloy used only in Tibet. That was mildly interesting but what was much more so was the expression on the Buddha's face which for once looked as though it really might have belonged to him. Michael bought it and it is one of the few objects that he possessed that I still have.

On another day we went in a *shikara*, the local wooden boat that transports everything from people to flowers, to the Shalimar Gardens. Laid out in Persian style with waterways and terraces, they were built by the Mughal emperor Jahangir in 1619 and are regarded as one of the most beautiful gardens in all India. There is a famous couplet by the poet Jami inscribed on the pavilion here which, translated, says "If there is a paradise on earth, it is this, it is this, it is this". Poetic exaggeration aside, Shalimar Bagh, with its elegant *chinar* trees, fountains and waterfalls, is certainly a lovely place but is it not the case that almost any garden is a reminder to fallen humanity of paradise? Not for nothing was Eden, our ancestral home and spiritual nursery, thought of as a garden. There is something about nature tamed and tended that recalls the peaceful security and lost innocence of our pre-dualistic world more perfectly than anything else.

Other than these two excursions and a walk to a nearby mosque where a hair from the head of the Prophet was a prized relic, we did very little sightseeing in Kashmir. I could easily have spent longer just drifting on the lake, eating curds and honey and watching the blue and orange kingfishers dart in and out of the water like little molten arrows, but the lotus eating phase of our trip was coming to an end and it was time to get back to Delhi.

On the last night of our stay the Masters came and spoke to me during meditation and I got an explanation for what had occurred at Varanasi airport. The gist of it was this. Back in February they had warned me that I **must guard against great joys as well as great depressions and keep an even keel at all times. I should also guard against negative entities which will attack when I least expect it in ways that I least expect.** My complete failure to control my emotions after the concert, stirred up to great heights by the music but then clung on to rather than let go, had opened the door to these negative entities. By succumbing to anger and irritation I had broken the seal in my aura allowing them entry, and because Michael and I were linked, as the Masters had many times described, they had got into him too[12]. In fact, because of his mediumistic nature they had got much more of a hold in him hence his extreme reaction to my admonishments. He had actually become possessed and it had taken the Masters a while to get rid of the invading entity. Naturally when I heard this I was deeply ashamed of myself. It made perfect sense in the light of what I had previously been told and I had to face the truth that the lapse that set everything off had come from me, and had done so in spite of the many warnings I had received. The Master was kind and did not reproach me at all but asked me to learn my lesson. He said that they allowed this sort of thing to happen because, by observing and becoming aware of the process, I could learn to master my reactions. He told me to have no fear as they would never let it go too far but also to make sure it did not happen again. Of course I said it wouldn't.

Unfortunately my optimism in that regard was to prove unjustified.

From Delhi we went on to Agra. Kashmir had given us a preliminary taste of the magnificence of the Mughal Empire but nothing there could match up to the peerless beauty of the Taj Mahal. The exquisite harmony of its proportions, the dazzling whiteness of its marble exterior set against the clear blue backdrop of the Indian sky and the serene atmosphere conjured up by its ornate gardens and water channels make of it one of the few things in the world that truly lives up to its reputation. So much modern art is subjective and according to taste hence it will pass. The Taj is one of the most sublime examples of objective art, art that brings out the same response in everyone. It is irrefutable and stands as a monument to pure geometrical beauty.

We stayed in Agra for a few days and went back to the Taj several times, the last of which was my 24th birthday. After leaving its grounds we walked back to our hotel through the bazaar. Michael bought some joss sticks, the smell of which I thought too over-powering, making them unsuitable for meditation purposes. Somehow or other an initially mild disagreement escalated into a full-blooded argument and before I knew it we were back to a situation approaching that at Varanasi airport. I was dismayed. I had disagreed with him about the incense but surely I hadn't been as aggressively indignant as before? Fortunately things didn't quite reach the point they had earlier but Michael became so enraged that there was no doubt something had got into him. You may be sceptical of this and think I am making far too much of an ordinary loss of temper, and trying to find an exotic reason for a perfectly normal everyday occurrence. I would not blame you for your scepticism. However I have to say that my experiences have made me quite able to tell the difference between loss of temper, reasonable or unreasonable, and demonic possession. It wasn't often that the latter happened with Michael but, on a very few occasions, it did happen and this was one of them.

That evening as we meditated in our hotel room I felt something on my shoulder. Opening my eyes I saw an extremely large grasshopper perched there. It placidly looked back at me. What's the correct procedure here, I wondered. Do you ignore it and carry on meditating or do you brush it off? I tried the former but my meditation simply consisted of thinking about grasshoppers so I gave in and brushed it off. Just at that moment a Master spoke through Michael. **Did you like our present to you?** he asked. I had to express my ignorance as to what it might have been. The grasshopper? No. **Our gift on your birthday was your argument with our brother.** By this time I knew the Masters well enough to venture a small joke. I thanked him kindly but said it wasn't the best present I'd ever had. He explained. I may have thought I had not succumbed to negative emotions when I expressed my disagreement with Michael about the joss sticks but it was no good suppressing an external reaction if inwardly I was giving way to anger or egotism, which I had been. Did I think that I could conceal what was in my heart from them? Did I even want to? He told me that the passing of one test simply moved the lesson on to a new level, and that one should always be on the alert for new tests, never thinking one could let down one's guard. **Observe yourself,** he said, **stay awake and do not try to hide anything from yourself. The greater part of you remains with us and I can assure you that you wish this training to take place however difficult it may sometimes seem.**

What does it mean, this statement that **the greater part of you remains with us**? It refers to the fact that when the soul takes birth only a fraction of it descends into the physical world to animate the mind and body of the incarnate person. The **greater part** remains on its own plane, which accounts for the feeling many of us might have that there is more to us than the self of which we are normally aware. The soul is the sum total of all our experiences, physical and spiritual. It holds all that we are and all that we have been since it was created. It is a far nobler being that its earthbound little cousin. And yet even this soul, this magnificent creation, must eventually be sacrificed. Our final test, symbolised by Christ's crucifixion, consists of giving up the soul and the fruits of our long incarnationary experiences in the phenomenal worlds, and renouncing all that we are, our very self. However it is this renunciation, this absolute emptying of self, that constitutes our true entry into the Kingdom of God. This is not the destruction of individuality but its transcending as the focal point of consciousness.

During our stay in Agra we also visited the abandoned city of Fatehpur Sikri and, a place that made a particular impression on me, Akbar's tomb at Sikandra which is about five miles from Agra. The emperor Akbar was the third and greatest of the Mughal emperors. Deeply interested in all religions, he held debates with Hindus, Jains, Christians and Zoroastrians and, unlike many other Muslim rulers, allowed them to practise their religions freely. By all accounts the possessor of a genuinely noble character, many see him as an example of the ideal ruler. The Theosophists even claim him to have been an earlier incarnation of one of their Masters which is interesting if unverifiable.

I wasn't aware of that claim at the time of my visit but as I walked up the broad approaching pathway, fringed by elegant palm trees with squawking green parrots darting between them, and made my way to the entrance of the tomb, I had a sense that this was another place the Masters wished me to link up with. Again, I make no far-fetched claims for any Mughal connection. I simply report what I felt which was that something inside me responded to this place. Perfectly reasonably, though much to my annoyance, Michael had taken photographs of me at various times on the trip and the one he took here is the only one in which I am smiling.

As we entered the mausoleum there was a feeling of regal dignity that one would naturally associate with a figure such as Akbar. Kings and queens are not much in fashion nowadays but they embody a true 1st ray archetype as God's stewards on Earth, figures of command and authority who exist not only to rule but to serve their people. Outmoded they may be today but the figure of a monarch stands for much more than worldly rule or political power. It is a true symbol of a spiritual reality. Of course, the symbol as manifested in the past was very often a poor reflection of that reality. Not so, one feels, in the case of Akbar.

An attendant inside the mausoleum gave the opening part of the Muslim call to prayer, *Allāhu Akbar* – God is most great. It echoed and resounded around the burial chamber creating an atmosphere of solemnity and piety that was extremely affecting. I was reminded that all religions teach that "In the beginning was the Word", the creative sound that woke the sleeping Mother of undifferentiated substance and began the whole process of manifested life. Here in the darkness of the tomb, it was as if that moment was being recreated on a tiny microcosmic scale. I could imagine the worlds being called into being by the fecundating sound as it filled the surrounding space and made of the tomb of the dead the womb of life. But then it died away and all was as before. Was my idea so fanciful, though? Many ancient cultures have worshipped the Mother in caves and underground places, whether natural or man-made. Such localities were regarded as at the same time tomb and womb, places of death and rebirth, ancient peoples being well aware that these are but two sides of the same coin. In fact, whether they were burial chamber, crypt, cave or just an empty hollow, what these places all represent is the universe as it was prior to manifestation when "the earth was without form, and void; and darkness was upon the face of the deep." Alone but for the now silent attendant in the deep stillness of the vaulted chamber of Akbar's tomb that time before time seemed somehow to be made present.

There is a profound saying inscribed on the main gateway at Fatehpur Sikri. It says, "Thus spake Jesus upon whom be peace. The world is a bridge, pass over it but build no house upon it." Christians won't recognise this saying from any of the Biblical scriptures but Jesus is a prophet in Islam too, and though I don't know the provenance of this quotation or whether Jesus really did say it, that doesn't matter. It is the sort of thing he might well have said, and is an excellent piece of advice for the pilgrim soul. How many of us heed it though?

Fatehpur Sikri was built by Akbar to commemorate the birth of his son Jahangir. Two of his children had recently died and, naturally concerned at the lack of an heir, he consulted a Muslim holy man who lived in the district. His name was Salim Chishti and he predicted that the emperor would have a son if he came and lived at Sikri, then little more than a village. So Akbar did and nine months later, runs the story, a son was born. Seeing Sikri as a place of good fortune, Akbar made it his new capital and over the course of the next few years he built the beautiful city that remains to this day. One of the reasons it remains in such an unspoilt condition is that it was abandoned after a brief seventeen years of occupation because of a water shortage due to a rapidly expanding population. Such, at any rate is the usual explanation. However there is another, more poetic but probably apocryphal, story. In this version the city was abandoned because Salim Chishti told Akbar that its noise and worldly atmosphere were interrupting his spiritual practices so either he or Akbar would have to leave. Akbar's magnificent reply is said to have been "Then let it be your servant, I pray."

The Mughals came to India as invaders but they left a legacy of beauty that hugely enriched the sub-continent, most notably architecturally but culturally too, for example in the fields of painting and music. Now it's hard to think of India without them, and they perfectly illustrate the fact that everything that comes into India's orbit affects India but in its turn is affected by India. The country is big enough to absorb a myriad of influences and yet remain eternally itself. In the same way I don't think that anyone who goes to India stays untouched by the place. As we left Agra to go back to Delhi I knew that I had succumbed to the same love for India shared by so many others and that Michael certainly had too. This was his fifth trip there, some of which had been extended stays, but as we boarded the plane to go back to London he turned and looked around him in silence for a while before saying "Goodbye dear

India. I don't suppose I'll ever see you again." What does anyone ever know of their future?

Chapter 22

"Earth is a School."

The Masters had spoken to me in India on several more occasions than the ones I have included here but I had not taken the notebook in which I normally wrote down their talks, and only jotted down a few of them. However, once back in England, I resumed my secretarial habits, and almost immediately after our return they came and spoke the following words. It will be clear that, the holiday concluded, it was now back to business as usual.

October 2nd 1979
The Master said he was pleased that I was learning submission. I must not attempt to subjugate Michael but should subjugate myself. It did not matter if I was right or wrong in what I thought or said. The lesson being taught now was humility and submission. I should never allow myself to be irritated by Michael's behaviour. I should ignore it and it would cease. They permitted him to be like that precisely so that I could overcome this weakness in me. If I concentrated on the higher and ignored the lower then in time that would dissolve. He repeated and emphasised "You must accept and you must submit. We realise this is a difficult lesson for you but it is the key to true spiritual knowledge, and without learning it you will be no better then those, and they are many, who use the sacred teachings to advance themselves."

He continued. "The best colt can win no races until it has been well-trained. The student may eventually exceed his trainer but first he must learn from his practical experience. No potential can be realised except by submission to a trainer who teaches you how to make best use of it. If the student feels arrogant about his inner potential and disdains practical training on that account then he will achieve nothing. He needs the trainer to realise his potential and, while being trained, must submit totally to the trainer and accept what he says without criticism or superiority. So listen to our brother who speaks with our voice."

Reading this now it might appear I was fairly insufferable with a rather too high opinion of myself but I don't think I was quite that bad. I cannot deny that I did, at times, have a superior attitude towards Michael, or that I lacked humility, but perhaps the Master's words could apply to many people today who are at a particular stage of the path; people of an advanced sensibility who have a rapidly developing intuitive sense but who, like me, may still have much to learn of practical spirituality. The opening up they have experienced might lead them to think that they have progressed further on the path than is, in fact, the case. It is a common error to appropriate insights that come from beyond the self to the self - 'I know this therefore I am this' - but the true knower knows that he is nothing. I did not know this. Oh, theoretically I did. That's easy. But I did not *know* it.

Here's an equation quite as correct as any mathematical one. Spirituality = submission + surrender + sacrifice. You could add service and selflessness to that list but I think the point is adequately made without labouring it. The point being that spirituality is about one thing and one thing only, the removal of the ego. This was the fundamental message behind all the Masters' teachings. I may have had a certain amount of spiritual knowledge but that was of very little account to them as long as it was filtered through the ego. Hence their constant insistence on the need for me to submit and surrender. Sometimes in the modern spiritual world the necessity for this is forgotten and greater emphasis is laid on more attractive aspects of the path such as joy, peace, wisdom, enlightenment and the like but these are the fruits of the path and the fruits will never grow if the plant is not adequately watered by the tears of the sacrificed self. Anyone who follows the path for what they hope to get from it will not reach its conclusion. You may deceive yourself, you may deceive the world but you cannot deceive God. We need to realise that the spiritual path is not about acquiring things but renouncing them and that the more we let go, the more we are required to let go until finally we must let go of everything.

I have mentioned suffering as a part of the spiritualising process. There is certainly nothing inherently good or valuable about suffering *per se* but it is the fire that burns out the fallen aspect of its nature from the soul. It would be counter-productive to actively search to suffer in the way of some medieval mystics but, at the same time, as is often said, those whom God loves, He chastises[13]. He does so because such people have dedicated themselves to Him and He wishes to remove the obstacles that prevent them from being one with Him. The main obstacle, the source of all the others, is the ego, and suffering is that which loosens the ego's grip on the soul. It removes our attachments and our pride, it cleanses our heart and it clears our vision. It should not be sought but, when it comes, neither should one seek to avoid it. Naturally I am talking about suffering as a spiritual purifier here. Nothing I say should be taken to mean that it is not every individual's duty to attempt to remove or alleviate suffering in others wherever he or she may find it. The fundamental law of life is love and this law takes precedence over all others. Having said that, as any parent knows, sometimes the greater love allows apparent hardship in the short term so that a higher good may come in the long run.

A few nights late the Master was back and spoke at length on various subjects. I should apologise for the somewhat disjointed nature of my transcription of this talk. As always I had to write the notes down quickly before I forgot the talk and whenever, as here, it was quite a long one, I tended just to include the salient points. So if I give the impression that the Masters jumped randomly from one subject to another, it's my fault not theirs. They never spoke anything other than articulately but I decided not to attempt to restore my notes of these talks to what might have been their original form so as to leave them as truthful i.e. unedited as possible. They are as I wrote them just after they had taken place.

October 8th 1979

The Master said that at night we should attune ourselves to the higher planes by meditation or prayer so that when we left our bodies we could go there quickly and easily. He said that music was a wonderful medium but I should not listen to it to excess as it tended to make me listless and dreamy. Earth is a school and I have work to do here. The wish to experience the glories of the higher planes was understandable but should not be indulged or the reason for being on Earth would be neglected. Now I needed to be earthed and that was one thing that Michael was there to help me with. For the time being he and I were linked and if I want him to overcome his lower self then I must first overcome mine. If he fails it is because I have and if he succeeds it will also be because I have. The ball is in my court. "Choose your shots with care!" he said.

He told me to be more simple and childlike, stressing he meant simple in attitude not mind then clarifying further. "Do not be as those who seek to penetrate to every corner of the universe but do not know themselves. It is not necessary to chase after the many mysteries of existence. Live simply in the heart and all mysteries will in time become known to you." I asked how I could pray more from the heart and less from the head and he said that I should concentrate on the heart centre and this would come. "Reason less and accept more then you will open up". He went on to say "Do not react to evil. It cannot harm you if you ignore it so do not react to it and like an irritating small boy of whom you take no notice it goes away."

I've written enough about evil so will only say here that this is excellent advice. What you pay attention to, you give energy to.

Withdraw attention or, as the Master said, **do not react** and it has nothing to feed on. The near identity of these words with those of Jesus on the same subject will not have escaped the reader's notice. Perhaps I should just add, to clarify the position for those who might imagine that not reacting to evil will allow it to triumph, that the reaction or non-reaction referred to is an inner one. Sometimes it might be necessary to confront evil (as in "wrongness") directly as Jesus did when debating with the Pharisees. At others it may be sufficient simply to demonstrate truth in the silent manner he did at his trial.

The Masters told me on several occasions that while we slept we were taken to higher planes for further instruction. They added that if we were in the right frame of mind before we slept, our transition there would be the more rapid. In the spiritual world like, in the sense of similarity of vibration, really does attract like hence their recommendation to attune ourselves at night-time.

The concept of higher planes is now well established in Western esotericism. These are usually thought of as interpenetrating the physical world so not somewhere far off as in the traditional idea of heaven but all around us here and now, co-existing in the same space but separated by their rate of vibration. All planes are composed of the one substance (we can think of it as light) vibrating at different levels of intensity. Thus everything from the highest level of pure light right down to physical matter is made of the selfsame substance. There is no ultimate separation between these planes but, practically speaking, they are divided at certain frequencies. A helpful parallel would be the notes in a musical scale or, maybe, different scales themselves.

For the esotericist the material world is not just the physical universe. That is merely the part of it that is perceived by the physical senses. Above it are the worlds of feeling and thought, and then one corresponding to what is called the causal or identity body which is the repository of memory (the memory of all our incarnations, not just the current one) and where our sense of self is stored.

This is usually seen as part of the mental plane. All these are definite worlds made of their own type of matter. Beyond these planes of form are higher planes comprising the spiritual world proper, which are only fully accessible to those who have transcended duality but may be dimly sensed by anyone who is awakening to what lies beyond self.

A plane is a place is a state of consciousness. Anyone can travel anywhere horizontally in the physical world but you can only go to a plane in the higher worlds to which your consciousness corresponds. We may all have aspects of our being existing on higher levels but that does not mean we are awake at those levels. The aim of life is to become so. **Earth is a school** and the experiences we have here are designed to teach us to become aware at higher levels. That is why we are here.

The Masters never specified exactly what they meant when they referred to higher planes and I don't doubt that they would have regarded speculation thereon as profitless. As they said, **it is not necessary to chase after the many mysteries of existence.** The Buddha is reported to have said much the same thing when asked about metaphysical matters. Likewise Jesus told us to seek first the Kingdom of Heaven and all things would be added to us. However it is clear that the levels at which the Masters operate are normally those beyond the material world, the lowest of which, the first of the spiritual planes, is generally designated the plane of intuition. When you consider that the term 'physical plane' describes everything we normally know, everything known to modern science, this really doesn't tell us very much but we can be certain that this is a level at which thinking in the conventional sense is transcended and knowing takes place as direct insight. Here there can be difference but no possibility of separation so it is a plane of universal love. At even higher levels as one approaches the unmanifest source of all, there is increasing unity until form and time and space themselves disappear into the infinite eternal absolute.

I had always been fond of music and at the time these talks took place I was expanding my knowledge of the classical repertoire through the good offices of the Bath public library. Perhaps I also used music slightly as an escape. Such, at any rate, seems to be the implication of the Master's words. He never said I should not listen to music but advised me to be moderate in my consumption of it for the reasons given. It's a hard truth but one that must be borne in mind by all spiritually sensitive souls who might shrink from the coarsenesses and vulgarities of the world. We are here on Earth to learn the lessons of Earth. **The wish to experience the glories of the higher planes is understandable but should not be indulged or the reason for being on Earth will be neglected.** This does not just apply to music lovers. Attempts to flee the world in any form, whether through art or the chasing after higher states of consciousness or even the retreat to a monastery or ashram, all these, if indulged too far, could lead to **the reason for being on Earth being neglected.** I don't mean by this that no-one should ever join a monastery. Each individual must decide his or her own path. What I do say is that in the current age such a life has its drawbacks and might be suitable for a limited period but not necessarily a lifetime. Now we are called on to lead spiritual lives in the world, not, as might have been done in previous times, to separate matter and spirit but to make the two one though always seeing matter in its true role as a manifestation of spirit rather than something real in its own right. You might say that the phenomenal world (*Maya*) is illusion when seen as itself but real when seen as the manifested expression of spirit (*Brahman*). Or, in Buddhist terms, *Samsara* (becoming) and *Nirvana* (being) are one but only truly so when seen in the light of *Nirvana*. Likewise, in Christian terminology, God created the world and saw that it was good but it is only really good when recognised as the creation of God and not looked upon as something self-subsisting and independent of its maker.

So the modern mystic should not seek to flee the world to find heaven but aim to bring heaven down into the world.

If I had to make a list of sayings that encapsulated the essence of the Masters' teachings, near the top would be the instruction to **live simply in the heart**. This is something they never tired of repeating and the reason for that is that it is something extremely difficult for the modern Westerner to do. Our minds are too cluttered, too active. Moreover we are deeply fearful of letting go of our intellectual grip of things. But what it amounts to is only this. We should live in the moment and without being the slave of analytical thought. We should live without calculation.

Then would come a phrase they also repeated to me many times, so many in fact that I'm surprised I have not mentioned it before now. It's really just another way of saying the same thing but coming at it from a slightly different angle, always a useful approach to refresh an idea and open it up so that you avoid reducing an insight to a concept. It is this. **Have inner calm and be centred in God.** You might think this is obvious for a spiritual seeker and so it is but often the obvious is neglected in favour of the more recondite. How do you have inner calm? You observe yourself and your emotional reactions and then stand back from them without identifying with them. From a purely practical perspective you focus on the breath, breathing slowly, deeply, rhythmically. You see the changelessness that underlies change. You have implicit faith that behind the veneer of apparent disorder there is goodness and truth which are gradually working themselves out into full manifestation. How do you become centred in God? Through imagination, through love, through faith, through humility. You forget yourself, you open your heart, you bow your head. To be centred in God is to be aware that there is a higher power and then submit yourself to that power.

Chapter 23

Further Thoughts on the Masters

People often ask why it is that if the Masters exist they do not reveal themselves. In a way this is just rephrasing the old question of why God does not reveal Himself. The answer to that is actually quite simple and it is that God is revealing Himself all the time. It is we who have blocked ourselves off from Him by falling into the duality consciousness. God is not hiding from us. We have hidden from Him. We have separated ourselves out from life by creating the ego and identifying with that. The moment we give up this false identification then we will be aware of God or, if you wish to put this in more impersonal terms, we will be aware of the divine power that is present in every atom of the manifested universe while, at the same time, transcending all manifestation.

Incidentally, don't read anything into the pronoun here. Him, her, it, it doesn't matter. These are just words to describe the indescribable. There is metaphysical justification for describing God the Creator in male terms (in contrast to Mother Nature), and spirit as the positive aspect of the One Reality with matter as its negative polarity, but really God is beyond all gender, as we think of it in a human sense, as He is beyond all distinctions. These come later. The attempt to define God in gender terms is for children who limit themselves to their appearance. You may be a man or you may be a woman but do you think your fundamental being is male or female? I am not here disputing the doctrine that we, as souls, have a masculine or feminine quality. I think we do and I think that that endures. But essential being is beyond any manifested characteristic.

In the case of the Masters the answer as to why they do not reveal themselves is similar but we can express it differently. The Masters do not walk about the world teaching openly for various reasons, one of which is that we are not yet spiritually developed enough to benefit from their presence. Another has to do with free will. They would come if they were wanted but, strange as it may seem, we do not actually want them. At least not enough of us want them enough. To be sure, many people would love to fall at their feet and others would gladly benefit from their wisdom, but we do not want what they would bring which is the need for self-transcendence together with the sacrifice that entails. We are not prepared to give up what we have for them. What they would bring would be the fire that burns out self and we are not ready for such intense purification, not in the mass anyhow.

For thousands of years the Masters have removed themselves from the world to allow it to develop in such a way as would not have been possible if they had been there holding our hands. They have let us find things out for ourselves and we have done that, in the process developing the rational mind to an extent that we could not otherwise have done. It could be said that we have gone too far in that direction but the many predictions about this time, for example those concerning the Kali Yuga of Hinduism, the latter days of Christianity and the prophesies of Hermes, supposedly coming down from ancient Egypt, along with others from cultures all around the world, imply that this was not unexpected. Humanity was intended to develop its sense of self in order eventually to become conscious co-creators with God and for that to happen a period of withdrawal by its spiritual teachers was necessary. A parallel can be drawn between this and the stage in a disciple's life when his teacher withdraws leaving him to depend entirely on himself. He does this because to become a Master you must master, which naturally you cannot do if you are supported by something or someone external to yourself. To transcend duality you must transcend the division between master and pupil. To discover God within yourself you must give up the idea of a separate external being. And so, in a similar way, our teachers left us to find our own way in the world and learn from the experience of self-dependence.

Thus you could say that, notwithstanding exceptional appearances here and there, the Masters have not showed themselves since historical records began to allow us the room to grow in this cycle in which the mind was to be developed and the material world thoroughly explored. But also because we have not been spiritually mature enough. The light they bring would dazzle undeveloped eyes.

Having made that point, one must go on to say that actually the Masters are now revealing themselves. Even this book might be considered a small part of that. In the late 19th century the renowned or notorious (depending on your point of view), Russian occultist Madame Blavatsky brought the idea of men who had transcended the normal human state to public attention. This may have been known by isolated individuals and the odd secret society in the past but it had not entered the mainstream until Madame Blavatsky rather colourfully put it there. Her presentation of the Masters may not have been perfect but it was better than that of her immediate successors, who promptly personalised the impersonal (hence the reaction of Krishnamurti), and considerably better than many of those who followed on from her.

It is likely that the Theosophical Masters were in the nature of what are called magical personalities which were constructed by the concentrated thinking of Madame Blavatsky and others, and strengthened by the devotion of many acolytes. This doesn't mean they were false but that the form they took was a created one albeit possibly based on something real. That form could then be used as a means to transmit knowledge by genuine spiritual beings but, once established, it could also take on a life of its own. Nowadays it must be recognised that there are potent thoughtforms of the Masters on the astral plane and these can be utilised by spirits of varying quality to transmit teachings of varying quality. Some of these teachings could contain much that is valid but, because of their origin, they will be somewhat 'contaminated' and so there will always be illusion and opinion mixed in with the genuine and the true. As I have said, the Masters prefer to work mind to mind on intuitive levels but, at this early stage of their introduction, it was deemed necessary to give them the appearance of some sort of personality to enable people to get a grip on them. A problem no doubt anticipated and thought worth the risk is that there are many more people who can raise their consciousness to the level of the astral thoughtform than there are those who can to that of the soul, where the Masters are truly to be found. That explains the numerous spurious communications that have bedevilled the esoteric world ever since Madame Blavatsky's day. It can't be denied that this has thrown the whole subject of Masters into disrepute amongst many intelligent people but it is a necessary phase to be gone through, and also serves to test our spiritual intuition so has a positive aspect even if it can cause confusion as well.

Over the last three decades I have met people who find the notion of a spiritual hierarchy of Masters ridiculous, even infantile, and I have met others who embrace it wholeheartedly but lack sufficient discrimination to discern the real from the unreal. I have come across a few teachings I regard unequivocally as emanating from a high spiritual source but many more that are either a mixture of truth and half-truth or else just plain fantasy. At one time I used to allow myself to get irritated by the number of false Masters, both channelled and self-proclaimed in the world, but I was told not to be concerned as this was inevitable in our day and would pass eventually. It was also pointed out to me that my reaction stemmed largely from lack of self-confidence and attachment to my own ideas, and it might be better if I looked to myself rather than worrying about others.

In the 21st century esoteric teachings from many different traditions are readily available for anyone who wishes to become acquainted with them. Virtually everything that might have been secret in the past is now out in the open. It is true that along with this cornucopia of riches there is a flood of less enlightened material but the point is that the truth is there for anyone desirous of finding it. The Masters have begun to reveal themselves through their teachings. The fact of their existence is also known and, in addition, there is the possibility of forming a closer relationship with them for any individual who is prepared to take the necessary steps to qualify for that. Contact with the Masters may not necessarily be registered in the everyday waking consciousness but we have been assured that they will notice anyone whose ardour for spiritual awakening is sufficiently strong. "Seek and ye shall find" remains as true as it has ever done as does the nowadays almost equally famous saying, "When the pupil is ready, the Master appears." This book, if it does nothing else, can at least bear witness to the truth of those statements.

In spite of what I have just written I can imagine the following objection. "This is all very well but it doesn't actually amount to anything more than a lot of words. If there really are such beings as enlightened Masters, why do they not appear in the public eye and simply prove to everybody that there is a spiritual purpose to life? Then we could happily give up our selfish, materialistic lives and fulfil ourselves in the way you say we are meant to. Why don't they reveal themselves in such a way to convince even the most diehard of atheists?"

When Jesus said that "it is a wicked and adulterous generation that seeketh after a sign" what he meant was that you cannot prove the truths of the spiritual world by material, that is to say, by external, means. You might be able to demonstrate some sort of higher reality but it would not make a fundamental difference to the people witnessing it. They would not really be changed in any way. True proof comes from within and it comes from a change in awareness. Change must grow organically from inside a person rather than be imposed on that person from outside if it is to be real. You might even say that it must come about through an inner necessity which is why it is usually left to the ordinary experiences of life to bring it about. It is true that Jesus did perform miracles sometimes (though often he refused to do so), but his mission was of an extraordinary nature in that it was intended to set the tone for a whole age. In the normal way of things any sort of conversion must come from within if it is to be deep rooted and not superficial.

If the Masters were to appear *en masse* at this stage of human development, they would be interfering with free will. They would be forcing us to believe. You might consider that if what we were forced to believe was the truth, the way it was brought about would not matter much but that is not so. We would not be believing it because we had become aware of it ourselves through our own intuitive capabilities and connection to the soul but because we had learned it as a fact. In other words, we would know it mentally not spiritually. Of all the facts you know how many do you really know as part of the fabric of your being? I would submit that the answer is very few. Spiritual things must be known spiritually if they are to be known truly.

As for persuading atheists of the reality of God, I once, in a fit of missionary zeal, asked the Masters how one could talk to confirmed materialists and convince them of the truth of spiritual things. I was told that there was no point engaging people in debate or argument as what exists beyond mind cannot be proved or disproved by mind. Mind can argue for or against any point of view, spiritual or material, but truth can only be known.

Atheists are, if you will forgive the expression, a peculiar lot. One can understand agnostics and one can understand people who look askance at spirituality because their experience of it is limited to religions in their modern exoteric forms, all of which have been distorted by corruptions inflicted on them by their adherents (even though the truth is there if you know how to look for it). These people have had the misfortune to grow up in a world with no spiritual understanding, unexposed to any proper teaching and in the highly artificial environment in which we 21st century people for the most part live and that we take to be real. So they doubt. But dyed in the wool atheists are different. Atheists are in some sort of denial. They are either in flight from God or they are on some level angry with God. They like to see themselves as fiercely independent rational thinkers but many of them are actually highly emotional and irrational. They seize on the discoveries of science to bolster their own prejudices, not realising, or not wanting to realise, that these discoveries might be valid on their own level but tell us nothing about levels beyond the reach of scientific instruments or rational thinking[14]. I am a blind man and I cannot see therefore light does not exist. Is that logical?

As a matter of fact, many of science's greatest discoveries have been made through a flash of intuitive insight and then confirmed through experiment afterwards. This is a time-honoured process in the mystical world. Scientists themselves recognise that this is a valid way to advance understanding and has often led to breakthroughs where the ordinary intellectual approach has failed. They are quite correct in their belief that intuition shows the way where rational thinking cannot go and can reveal things that the ordinary mind could never discover unaided. Many people have had an intuitive realisation that God or a transcendent spiritual force exists. Nobody has ever had an intuitive realisation that God does not exist.

An atheist would say that science has shown that we do not need God. Of course, even if we accept all the Darwinist claims in the matter of evolution (which we are by no means obliged to do, many of these being entirely conjectural), it has done no such thing. Life, consciousness, intelligence, love and the origin of the universe remain unexplained. All the things that matter, in fact. They claim that you can have a perfectly valid moral sense without God, and they would add that they are just as much able to appreciate beauty and mystery as the believer, because it is the human imagination which provides access to those worlds. What they utterly fail to grasp is that if there truly were no God, they would have neither a moral sense nor an imagination. Of course they have these things, or the potential for them, but only because of the presence of God within them who is there whether they believe in Him or not. What I would add to that is that if they allowed themselves to believe in

Him that would benefit their moral sense, their imagination and their power to respond to beauty and mystery immensely.

If you don't believe that God exists, do you believe that you exist? I mean do you believe you exist as an individual creature with free will? If you do then you cannot logically follow the atheist's creed and hold that life evolved out of inert matter because that demands you to be fundamentally no more than a predetermined, pre-programmed machine. If you don't then you don't believe that anyone else exists either so the only reason you possess any kind of moral sense is for the benefits that might bring you. Following your belief to its logical conclusion would mean that you can have no concern for any other human being, all of whom exist only for you to exploit as best you can in the quest to fulfil your appetites. Is that what you think? Perhaps it is but I doubt it. Only the most deluded of psychopaths has sunk to that level of denial. No doubt many self-professed atheists are as moral as a lot of religious believers but they don't recognise the logical inconsistency of their position. Atheists believe we can have morality without religion not realising that they may deny God but God does not deny them. Their conscience, which is the true source of morality rather than some intellectual theorising or evolutionary cultivation of cooperation to mutual advantage, is the voice of God within. Atheists fail to appreciate that by denying God they are denying their own reality. Without a divine source we would be no more than mechanical beings without free will[15] or true substance. Do atheists love their children? Why, if they really believe what they say they do? Human love is based on the unique individuality of the loved one but if that individuality is formed by a purely mechanical process, it is mechanical itself and has no true centre and so no intrinsic reality. Atheism denies love (atheists may not but again that is their logical inconsistency) except of the purely self-interested kind but then that is not love at all.

I have met people who say "I do believe in being a good person but I don't need God for that" but this is a simplistic point of view. You may not need the idea of God to be a conventionally decent sort of person who (in most circumstances) doesn't harm anyone and wishes everyone to be happy but true goodness runs so much deeper than that and can only come from a realisation of one's divine source. Without God there is no love, without love there is no goodness.

I realise that I may seem to have disregarded the Master's advice not to try to engage in debate with those of an atheistical disposition but my hope here is not to convince atheists of the absurdity of their position but to help those who might be bamboozled by their arguments. My intention in the paragraphs above is to try to assist prospective believers in a spiritual reality to find a way through the boggy morass of atheistic argument. In the modern world, it can be hard for anyone awakening to spiritual truths to protect the fragile flower of their new awareness from the icy blasts of the predominating materialistic ethos.

Lest it be thought from the preceding that I am arguing in favour of a return to religion such as it existed in earlier times, let me say that that is not my intention here. Atheism is a denial of truth and, if left unchecked, would completely cut humanity off from its source and plunge us into darkness and, possibly, destruction but conventional religions that teach a God in the sky, separate from his creation belong to the past. It is time to move on from that approach which would satisfy few people nowadays anyway. I am not arguing for religion as opposed to atheism or, at least, I most certainly am but for a religion that sees Creator and creature as ultimately one not an outer religion of rules and dogmas. Undoubtedly such religions have served us well in the past and without them the human race would be even more benighted than it currently is. However we are now capable of greater understanding and not just a few of us but a critical mass who can carry the rest along with them.

It's a strange world we live in at the beginning of the 21st century. On the one hand the culture and mindset of all Western countries, and an increasing number of Eastern ones (many of which held out a little longer but are now also rapidly succumbing to the seductions of consumerism), are thoroughly materialistic. Our near total reliance on machines underlines that point. The fact that we are rapidly emptying ourselves into outer things, a process that started innocently enough when books replaced memory but has now reached almost epidemic proportions, is further confirmation if it be needed that we have lost touch with the centre. On the other hand there might be said to be a spiritual awakening of sorts, and although this frequently leaves much to be desired, it is the commencement of something that has the potential to transform the human race if managed correctly.

To support this awakening people search wherever they can and some like to bring in science, previously chief spokesman for the prosecution, as a witness for the defence. Hence it is often said that modern science is confirming the insights of ancient mysticism, particularly in the fields of quantum mechanics and related theories of the structure of matter. This may well be the case but not that many scientists seem to think it at the moment, and even if they did it should be remembered that science is an intellectual pursuit which in no way can lead to mystical enlightenment. I am not attempting to belittle science at all, merely cautioning those who make rather too much of any slight link it may have with the world known by the sages and mystics of ages past. These knew what they knew by raising their consciousness and we must do exactly the same if we are to know what they did. The way to do this remains what it always has been and it is the way taught by the Masters. It is arduous and it requires sacrifice and because of this many people throughout the centuries have sought shortcuts. A number of these are promoted as legitimate paths nowadays but, as St Paul has it in his epistle to the Galatians, "God is not mocked" and if you try to enter His kingdom without leaving yourself at the door, the best you can hope for is disappointment.

The transcendence of self is what the Masters teach. The reality of it is what they demonstrate in their persons. One day they will return but they will not do so as saviours come to extract us from our self-created predicament. Rather they will come when we have reached a point at which we can benefit from their guidance to take the steps necessary to become Masters ourselves.

Chapter 24

Idle Dreaminess and False Prophets

If I had thought that the holiday in India might be the precursor to a more rapid development on our return, I was mistaken. Life continued in much the same vein as before, revolving around working in the antiques market during the day, punctuated by occasional buying trips further afield, and meditation in the evening. Outwardly it was a fairly dull existence with little excitement and no social life to speak of. That, though, is a basic requirement if one is truly to dedicate oneself to spiritual practice. An interior life must go hand in glove with the minimum of external distractions if it is to bear good fruit. That does not mean one cannot lead a spiritual life in the world but it is harder and results will take longer though I should add that, as always, everything depends on the individual and his or her karma. That notwithstanding, in general terms, the point stands. Serious spiritual practice demands one's full attention.

I have mentioned the higher Masters before. That is not my description of them. It is what the other Masters called them. Although all life is one and no-one can enter the spiritual kingdom who has not fully realised this, there is a hierarchical structure to that kingdom. Since we know that hierarchy asserts itself everywhere, even where it is denied, that should not surprise us. It is a fact in nature and that is a reflection of the reality in the spiritual world. Evidently spiritual hierarchy is not about the higher oppressing the lower or the lower serving the higher in any way. In fact, it might even be said to be the precise opposite, as demonstrated in the life of Jesus. The higher loves the lower, seeing no innate difference between that and itself. Nor is there one. The difference is merely one of greater unfoldment of divine consciousness. At the same time, where true values obtain, we always find that the lower has the utmost love and reverence for the higher, and why would it not since it recognises the greater development and aspires thereto? Where there is no ego there is no risk of a hierarchy degenerating and it will work in the way it should which is to the benefit of all units belonging to it.

The higher Masters came rarely but when they did they left a very powerful impression. I felt like a small sapling in the presence of a mighty oak, and any egotistic pretensions I may have harboured were completely dispelled, for the time being at least.

October 9th 1979

First of all one of the higher Masters spoke to me. He said that I must conquer arrogance and laziness. These were my besetting sins and the reason for my coming back to Earth was to overcome them. He told me that one day the Masters would speak to Michael and me together, not separately as at present, and all secrets would be revealed. He stressed that I should not allow myself to become irritated or annoyed at things but always be mature and tolerant. I should not let myself be disturbed by anything that happened outwardly. What took place outwardly was not my responsibility but what happened within was. No matter how wrong I thought something was, no matter how contrary to the good and the true I considered it, I should not react to it inwardly. Perfect love at all times was the way of the Masters and I should follow that way too. He then said that my love for Michael had exceeded their expectations and I should keep it up. When he left he sounded the OM and it was so long and deep and strong that it ceased to sound like a voice at all but became like rocks crashing down a mountainside. It was extraordinary.

Then my usual Master came and spoke to me. I asked him about false prophets and he said that there were many teaching half-truths at present. They were not all evil but they were not very evolved. Some were doing work at their level. I should remember that men were by no means equal on the Earth plane but at the same time not let that be a cause for dismissing anybody. He then warned me that evil entities would seek to influence my thoughts and might even try to occupy my body but they could be banished by love. I asked him what these evil entities were and he said that they were erring souls but would say no more than that. He told me not to have fear of evil or dwell on it but to be aware than it existed. "It has no power over you unless you give it power" he said.

We talked about the conditioning caused by my earlier life and he made the point that human beings are all narrow-minded in one way or another. Even those who are convinced they are not. He said that conventions and traditions had their place in the world, some good, some not so good but still valid at some level and, whilst most of them would be outgrown in time, they should be understood before they were rejected.

He then told me that the drugs I had taken in the past had done me some harm but that slowly and surely the damage was being repaired. Drugs had made my brain sluggish and lazy which made me inarticulate and that in turn caused me frustration. This would be corrected by concentration and meditation and also by speaking more often and attempting to communicate my thoughts to others. Drugs had made me retreat into myself, which was a tendency I had anyway, and they had conditioned me to a certain way of thinking. I needed to come out of myself and to understand that by helping others I would help myself. He told me not to be alarmed by what he said, as the problem would be rectified but that I should be aware of it and work at overcoming it. He then told me to be humble, hardworking, positive and active. "Be self-assured, stay mentally alert and be thoughtful of others" he said. "Avoid idle dreaminess!" Finally he stressed the importance of tolerance of the faults of other people and pointed to Michael as an example of someone who was naturally tolerant because he loved.

Earlier I had asked the other Master if I could speak to Michael about his faults. He said that this was intended but I should do it with love, forbearance and humility. I was young and youth always wanted to rush ahead but I must learn patience. He told me that Michael was the person it was ordained I should spend much of this lifetime with. This had been agreed before I was born in the world. Finally he said I could trust my intuition but should be careful not to confuse it with wishful or conditioned thinking. When I asked how I could be sure which was which he said "You will know" adding that if personal desire or attachment were involved then that would indicate the latter.

Once again my notes of these talks are slightly rushed, not properly reflecting their tone and rather dashing on from one subject to the next. On this occasion there was a lot to get down after the Masters had left and in my haste not to forget anything of importance I had to leave out some of the less relevant material. I often found that if I had forgotten something when I first wrote my notes down it would come back to me the next day or during a meditation and then I would add it. These insertions sometimes cause the notes to read a little clumsily.

I was never a heavy consumer of drugs but between the ages of 16 to 21 I took LSD a few times and smoked marijuana quite regularly. In retrospect it seems foolish but part of the reason for this was down to the times (the early to mid seventies) and part of it was a direct result of my then perception of the world as a spiritual wasteland. If there had been any proper guidance available to me to explain why I felt such an emptiness, what its cause and the remedy for it were, I might not have wasted time with drugs but there was none so, like many others, I did. At least my experience with psychedelics opened my eyes to something beyond the banalities of mundane existence but any slight benefits were outweighed by the adverse effects as described by the Master so let me say something here to anyone tempted to utilise drugs as a means of exploring or expanding consciousness. Don't. Anything you might learn through drugs you can learn far better through spiritual practice and they, the drugs, will inevitably exact a price. I was fortunate in that the Masters helped in repairing the damage done to the brain (and they were quite specific that it had damaged the brain) but why run the risk, especially as drugs will show you as much illusion as reality? There are advocates for psychedelic drugs who claim that these can be spiritually beneficial under certain controlled circumstances. Do not be deceived by their apparent plausibility. These people may be sincere but they are mistaken and have no backing from the spiritual hierarchy that guides humanity's progress.

Above all else the Masters were practical. Indeed, practical mysticism is not a bad definition of what they taught. When they told me to **be hardworking, positive and active** and followed that with instructions to **be self-assured, stay mentally alert and thoughtful of others** it rather sounds as if they were just reeling off a shopping list of virtues, most of which have no specific relevance to the spiritual path (though, of course, in a broader sense, they do) but at this juncture they needed to bring me out of myself and make me more outgoing. You take the pupil where you find him and bring balance where it is lacking. Because I leaned too far on the side of introversion, even passivity, they had to emphasise the other side of the coin in a way they would not need to have done if I had been more balanced to begin with, and would not necessarily have done with someone else. Having said that, I believe (and it's the reason I mention this) that many people attracted to spirituality might share some of my dreamy characteristics and need similar advice if they are to progress from vague intuitions to real attainment. Receptivity to the inner worlds is fine but it needs to be earthed and shared. Hard work is essential for anything to be accomplished, in the spiritual world as much as any other, and the true master is one who combines complete inner awareness with the ability to express that outwardly. This is the only way that fire from heaven can be brought down to Earth.

Avoid idle dreaminess! Alas, I was a bit of a dreamer, a tendency, as the Master said, exacerbated by drug taking, but with a conjunction of Mercury and Neptune in my natal chart (though luckily not in Pisces) what could you expect? My serious point here is that we all have the defects of our qualities. I was naturally intuitive with an innate attunement to the spiritual world but the downside to this was a proclivity for what the Masters called **idle dreaminess** and I had to get to grips with that. My astrological reference is made with a serious purpose too. If we can understand our psychology, as potentially revealed by the birth chart, we can cultivate its good points and, through becoming aware of them, address the negative aspects. "Know thyself" is the famous aphorism inscribed above the entrance to the Temple of Apollo at Delphi. An understanding of astrology can assist us in this essential task. It can be an excellent tool of self-knowledge, even helping us to heal those elements of our psychology that are wounded or damaged, which we all have as a result of either this or previous lifetimes' experiences. I am not saying that astrology is obligatory to do this but it can be a help. I knew nothing about it at this stage of my journey but the impersonal nature of a birth chart can be easier to learn from than, say, another human being because of its objectivity. It is what it is, a pure fact as reflected by the position of the planets at birth. It may be open to misinterpretation but essentially it is something undeniably real, and any interpretation must be within the confines of the astronomical data. Incidentally, if we wish to know where we are wounded, we have to look at what causes us fear and what we shy away from, and if we wish to heal ourselves of that wound then very often we must experience what it is we wish to avoid. Astrologically, it is a good idea to see what Saturn is up to.

Healing a damaged psychology is essential before any real spiritual work can begin. That is why self-knowledge is so important. Unfortunately the escapist nature of a certain sort of misconceived spirituality is very attractive to some people who wish to flee either the world or themselves, which is why we see so many people of that type in spiritual groups and organisations. But if you seek to use the spiritual path as an escape from reality you will fall further into illusion, an illusion from which one day you will have to awaken. That's unavoidable and if you don't do it of your own accord, life will make you. Healing your psychology is facing up to the truth of what you are, and if you practise meditation or some other spiritual technique without addressing this aspect of things then you are largely wasting your time. You may think you are progressing since certain experiences of a psychic nature may come to you. You may even find a degree of peace but that won't alter your fundamentally disordered inner state. At root you will remain a fragmented human being. No amount of meditation can bring order where there is inner disorder. You need to know yourself to heal yourself.

Odd as it may seem, one of the best ways to do this is to forget yourself. This is because if you truly do forget yourself, you transcend the wounded self so you transcend the wounds. If you no longer identify with them, they are gone. One of the reasons the Masters emphasised love and humility so much is that these heal the damaged psyche better than anything else, and they do so precisely because they bypass the ego which is the fundamental wound we all suffer from.

I hope I haven't made this sound more complicated than it is. We tend to obscure things with an intellectualising approach but the truth is very simple. We all carry wounds. You heal yourself first by knowing yourself and then by forgetting yourself.

I must comment on the expression used by the first Master that **all secrets would be revealed.** My method of writing here is to go through my old notes in date order, putting down what the Masters said on each occasion and then adding whatever comments I might be inspired to make now. When I came to this section, I briefly thought of leaving these words out but didn't because I had made the decision when I first started to write this book that I would include everything I noted down after the Masters' talks, adding nothing and taking nothing away. I wanted to make this as authentic a record as possible. Therefore, as he said it, so I include it.

One reason for my initial hesitation was that, on the page, it might look somewhat melodramatic, just the sort of thing a discarnate *poseur* would say to a gullible individual to give himself importance. I can assure the reader that it did not sound like that at all when it was actually said. This Master had a solemn dignity about him that completely silenced any doubts as to his status, and these words when he spoke them conveyed the impression that they were coming from one who did indeed know **all secrets**. The mysteries of the universe were as an open book to him. A higher Master is conscious at loftier levels than even a Master, levels of which we cannot comprehend. He is approaching god-like status and can speak in a god-like way, giving the words he utters their fullest meaning.

The second reason is that all secrets have not been revealed to me. That is a pleasure I still await. Of course, what the Master probably meant was no more than St Paul when he wrote that "Here we see through a glass darkly but there we shall see face to face". In time all secrets will be revealed to us all. As sons and daughters of the Most High, that is our birthright. But there is another way of looking at this. Secrets are only secret because we are not able to understand them. Everything there is to know is there in front of us all the time. There is nothing hidden except insofar as we are unable to see it and, just as a child cannot comprehend many things in this world until he has developed his mental apparatus sufficiently, so there are many things of a spiritual nature that we cannot comprehend until we have developed the necessary faculties to the appropriate degree. Secrets are revealed when we are developed enough to receive them.

When this Master departed he sounded the sacred syllable OM. I have mentioned previously that this was the usual manner in which the Masters announced their arrival and normally they departed in the same way. Michael on his own could not sound the OM any better than the average person but the Masters, through him, attained a volume, power and prolongation that just would not have been possible for a normally constituted human being. I have heard people chant and I have heard recordings of Tibetan monks. I have never heard anything that approaches the Masters' proficiency in this field. This particular Master surpassed even that. Far deeper than Michael could manage, it was loud without being noisy and resonant without booming. It remained on a single note which swelled and expanded and filled the room. It brought to mind the origin of all things and left in its wake a sense of absolute peace. It was one of the few overt signs the Masters gave of their superhuman powers.

When the next Master came he asked me if I had any questions. As somewhat of a perfectionist I had long been troubled by the many, to my way of thinking, desecrations that spiritual teachings were subjected to in the modern world. I was aware of the prediction of Christ that "there would arise false prophets", and while I imagined there always had been such, it did seem they were more prominent than ever at that time. The situation has scarcely improved since but then there were several gurus in the public eye who were, shall we say, of doubtful pedigree.

Nowadays the phenomenon of the abusive guru is well known and the conventional view is that this is someone with a strong, possibly charismatic, but disordered personality who preys on his devotees in ways sexual, financial or whatever else they may be. He might be a power crazy individual or he might simply find that this is the best way to get what he wants. This is one form, a rather obvious one, of false prophet. He deludes but he is not necessarily self-deluded other than in thinking he will always get away with this behaviour.

Human beings seek power or rather the human ego seeks power. It also demands validation. To be perceived as a purveyor of wisdom is one of the highest forms of validation. For some it is an irresistible temptation. It may even be a temptation that we all experience at one time or another. There is a stage on the path after one has gleaned a certain amount of knowledge and experience of the spiritual world when one can legitimately become a teacher. It is not necessary to be enlightened to be a spiritual teacher. If it were, there would not be many of them. How you then present yourself is the question. If, because of your greater knowledge, you fall victim to a swollen ego you may project a false persona and assume a higher status than you merit. You may believe in this persona or you may simply want to believe in it. The end result is much the same.

The Master said that there **were many teaching half-truths at present.** On another occasion I was informed that this is something that has always existed to an extent but has become much more widespread since formerly esoteric teachings were made public around the end of the 19th century. When the sacred is revealed it is often profaned and, although this is regrettable, it was thought more important to release the teachings since there were many who could benefit from them.

There are many teaching half-truths at present. The Master may have said this thirty years ago but the situation is the same, if not worse, today. These are those who have begun to understand spiritual truths and mistakenly present that understanding as complete. They may have a developed intellectual comprehension but are not yet able to embody in themselves what they know conceptually. Consequently there is a gap between what they know and what they are. Alternatively there are some who may have had certain experiences which lead them to mistake partial for full initiation. The majority of these teachers probably have excellent intentions but they have not yet fully negotiated the pitfalls of *samsara*.

Curiously he went on to say that **they were not all evil but they were not very evolved** thereby implying that some were evil. I had not been thinking of that when I asked the question. Evil is a strong word and not one I would normally use about anybody. However all religions teach that there are powers of darkness who seek to subvert and derail the spiritual progress of humanity and one of the ways they effectively do this is by corrupting spiritual teachings. Of course, they have many strings to their bows and through the fomenting of war, materialism, atheism, the vulgarising of culture, the over-stimulation, through advertising and marketing, of desire in all its forms and so forth, they mount a multi-pronged attack. But to distort spiritual teaching would naturally be high on their agenda. Certain esoteric traditions speak of fallen angels, evolved beings who have fallen because of their defiance of God. One can speculate that it is beings answering to this description who are the source of the evil spoken of by the Masters, though presumably these would not be the **erring souls** alluded to, who would more likely be human souls who have succumbed to the machinations of the fallen angels. Needless to say, these are **erring souls** too as they are pursuing a path of pure illusion but it is quite conceivable that they are highly evolved along certain lines.

I don't think it's wise to speculate on which individuals fall into which category. I certainly don't think it's helpful to attempt to brand anyone as 'evil'. In fact that would just be playing the game of the fallen powers who thrive on division, dissension and antipathy. Infighting between rival spiritual camps has a long and shameful history and it's not a good idea to contribute to that even if one has good intentions. We all know what they say about those. It is much better just to seek to be aware of spiritual truths and concentrate on demonstrating those without setting oneself up against anyone else. Sometimes that might be necessary in order to expose falsehood (witness Jesus and the Pharisees) but, generally speaking, one should leave the misguided to God and the Masters who you will help best by eradicating evil within your own heart.

Don't let this talk of false prophets deter you from seeking a teacher if that is your desire. Yes, false prophets exist and it's as well to recognise the fact but there's fake money around too. That doesn't mean there is no genuine coin. You simply have to examine the article carefully before you accept it.

It is slightly disconcerting to be told **that evil entities might try to occupy my body.** I was never aware of this as regards myself but

I did see it happen to Michael, as for example during our holiday in India. There were other times when it occurred including once after meditation when something really unpleasant got into him and actually attacked me physically. The reader brought up in the modern age might wish to look for alternative explanations for this. Superstition exists and I am not saying that everything described as possession always is so but there is no doubt that these things can happen, particularly if an individual is of a mediumistic nature as Michael quite evidently was. Full possession might be rare but a partial overshadowing, of which the victim might be quite unaware, is much more common and is all the more reason for us to learn to control our emotions. Giving way to negative emotions opens the doors to such beings who conversely, as the Master said, will be **banished by love**. As a matter of fact, the Masters once told me that the best way to get rid of these dark shadows if I felt their presence attempting to influence my mind negatively towards Michael was to give him a hug! Being of a fairly typical English temperament I did not attempt this too often but when I did it seemed to work. As I have mentioned that Michael was homosexual it might be suggested that he somehow manipulated this instruction, on an unconscious level at least, but that would be quite unfair. His cultural upbringing was even more traditionally English than mine and he was quite taken aback the first time I did hug him.

I like the point that compared to enlightened beings we are all narrow-minded. That doesn't mean we should be more broad-minded. At least not in the way we would normally understand that term. It means that we are all bound by our conditioning and even broad-mindedness and tolerance can be forms of conditioning. Which, of course, does not mean that we should not be tolerant. We need to rise above any sort of 'mindedness' at all, above any precon-ception, prejudice or opinion (whether a narrow-minded or a broad-minded one) and learn to see things as they are without the inter-ference of emotion or thought. We are all conditioned by our upbringing even if we react against it. We are all conditioned by our temperamental predispositions. These might cause us to accept conventions and traditions or they might incline us to reject them as outmoded and belonging to the past. Either way whatever we do we should do it with full understanding and not out of prejudice or reaction. It is not easy to escape one's conditioning and the effort to do so can often just lead to a new form of conditioning. The way taught by the Masters is that of self-awareness coupled with surrender to a higher power.

Some Buddhist teachers advocate what is called choiceless awareness to escape conditioned thought in which one observes without judgement. This can be effective but, as almost anything can be perverted, there is also a possibility that it can descend into a mental exercise. Without love and surrender no spiritual practice is complete. Without **remembering the Creator** (which does not necessarily mean fixing one's thoughts on a personal God but does mean humbling oneself before the creative source of the universe), practices such as choiceless awareness can potentially become mere intellectual navel gazing which may bring a degree of stillness to the mind but will not lead to a truly spiritual awakening. I am not decrying choiceless awareness as a spiritual practice but I am saying that on its own it is not enough and risks being no more than a psychological tool. As the Buddha himself might have said, it must be right choiceless awareness.

Conditioned thinking is something we all need to escape from and not just seek to replace one form of it with another even if that be a 'higher' form. In order to do this we need to develop the intuition and that we do by learning to be properly receptive. Important as it is I haven't written much about meditation here because there are so many books on the subject and it's not something you can learn from books anyway. To be sure, you can pick up various techniques that may or may not be helpful but the essence of meditation is extraordinarily simple. It is being receptive. It is opening oneself up to silence and seeing what can be learnt from that. The basis of meditation is that there is a level of being above thought that transcends our normal time bound existence. This is the level of the intuition. Conventional mystical teaching says that we can access this by emptying the mind and this is good theory but in practice for the modern Westerner with an overactive mind, it can be problematic. We are trained to activity and achievement. We are taught to believe that if we want something we can go out and get it. All we need do is make the necessary effort. Meditation doesn't work like that, not proper meditation anyway. The perils of seeking to empty the mind by means of the mind are well known nowadays chiefly, I believe, through the efforts of Krishnamurti, whose influence is far wider than just among those who follow his teachings. There can be few spiritual teachers of the last fifty or more years outside conventional orthodoxy who have not been influenced by and (often without acknowledging their source) borrowed from him.

So, for the student whose education, cultural background and environment make emptying the mind difficult, either because arresting the processes of thought is just too hard in this modern world or else because he cannot get round *trying* to empty the mind, i.e. using the mind to empty itself, an obviously futile task, I would suggest a form of meditation that the Masters suggested to me. Forget the head and focus on the heart. Meditation on the heart centre helps us to bypass the thought making activity of the mind altogether. It is especially beneficial for those who are, as many are these days, rather too intellectually polarised. Somewhat helplessly I asked the Masters how best to focus on the heart centre and was told that it didn't really matter how one did it although visualising it as a flower or star would be effective as these were objects in nature that reflected higher realities. Still, the important thing was to attune oneself to the heart and not become preoccupied with a method. After having flirted with a star and the sun (I know they're the same but we don't see them as the same) I eventually chose a pink rose gradually opening as the form in which I could most easily visualise the heart centre. The rose is the Western version of the lotus and has a long and distinguished history as a symbol of spiritual perfection. As it opens from bud to bloom it represents the unfolding soul. Pink is the colour of selfless love, something I knew I lacked, so it made sense to try to build that colour into myself through its visualisation.

The Master's description of flowers and stars as objects in nature that reflect higher realities is a good definition of a symbol. A symbol is the manifestation in form of an archetypal truth and it serves as a vehicle through which one can access that truth though only to the degree to which one's imagination is open. At the same time, meditation on a symbol can help to develop the imagination because it is a physical object, or representation thereof, that acts as a channel to the world of meaning. A true symbol will have many levels of meaning, some of which will be apparent to anyone while others will only be perceptible to those whose intuition is sufficiently awake. These are not always definable or expressible in words but a symbol's meaning can never be exhausted by a verbal description anyway. That is its beauty and its power. You can analyse a symbol but, although that might be of academic interest, it is not the way to extract the real benefits it has to offer. The precise value of a symbol is that meditation on it can take you beyond the analytical mind to the plane of pure ideas. It is using form to go beyond form, perfectly demonstrating the truth of the Hermetic axiom "As above, so below", an axiom so simple yet so profound and the key to so much if pondered aright that it is almost a verbal symbol in itself, if such a thing can exist. My use of a rose as a means to visualise the heart centre not only helped me focus on the heart, it also served to reveal to me what, spiritually understood, the heart actually is in a way that, say, a daffodil would not have done though that may have been just as effective an aid to concentration.

The heart centre is not the physical heart. It is more centrally situated than that but there is no need to be overly concerned about its corresponding position in the body. Its location is where you feel it to be. It is one of the chakras described in Hinduism and now a minor obsession with materialistic New Agers (materialistic because to focus on chakras is to focus on effects rather than causes), and it is the only one that the Masters taught that the spiritual aspirant should consciously focus on. Michael once asked them whether he should do anything to try to arouse my kundalini. This is the spiritual fire that lies sleeping, coiled like a serpent at the base of the spine, but rising, when aroused, through the psychic centres to the top of the head at the time of enlightenment. He was told quite categorically that that is something that should be left to take place when it does so of its own accord as a result of correct spiritual practice. On no account should it be forced or even encouraged.

The Masters do not advocate concentration on the chakras. They advocate purification of the centres, if one uses that terminology, but not the attempt to arouse the latent energy within and push that through them before they are sufficiently purified. Purification of the chakras means rising above desire, attachment and the ego, and if one attempts to stimulate kundalini before this is sufficiently advanced, one is courting trouble. The energy of kundalini (which is roughly analogous to the Christian concept of the Holy Spirit that descended on the disciples at Pentecost) inflates what it comes into contact with, and, if it passes through chakras in which there is not perfect purity, it will augment any faults to be found therein, stimulating unbalanced emotions and egotistic thoughts, in the worst case scenario to the point of mental breakdown. It is true that it may at the same time bring about experiences the subject regards as spiritual but, if he or she is not perfectly balanced and non-attached, these will not result in spiritual growth but instead lead to a reaction with corresponding lows following the highs. The attempt to arouse kundalini is basically motivated by spiritual greed, the desire for experience, which can in no wise lead to spiritual growth. Fortunately most people who do attempt to do this lack the ability to take it very far but sometimes a premature and partial awakening of kundalini does take place spontaneously. This should not be mistaken for enlightenment though very often is by the inexperienced and over-ambitious who might see spirituality principally in terms of its outer effects. But those whose concept of spirituality is limited to what they hope to get out of it have a lot to learn.

If we would get to grips with meditation we must acquire the art of inner listening. The Masters constantly told me to listen to my intuition. However they were well aware that people tend to attribute to intuition all sorts of impressions based on and arising from **personal desire or attachment** which is why I was told that I **should be careful not to confuse it with wishful or conditioned thinking.** The reply to my question as to how to tell the difference was interesting. **"You will know"** the Master said, implying that, if we are true to ourselves, we will know the truth. After all the truth is in us as our real nature and all that prevents its full flowering are the prejudices, desires and attachments of the self.

Chapter 25

An Initial Look at the Spiritual Field

In the antiques market in which Michael and I had our shop selling pottery and porcelain most people knew that we were interested in spiritual matters. We never mentioned the Masters to anyone but people were aware that we were vegetarians and that we meditated and believed in such curiosities as reincarnation and higher planes of existence. Some of that is fairly mainstream now and was becoming so even in 1979, but then it did put you a little outside the norm not only to believe in a spiritual world but actually to live your life as though you did as well. For Michael the growing acceptance of ideas of which he had been a partisan for decades was something of a two-edged sword. He was glad to see the increased openness to these ideas but regretted the "hippiefication" of them which he felt presented them in a somewhat disadvantaged light. One could argue for a long while about whether the trivialisation of esoteric ideas is justified by the fact that they are more readily available to enquirers. I don't know what the answer is to that. Possibly it depends on the extent to which that trivialisation is taken.

Because we were in a public place and it became known that we were followers of the spiritual path, a range of people would drop by our stall to talk, some interesting, some odd, some lost and some quite normal. I remember one individual, of a fundamentalist Christian persuasion, who came to save us and got quite worked up when we declined his offer. Another visitor was a Catholic priest who accused us of being misguided and even arrogant for choosing to follow our own path rather than submit to a religion that had been good enough for millions of others. I had some sympathy with him because following your own path can be misguided and arrogant but couldn't forbear pointing out that Jesus had followed his own path as had the Buddha, at which I was accused of trying to put myself on the same level as those two. I demurred and said I was only following their example as they themselves had recommended one should do but it was no good. When someone has committed themselves to a belief system they don't want to hear that it is only a belief system. The priest, who had come because he had heard that Michael was an ex-monk, shook his head at our foolhardiness at thinking we knew better, as he put it, and told us that you cannot have spirituality without religion. I responded that for me spirituality without religion did not mean taking the bits that I liked or found personally agreeable and throwing out the rest. If it did then I quite agreed with him but I did not see how being bound to anything could set one free.

In saying that I am not for a moment disputing that adherence to an orthodox religion is very beneficial for countless numbers of people. Religion provides guidelines, structure and direction that "spirituality without religion" frequently lacks particularly when that is the vague sort of belief or practice adopted as a kind of lifestyle choice that makes minimal demands and which is more concerned with benefits it hopes to receive than the pursuit of saintliness. Ultimately, though, I do believe that organised religions are restricting, especially at this late stage in their cycles when they all have either been outgrown in the forms in which they originated or else been so damaged by unenlightened tampering that they have lost their transformative power. Perhaps this is the essential point. There is no religion that has not succumbed to the natural and inevitable effects of decay and decline. That is not to say that there is not an enormous amount to be learnt from religions, from their scriptures, their practices, their art and symbolism and the lives of their founders and saints. I would never reject any of that as an invaluable repository of spiritual knowledge, moral guidance and wisdom. But I would not nowadays choose to identify myself with any of it either.

A regular visitor to our stall was a young man called Tim. He had

had some problems at home and was currently living with his uncle where he helped look after the uncle's young family. He had no job other than that so had a lot of free time which he spent in wandering around town and reading books on occultism, as a consequence of which he had far too much ungrounded theory buzzing around inside his head which did not help his already rather unbalanced state. Recognising in Michael someone who knew something about the subjects that interested him he used to come along and talk. Michael saw that Tim was directionless and confused and tried to help him by *not* discussing spiritual subjects but that's all Tim wanted to talk about. Mostly he wanted to air his theories. As we were of a similar age, Michael thought it would be a good idea if I befriended Tim and we would take walks together but it soon because clear that he was one of those people who don't really see others as existing except in relation to themselves. There was nothing mean or nasty about him, in fact he was rather sweet-natured, but he was utterly self-preoccupied. The habit in the antique market was that if you were talking to a stall holder and a potential customer appeared you would discreetly withdraw to enable business to be transacted. Tim was totally oblivious to this. He could be chatting to Michael and someone would ask about the price of a plate or some such item but Tim would sail on regardless, occasionally even causing the customer to give up and walk off. This did not endear him to Michael. Still, he saw that Tim was in need of help and wanted to do what he could.

Tim's favourite writers were Jung and Gurdjieff and he tried to convince me of their virtues but I did not feel much sympathy with the work of either of them. In neither case did I detect a truly spiritual tone even though the subjects they concerned themselves with were, broadly speaking, spiritual. At the time I had read a certain amount about both men but what I had learned did not make me want to explore further and so I had not read anything actually written by either of them. I still have not read any Gurdjieff and only a couple of books by Jung so feel free to discount what I have to say on the grounds of ignorance, but I believe I am familiar enough with their life and work to stick to my original impression. They were both highly important figures in 20th century thought, no doubt about that, and they both had a great deal of knowledge as well as, in Gurdjieff's case, power. They attracted intellectuals and artists. But did they speak from the level of the soul? I don't believe they did. For me what Jung basically did was to reduce the spiritual to the psychological thereby bringing God down to Man, which is the reverse of what should take place. I don't deny his many insights but he appeared to view the goal of life as self-actualisation rather than self transcendence. In practice if not in theory. And his preoccupation with the subconscious shows an insufficient appreciation of the fact that human beings are spiritual beings descended not material ones ascending. In a sense he was the perfect prophet for modern secular humanity because he demoted the spiritual powers to psychological principles so, although he is regarded as having reintroduced certain esoteric ideas to a materialistic world, the way he did so presented them in too much of a misconceived fashion for them to be of genuine spiritual use. Jung speaks from and about the psychic and mental levels and so his teachings do not take one beyond the multiplicity and confusion of the phenomenal world to the perfect clarity of the divine realm.

As for Gurdjieff, he clearly had abundant occult knowledge and was a powerful magician of sorts but that does not mean he was a spiritual person. His supporters might not regard that as important, seeing him as somebody who was awakened, but the best you can say of the level of his awakening is that it was a magical rather than a mystical one, by which I mean he had not transcended the ego or even, it would appear, begun to. I know he utilised many techniques (though tricks might be a better word) to expose the egos of his disciples and some of these had some basis in traditional esoteric practice, of which he had an extensive though, I would say, garbled knowledge, but the confused context in which they were used rendered them ineffectual. There are some actions and practices of a true Master which may be valuable when coming from him but, if employed by an individual of a less illumined state, in whom the ego is not yet dead and who is not motivated entirely by love, can have precisely the opposite effect to that intended. The temptations of flouting convention and seeing oneself as "beyond good and evil" are strong but only he who has truly transcended identification with self is beyond the pairs of opposites. That, by the way, does not mean seeing good and evil as being of equal significance or insignificance in the relative world. It does mean taking one's stand in the formless absolute and seeing what is relative as relative, but that does not imply regarding all that takes place in the world of duality as being equally in tune with reality and divine law. Far from it.

Gurdjieff was undoubtedly a man of extraordinary will and mesmerising character, and some of Jung's insights into the worlds of mythology and dreams were profound but both of them were on the outside looking in. Gurdjieff drew power from somewhere but it was not from the same source that the Masters draw theirs. Jung uncovered a path that potentially leads beyond this world but that path does not reach up to heaven. Neither of them knew enough about love.

Tim's uncle was a follower of a spiritual practice called Subud which was quite popular at the time largely, I believe, because a lot of ex-Gurdjieff disciples were interested in it. It had the usual charismatic leader though, unusually, he came from Indonesia. The main focus of this religion, if that's what it was, it was never quite clear, was something called the latihan, and Tim's uncle was keen to persuade Michael and me to try it. I may be doing it an injustice but his description of it as a kind of letting go of all inhibitions in which you might cry, shout, jump, dance or make strange involuntary sounds and movements did not appeal to me in the slightest. This was not because I was too buttoned up or emotionally repressed. I did not feel myself to have any particular inhibitions or suppressed memories or whatever it was everyone was supposed to have, and, even if I had done so, I would not have thought that this was the way to overcome them. The road to spiritual enlightenment is not taken by behaving in a way totally at variance with it. But Tim's uncle was very pressing. Like many converts he wanted to spread his new faith and Michael, more out of a desire to please than anything else, said he would give it a try. I was more resistant. For me the holy life was found through silence and stillness on the one hand and service and prayer on the other. The soul could be contacted by rising above emotional reactions not by giving way to them, and I did not believe the theory that freedom from psychological problems could be gained by unbridled expression of them. With the arrogance of youth I even told Tim's uncle, some 25 years my senior, that his chosen path, far from leading to any spiritual opening, was more likely to cause psychic imbalance. He forgave me my lack of understanding and gave me the beatific smile of one who knows. The latihan was surrendering to God, he said. To me it sounded more like rendering oneself open to any passing psychic influence which could as easily be negative as positive. Letting go is not the same as letting oneself go.

One session was enough for Michael. He felt that he had witnessed men and women behaving in ways that did no credit to their dignity as human beings. He had been told to open himself up to whatever came but, being a sensible fellow, realised that just as you wouldn't necessarily leave your front door open for all and sundry to walk in, it might be prudent to retain a degree of control over what took place within your psyche. Obviously not all his fellow practitioners were quite so wise. Some had run about yelling, others had howled and danced as though possessed while yet others had wept uncontrollably. In his view what took place was a confusion of the non-physical with the spiritual, a common mistake that is the result of failing to discriminate between the psychic (imagination, feelings, subconscious) and the truly transcendent, that itself being the result of ignorance of the various planes of existence and the inner anatomy of a human being.

For millennia human beings, unwilling to submit themselves to the proper discipline of the spiritual path, have sought other avenues in an attempt to access higher states of consciousness. Drugs are an obvious example but there are numerous techniques and exercises which can, to an extent, rend the barrier between our normal everyday consciousness and states in which the mind is temporarily liberated from the constraints of the material condition. But the barriers in place exist for a reason. If you try to take what you have not earned, you will have to pay a price and if a vessel is inadequately prepared for a sudden influx of higher energy it can break. Moreover there is an infernal domain as well as a supernal one and if you remove the natural barriers between this world and the next you can't always guarantee which one comes through. Tim's uncle reported feelings of great exhilaration after the latihan assuming that these indicated some kind of spiritual opening but, setting aside the question as to whether the spiritual path is about the search for peak experiences and self-gratification or about purification and self-forgetfulness, the fact remains that the emotional agitation the latihan can encourage, like that of some fundamentalist church services and, for that matter, rock concerts, might lead to a sudden high but in no way touches on the calm serenity of true spiritual perception.

Curiously enough, just after this incident I bought a book of letters written by Wellesley Tudor Pole, possibly the foremost English sage of the last century, responsible amongst other things for Chalice Well at Glastonbury, to the author Rosamond Lehmann in which he says about Subud that "The method as practised over here is dangerous, unenlightened and full of pitfalls"[16]. I appreciated the Masters sending me this confirmation of my feelings. As any seeker knows, the powers that be often manifest their presence through apparent coincidence. I had actually asked them about Subud when the matter as to whether we should look into it or not came up. I knew what I felt but I suppose, lacking confidence, wanted their sanction for my view. They declined to give it, other than to say, as usual, that I should follow my intuition. They were not interested in telling me what to do and I should have known better than to ask them. At the same time I had asked them whether I should try to dissuade Michael from attending a latihan and they did tell me that they were not in favour of it, as they wished us to tread the same path but that I should not be concerned as he would learn from the experience. And so it turned out.

I am not suggesting that any long term damage is necessarily done to people who have engaged in practices such as the latihan but I don't think there are many spiritual benefits either, and, as Tudor Pole's words make clear, the potential for damage exists. The 1960s and '70s were a time of spiritual ferment and many people were seeking a deeper awareness of life than they thought could be found in orthodox religion. Many groups and cults sprang up to cater to this thirst. A lot, possibly the majority, were of dubious value and sometimes people would have been better served by exploring the religions of their birth more thoroughly, but it is a stage on the path to seek the way through false routes thereby honing one's powers of discrimination and, by finding out what is wrong, learning what is right. We lost contact with Tim's uncle not very long after this but he was a genuine enquirer after truth and I don't doubt that sooner or later he would have moved on from this, in my view, illusionary stage of his spiritual journey.

As for Tim, Michael continued to try to get him to find some focus and direction in his life but he was a classic example of the spiritual dreamer and seemed unable to apply himself diligently to anything for long. I recognised the potential for that in myself and often thought that there, but for the grace of the Masters and Michael, went I. But in fairness to myself I would never have drifted quite so aimlessly as poor old Tim, who would get sudden enthusiasms for new philosophies and paths and then completely lose interest in them after a while when it became clear that they were not going to bring him instant enlightenment. He eventually went back to live with his father and, as we left Bath shortly afterwards, we lost touch with him too.

A colleague in the market was a devotee of Guru Maharaj Ji, the chubby adolescent who for some strange reason was taken up by a lot of people around this time. Anthony was an ardent enthusiast when we first met and, just like Tim's uncle, wanted to convert us to his cause when he found out that we were interested in spirituality. He claimed that his youthful guru could offer a direct experience of God and we should try him out. Again my instincts said no but I was interested in seeing how these new spiritual movements, which to me were more parodies of spirituality than the real thing, worked so I went along to a meeting as a detached observer. The guru himself was not there but his lieutenants were and they gave a presentation. You might almost say it was a pitch for their business. Outwardly it pressed all the right buttons, love, peace, bliss and so on but behind the façade I felt a coldness that made a mockery of these words. Having the Masters as a spiritual touchstone, not to mention the timeless examples of Jesus, Buddha and the host of other genuine enlightened saints and sages of the past and present, showed this group up in its true light, and I would advise anyone in a similar position to me at this talk to go beyond the words spoken and sense the vibration behind them because the quality a teacher transmits is as important as what he says. Anthony himself eventually became disillusioned with the group, citing jostling for power amongst supposedly god-realised people as a prime eye opener, though the worldly lifestyle of the increasingly wealthy guru must have helped too. It is hard to leave a movement in which one has invested a great deal of oneself but he was philosophical about it treating it as part of the learning curve, which I thought showed a lot of sense on his part. Don't regret the past, just learn from it and get on with your life was his attitude, which is very easy to say but I was tremendously impressed at how completely he put that into practice.

As I understood it from devotees of this guru, his main claim to fame was his apparently ability to bestow an "experience of God" to his followers. Now I know very little of his background other than that his father was a guru of sorts and he was raised to follow in that tradition, but I do know that techniques exist in India which can induce in some impressionable sensibilities a temporary opening of certain of the psychic centres. To call this an experience of God, however, is stretching things a bit. Exceptional as it may seem to one unversed in the ways of the inner worlds, it is not a revelation of the divine. Once again we must distinguish between the psychic and the spiritual.

Why do I mention these things here, especially after comments I have made earlier? I have no interest in denigrating anybody but we live in a time of spiritual confusion, very possibly the time described by Jesus as one when there would arise false Christs and false prophets who would show great signs and wonders, and I have met many seekers deeply troubled by teachers claiming to offer the truth and seemingly giving teachings that do just that but in whom there is a discrepancy between what they say and what they are. In the modern world there is little spiritual education so when we are exposed to apparently profound teachings of liberation and enlightenment our lack of experience, even in those wise in the ways of the world, can cause us to go astray. All that glitters is not gold, in the spiritual world as elsewhere.

And yet, having said that, I would add that there is a sense in which you *can* judge a spiritual book by its cover. You have to know how to look though. As you begin to develop the single eye of insight, you start to see that we do all in some way manifest our inner spiritual state. Great souls have their realisation written in their faces. Others may appear charismatic or powerful but when you look into them you cannot see past them. A truly enlightened person is transparent. You can see through him.

Of course, there is a wide range of teachers between the fully liberated and the spiritual pretender and I am not saying that if you do not see total absence of ego in someone that person cannot be a genuine spiritual teacher. There must be a definite leaning in that direction though. It is also well to remember there is nothing perfect in this world and even in the greatest some shadow of the past will always remain whilst they are still in a body. As always, and the reader must be weary of me repeating this time after time but it is important, we must use our intuition in these matters.

Chapter 26

"Be Like a Tree."

The Masters' visits continued though less frequently than before. I felt that they were always present in our periods of meditation but they did not speak through Michael as often as they had. This was as it should be. They were expending a great deal of energy and effort to communicate with me, and Michael was also making the sacrifice of offering himself for their use. He did not wish to speak much of the effect this had on him but I could see that emotionally it was upsetting, making him very sensitive and highly-strung. This was particularly the case immediately after a session with the Masters but the effects could linger for quite some time. And there was not just emotional disturbance involved in all this. The Masters told me that the procedure was not without risk from a physical point of view as well even if they and their helpers had the situation under control.

The other reason for the reduction in the number of the Masters' visits was that they had no desire to spoon-feed me for long. They had made the initial approach and given me more than enough to work on and it was now up to me to take an increasing degree of responsibility for my spiritual growth. Often they stressed the importance of maturity. By this they did not just mean that I should grow up quickly but that I should be completely serious and disciplined in my approach to the spiritual life. You cannot make real progress unless you give yourself to the task with wholeheartedness and that requires assuming full responsibility for yourself.

October 14th 1979
The Master told me that a person was only given as much knowledge and grace as he merited and was able to take without

315

being overwhelmed by. I was not yet mature enough to be given it all at once and should be patient. I was warned to stay on my mettle and not get swollen headed as a result of what was happening to me as that kind of reaction would immediately halt all progress. He then told me that Michael and I had to learn to develop in ourselves what each disliked in the other so I had to acquire Michael's capacity for hard work, his practicality and enthusiasm. He went on to say that my mental sluggishness and apathy were partly due to karma and partly the result of the life I had lead before I had come under the Masters' direct control. Through hard work and concentration they would disappear. Then he gave his love and blessings as usual and reminded me that these were not simply words but that, if I received them correctly, they would act as the Masters' grace.

Grace. This is a concept completely at odds with the mainstream contemporary understanding of the world in which it has no place whatsoever. How could it when that approach to life recognises nothing beyond what can be detected by human senses or scientific instruments which are necessarily designed out of physical matter? However we have the Masters' word for it that grace exists. That and religious, especially Christian, tradition not to mention the experience, past and present, of thousands of aspiring souls. What is it though? Rather like the notion of blessing it has been reduced in significance, even amongst the religious, to a rather vague and insubstantial idea. But grace is a powerful spiritual gift, the reality of which has been attested to by many people. It is a descent from above of spiritual force that illuminates the recipient leaving him with a certitude that no amount of mental reasoning or argument could ever provide or, for that matter, erode. It is described as a gift because although we have to earn it we can never (*pace* the Master) really merit it so a gift is precisely what it is, a gift from a higher power. In truth we, as separate individuals, merit nothing but we can still remove some of the obstacles to grace which, like a form of divine sunshine, is always radiating out from the heart of God in a constant stream of light. Ultimately all grace does come from God but it can be channelled through a realised being who acts as a conduit through which spiritual power can be transferred. Think of the images of Christ or the Buddha with the right hand raised in blessing for perfect visual examples of this.

The Master spoke of being overwhelmed by too much grace thereby giving support to the notion that grace is in some sense equivalent to light, too much of which can dazzle or even blind the insufficiently prepared. He associated grace with knowledge but the knowledge he was referring to was not the intellectual sort which is gathered and stored by the brain. It was not the knowledge built up through time and experience. Nor was it something he was going to tell me. Rather it was the direct knowing of the mind beyond mind, the non-individual supra-rational overmind. You might call this insight if that word had not lost much of its meaning by being applied to a sort of intellectual perspicacity, and it is not that. Spiritual knowledge, that is, not knowledge of spiritual things but knowledge in a spiritual sense, is knowing with the whole of one's being. It is not knowledge based on conceptual thinking but on a state of awareness that comes from being one with reality. And just as too much light can dazzle so too much knowledge of this kind can destabilise the unready or immature mind. What is an immature mind? It is one that is identified with self.

I said that this kind of knowledge is not stored by the brain. By that I meant that it does not arise as a result of material processes as is the case with our normal modes of thought which are the fruits of memory and experience. It originates from outside the world of form, taking that to mean the phenomenal world perceived by the senses. It may be expressed through the physical brain but it does not come from it. It has become quite common nowadays to talk of the two hemispheres of the brain as though one, the left side, concerned with detail and linear reasoning, related to our ability to function in the world in a practical manner while the other, the right, which apparently perceives patterns as wholes rather than in terms of their constituent parts, was somehow a more "spiritual" form of perception. I don't believe this to be correct. I see these modes of cognition (the former functioning more in time, the latter in space) as complementary ones that you might loosely characterise as active and passive (as in receptive), and thus both belonging to the phenomenal world of dualities and both transcended by the direct, non-dualistic knowing of *buddhi*, a word I use here instead of intellectual insight to avoid ambiguity. *Buddhi* is the principle of spiritual knowing which transcends both left and right brain forms of perception rather as the point at the apex of a triangle does the two points at either end of the baseline.

So, while people more focussed in the right hemisphere of the brain, which synthesises rather than analyses information, do tend to be more creative or artistic than left brain types, that is not the same as saying that they are more spiritually aware.

On the subject of cranial hemispheres and the brain, the Masters once suggested that I try to meditate focussing on the back of the head. This was in response to a question I had asked about meditation which I had initially found relatively easy but which subsequently became more difficult for me. I know next to nothing about the brain and its structure and have not heard this mentioned anywhere else so pass it on simply as something the interested reader might care to investigate. I confess that when I did try to concentrate on the back of the head I found it quite unnatural to focus attention there at first (one's normal point of attention seems to be at the front), but after a while I noticed that ego consciousness was reduced on those few occasions when I managed to transfer attention to the back. But this was not a technique I practised for very long or can say very much about and I bring it up it here more as a curiosity than anything else.

It is going too far to say that I disliked Michael's capacity for hard work and practicality but at that time I did consider those qualities somewhat prosaic when compared to the more rarefied ones of imagination, intuition and sensitivity to the inner worlds. I realise that does not do me much credit but give some leeway to a young man who throughout his life had struggled to maintain contact with his inner vision in the face of outer disbelief, sometimes even ridicule. Excuses aside, I have to confess that I leaned towards being an impractical dreamer and two of the first things that the Masters wished me to acquire from my association with Michael were practicality and the willingness to work hard. In those days they regularly told me that I had come to Earth to learn the lessons of Earth and that required that I should, metaphorically speaking, get my hands dirty. Spirituality demands an awareness of what is beyond this world. At the same time that should not preclude the ability to function effectively in this world. For the aspirant to the mysteries, spirit and the inner life must always come first, but the external world is part of the whole fabric of life and the lessons it has to offer cannot be ignored or denied. This is especially so if one is to translate any spiritual understanding into a form that can help others, and there is little point in having spiritual understanding if one is unable to share it. This perhaps hardly needs saying but my predisposition of the time is not unique and if anyone thinks that spirituality is an excuse to avoid engagement with the world, they will need to think again. The spiritual person is in the world and must master it on every level.

The Masters generally spoke in very straightforward language with little direct reference to metaphysical or esoteric ideas. On this occasion, when discussing my mental sluggishness (in response to a question I had asked), they mentioned karma. I was naturally tempted to ask what I had done in a past life to cause such a karmic effect but knew they would say it was unimportant so refrained. I frequently noticed that the Masters would always give me the information I needed but not a jot more. They were not there to satisfy my curiosity. They did tell me that energy creates energy and laziness, or lassitude as they termed it, would also lead to more of the same, and they always encouraged me to avoid inertia, making clear that the contemplative life was in no sense a pretext for indolence; that it might not be doing but it certainly was not doing nothing. On this subject of keeping occupied and not falling into idleness, the Masters were, if they will forgive me for saying so, rather like strict but good-hearted nannies of the old school. On the face of it there may be nothing esoteric in the advice that **through hard work and concentration they (sluggishness and apathy) would disappear** but it is sound advice and does actually contain what has become an occult maxim, that energy follows thought.

Although the Masters confirmed that reincarnation is a fact, spiritually speaking it is an unimportant fact. That is because it relates to the being as it exists in form and a major aim of spirituality is to transcend identification with form. The Masters would occasionally allude to it in passing but only to make a larger point. If we are to know ourselves as spirit then all doctrines relating to the transitory impermanent planes and our transitory impermanent selves must be seen in their correct light as relative truths that have no reality from the standpoint of the absolute. That is why certain esoteric teachings can deny reincarnation while others can say that no individual reincarnates, there is only the One Self ceaselessly manifesting itself in multitudinous forms throughout the created worlds, so gaining the experience it needs to become ever more.

As for karma, this was not a subject the Maters cared to elaborate on either. They would mention it now and again, as in the talk above, but its details and workings were not something they thought necessary to share. Any preoccupation with the minutiae of esotericism they would regard as distracting. It serves no real purpose to know who one was in a previous life. Who you are now is what matters.

October 20th 1979

The Master said that I should listen to Michael. What he told me came from the Most High and I should not argue or criticise. Part of my lesson in humility was to accept teaching from an imperfect source, one than which I thought I knew better. "Be like a tree" he said "It just is itself and does not try to rule anything else. That is your task now. It is not your job to teach your brother. He will learn from you if you are humble. You do not have to say anything. At this stage you should not say anything but simply accept what you are told. Stop resisting, stop fighting and stop trying to run things. Let them happen and roll with the flow. At present you confuse yourself, thinking too much about too much. Keep things simple."

He then told me to love people's weaknesses and they would disappear. At the moment I was too critical but, if I continually strove to be uncritical until that became part of my nature, I would find that that which irritated me in others would cease to do so. I should accept Michael's weaknesses and learn from his strengths. The Masters had arranged this situation so that we balanced each other and could learn from each other. If I were with a paragon of virtue I would just be obeisant and learn nothing, he said. This way my lessons will be learned properly.

Here's an answer to those who think that if God somehow revealed Himself or perfect spiritual beings, **paragons of virtue,** appeared in the world, all would be well and humanity would enter a Golden Age of love, peace and brotherhood. It is possible that we might be stunned into some sort of goodness but it would be a false goodness, not one that originated naturally from within. It would be a goodness in some measure forced on us that did not arise from our own free will and so was not a natural part of us. We **would just be obeisant and learn nothing.** Thus when the outer stimulus was removed we would revert to what we had been like before, perhaps not immediately but certainly after a while. This does not mean one cannot be inspired by the example of great souls but there is greater opportunity for growth when one has to work for it. Let us note that it was only when Jesus left his disciples that they blossomed spiritually.

Whenever I heard the Masters speak of **the Most High**, I felt great reverence. They did not do so often but their occasional use of this phrase to describe the divine source seemed to me to convey more of its transcendent and awe-inspiring mystery than any other. Words can never capture truth but some can suggest it more effectively than others which is why they are important and should be chosen with care, the better to convey the meaning behind them. Traditionally language comes from the gods and in the ancient world its deterioration was regarded as symptomatic of a commensurate deterioration in thought and values. Today, in our largely relativistic and egalitarian culture, we would tend to dismiss that idea but, as we have lost all contact with the vertical dimension of life and have little understanding of the power behind words, we are not really in a position to judge. In the Corpus Hermeticum, thought to be a 2nd and 3rd Century A.D. presentation of what may have been ancient Egyptian teachings, the sage Hermes warns against the translation of metaphysical teachings into Greek, saying that translation will distort the inner meaning as only the Egyptian language has the power to convey the true sense behind the words. Very possibly there's an element of parochialism here (the Egyptians are said to have regarded the Greeks as chattering upstarts) but there is also a truth. Many traditional cultures which modelled themselves on a heavenly pattern regarded words as having magical power so that some really could express more of the reality behind them than others with an outwardly identical meaning. In like manner, some descriptive terms such as **the Most High** (Hebrew in origin but still powerful when translated) have great resonance that cannot be matched by more mundane counterparts. Ultimately this all stems from the basic fact that in the beginning was the Word. Sound is the creative force of the universe.

So the Masters made clear that what I was told by Michael was inspired by God. Actually, I would guess, it was inspired by them but as they had realised God within themselves that amounted to the same thing. What Michael told me was not complicated and largely echoed what the Masters said when they spoke to me directly in that it concerned the need for me to acquire humility but I was less able to take it from him. I did argue and I was critical about what I perceived to be his shortcomings. I was more concerned with teaching him than learning myself, and, looking back, I am chastened by the thought of his forbearance in putting up with me, especially considering the difference in our ages. I can make excuses for myself, some of which would have some justification, but the unavoidable fact is that I used his faults to avoid facing up to my own. That's something I had already been warned about. See for instance the talk of June 20th.

But forget my individual case which is not of any interest to anyone else. The point of these remarks is this. In life we are often taught lessons by unexpected and **imperfect sources**, by the people we meet or have relationships of one sort or another with. Doubtless such people are used unbeknown to themselves but they are used because they are the most appropriate vessels through which we may learn whatever lesson it is that we need to. We all learn through our relationships with others. These provide the necessary challenges and stimuli and there may be issues of karma too. They may not be our teachers in the conventional sense but we learn through them. In my case, being humble before the Masters was easy. Being humble before a fellow imperfect human being with many faults of his own was another matter and the real test.

We might all hope to have an illumined guru as our master. Sometimes our karma might give us just that but there is a downside. Do we become attached to the teacher? When happens when he is no longer there as will inevitably be the case? And do we use him to become like him or just to follow him slavishly? As the Masters say in *Towards The Mysteries*, is he a bridge or a prop? At a certain period in my life I had the good fortune to be taught by the Masters but they have not been my only teachers. Michael obviously was another and I have learnt from many of the people whom I have encountered over the course of my life. God sends us the teachers we need at the time we need them and we must always be open to learning from every situation we find ourselves in. What is the mark of an old person? Surely it is someone who has stopped learning.

Perhaps the hardest thing the Masters ever told me, both to understand and to put into practice, was **to love people's weaknesses and they would disappear.** Love weaknesses? How do you do that? At first I assumed it must mean love people in spite of their weaknesses. Focus on the good and ignore the bad and that will draw the good out and the bad will diminish or, at least, it won't be stimulated by you directing attention to it. There might be some people who are too far gone in wrong thinking and egotistical behaviour for this approach to be realistic but most of us are a combination of good points and bad which latter often arise from fear and insecurity anyway. And even the former type would benefit from this attitude more than from criticism of their faults even if we tell ourselves that such is meant constructively. So, this does not mean being naïve and turning a blind eye to reality but it does mean being motivated by love and goodwill.

That's what I thought at first, and it's not incorrect as far as it goes, but then I realised there was more. The Masters are always one step ahead and they mean precisely what they say. I had to think again. **Love people's weaknesses and they will disappear.** If you really do succeed in loving an individual's weaknesses, not for what they are in themselves but as a part of the reality of a human being, then these behavioural tendencies actually will disappear *in your perception.* That doesn't mean that the individual who manifests them no longer does so but to you they are now seen to be the surface blemishes, illusions even, that in reality they are. They are not the person, merely a condition that that person has mistakenly and temporarily identified with. But that should not mean that you identify the person with them. This truth is of a piece with the Master's statement which followed that (to paraphrase) if you **strive to be uncritical that which irritates will cease to do so.** Irritation is a major cause of criticism as I well know from personal experience

324

but criticism merely aggravates that which it criticises. It's like scratching an itch which, after initial relief, just makes it worse. If you don't scratch, the itch eventually goes away.

Sometimes the Masters would appear to take a more Christian approach to the spiritual life. Their unceasing and uncompromising emphasis on love and humility is an example of that. At others they would seem to be more Buddhist, Taoist even. I don't know who or what they may have been in their past earthly incarnations. It's irrelevant anyway. I do know that they had no religious affiliation when they spoke to me. They spoke from the plane of spiritual at-one-ment and their teaching had no religious element to it at all. In case of misunderstanding, let me elaborate on that a little. Of pure religion they were the living embodiment. To any particular religion they had no attachment. They were free from all limitation, free from identification with any kind of form and they viewed that which is directly without seeing it through the unavoidably distorting lens of any intermediary. At a certain stage a map of spiritual reality is a great help. After a certain stage it can be an obstruction because the description is never the thing itself. This is not to say that the Masters would not have had the utmost reverence for the founders, saints and sages of all the main religions. Indeed, they would almost certainly have been numbered amongst such light-bearing individuals themselves but religions are of this world not the next, and if anyone thinks Jesus was a Christian or the Buddha a Buddhist they need to study the lives of those great souls again.

Be like a tree is rather a Taoist statement. The suggestion that one should not try to be anything but just be, which is what, at root, that means, certainly has an Oriental flavour though, of course, it is not specifically Oriental. It is a simple key to the truth. It is so simple it can sound a little glib when repeated by those who, without having achieved that state, might seek to give themselves an air of profundity by association with it. I would prefer to avoid that trap so will just say that the statement may be simple but the enacting of it is not easy. Temperamentally I may have inclined more to contemplation than action but just to be without trying to be something was another matter. For what this really amounts to is to be nothing. Nothing at all. Truly to be is to be nothing. This is a concept completely alien to us today. We all try to be something whether that is something worldly or something spiritual. That's what we are brought up and educated to do. We seek success, we seek achievement, we seek fulfilment. But a tree doesn't try to be anything. **It just is itself.** Now, you may think this is absurd because how could a tree try to be anything other than what it is? It's a tree, for heaven's sake! Moreover, if I try to be like a tree, aren't I trying to be like something? But the tree is just a metaphor which need not be taken too literally and the recommendation is not that we should try to be like a tree but be like a tree. The difference may appear slight but it is essential.

If you find the advice to **be like a tree** a little too vague to get an effective grip on, the key part of that advice is given in more practical terms a few lines further on when the Master told me to **stop resisting, stop fighting and stop trying to run things. Let them happen and roll with the flow.** He was telling me to give up trying to bend life to the shape I wanted and just move with the current of life, letting it take me where it would. He was not telling me to be passive but to let go of the dualistic struggle, another difference which amounts to a good deal more than at first sight might appear.

October 24th 1979

The Master told me that I was being given a little more power to influence people. The Masters give their students power for several reasons, but the two main ones were so that they could help others and as a test to see how they handled it. I should bear that in mind and make sure I used it wisely, responsibly and in moderation. He then told me that there were many changes going on in my physical body at the moment due to the training I was undergoing and it was possible these might lead to illness in which case

I should consult a doctor as these were there for using. The training I was receiving took place at inner levels as well as outer, and, although I might not be aware of what was happening there, the effects would filter though to my brain in time. He then told me always to be true to my thoughts and never to shelve things but get them done when they were impressed upon me. The more I responded to impression, the stronger it would become.

I asked him how I could overcome my criticising tendency and he said that it mainly sprang from fear and defensiveness. I love the highest but this makes me critical of anything which fails to match up to that in my eyes. If I were confident that the highest was the truth and could not be touched or affected by lower vibrations then I would be less critical as I criticise to protect myself. The truth can never be pulled down or tarnished by anything, he said. It is inviolate so I had nothing to fear. I must also understand that what I thought of as the lower was still part of the whole and had its place in the whole. He went on to say that I had to learn that sometimes the less evolved could only advance through the loving sacrifice of the more evolved. He said "You have a perfect example of that in your world in the life of Jesus who humbled himself and spoke to simple people as one of them without any sense of superiority. He did not get irritated or upset by their behaviour but remained calm and loving and you must do the same for only by doing this can you teach others." He concluded "You may think of your lesson in this life as to learn to love your enemies. What do you think that means? I will tell you. It means to see God in all people whatever they might be like on the outside".

There are occasions when I feel I am leaving myself a little over exposed in these pages which is why I sometimes draw attention to my youth at the time the talks took place. But really my age is beside the point. My faults were not the faults of youth. They were the basic human faults, as filtered through my personality certainly but faults which, in one form or another, we all share. I was over-critical and I probably still am which leads me to wonder if we ever completely overcome our failings. We can become aware of them, we can strive to curtail their expression but I'm not sure we can ever completely eradicate a tendency towards them in this life. That doesn't mean that through constant effort we cannot reach the point where they cease to manifest themselves, and nor does it mean, since the faults are in the lower self, that we cannot transcend them through transcending identification with that self. But perhaps until we do that they will always be present in some form, even if it be a reduced one. If that seems a disheartening prospect, it really only implies the need to be ever vigilant but then that vigilance is the seed that will grow into the awareness which eventually releases us from egotistical domination.

What was this power of which the Master spoke? It was not power in the way we usually understand that word. It was not a charismatic personality or the gift of oratory or intellectual force, and it was certainly not a psychic power. I think it was the ability to reflect. Spiritual teachings are ten a penny nowadays and that is a good thing. At the same time what the world really needs is men and women of all nationalities and backgrounds who reflect something of the higher world in themselves, people who may not even be outwardly spiritual but who carry some kind of light. So I believe this power was the ability to reflect light. Evidently such a light will shine only to the degree that the individual stands back and lets it, in other words to the degree of his transparency, so it can never be regarded as a personal attribute. That doesn't mean that one is not aware of it hence the Master's words about it constituting a test and that the accompanying power to **influence people** should be **used wisely, responsibly and in moderation.** But it does most assuredly mean that it is not a personal power and will only remain to the extent that one can forget the personal self. Failure to do that will cause its disappearance even though the illusion of power might remain. If ever you think that the light that shines through you comes from you, that very thought is the shutter that will block it out.

I have to say that I was never consciously aware of any physical changes but it is interesting to note that the Master said these were taking place. Does that imply that as one treads the path one's physical body actually becomes more refined, more rarefied? It is widely accepted as part of traditional spiritual teaching that matter has not always been as dense as it is now and will not always be so. Do the atoms in one's body become heightened in vibration as one treads the return path to the source and purifies oneself through right eating, right feeling and right thinking? The ascended body of Jesus is said to have been made of light. Is that something that will happen to all our bodies when we reach his state, and does the process start when we begin to aspire towards the light? I was not ill, as far as I recall, but I did become increasingly sensitive, sensitive to noise, to dirt, to what you might call 'bad vibrations' in general. This always poses a problem for the developing aspirant. On the one hand, he is instructed to be detached, not to get upset over external things, not to react and to remain calm and perfectly poised at all times. On the other, his response to the disorder of the world becomes ever more acute. But this is just a fact that must be faced. It does become more difficult to deal with the world as you grow in sensitivity but you become a Master by mastering, by mastering the world and by mastering yourself. And the only way you learn to master is by facing difficulty, by meeting challenges and surmounting them.

An increased sensitivity to the imperfections of the world is something every aspirant is faced with. One of the hardest things for a spiritual person today is to see that practically everything in this world is out of alignment with divine reality and yet still love the world and one's fellow men and women, and not feel apart from them because you see something they don't. Nevertheless this absolutely must be done if we are not to fall victim to one of the many snares that the devil has in store for those seeking to escape his power. You must see the error held by those who deny God, either literally or by following one of the many false gods, but you must not identify those who hold or even propagate that error with the error. They are as much children of the one High God as you are. They are just not conscious of it yet. It might help to think of it this way. There are no wrong people, only wrong states of consciousness that people mistakenly identify with.

The Master said that doctors were there for using which may seem a rather unnecessary thing to say but followers of some spiritual paths have wondered about that, and certain religious groups have taken the avoidance of Western medical practice to extremes. One can sympathise with the attitude that sees a system based on purely materialistic principles as lacking in completeness but in matters such as this one must use one's common sense. The body must be cared for if one is to function properly in the world. That much is surely obvious. If it falls ill, it needs to be healed and doctors are there to do the healing. That also seems unarguable in the main but is it true under all circumstances? Here are some questions worth pondering. Is there a line to be drawn beyond which the person concerned with spiritual development should not go? Might it not be necessary sometimes to accept our karma? Is it right always to seek to extend human life? Are, for instance, organ transplants in accord with the truth that a human being is not just a body but a soul in a body? Wellesley Tudor Pole, who I have mentioned before, thought they were not. In one of his letters to Rosamond Lehmann he says, on the subject of organ transplantation, "artificial surgery of this kind may prolong life but it is *not* evolutionary, in the spiritual sense."[17] I would tend to agree with that but I don't think there can be a hard and fast rule that applies to everybody at all times. Each one of us must make up our own mind and decide what is right for us at that particular point on our path. However when we do this we should remember that just because something is technically possible and culturally accepted does not mean it is spiritually correct, especially when it has been developed in a culture that either denies spiritual reality or is ignorant of its nature.

There are many things in our contemporary world that are regarded as perfectly acceptable but which from the spiritual point of view are quite out of harmony with reality. Enormous advances in technology have given us hitherto undreamt of powers. We assume that because things are there it is always right to use them. I would say, don't make that assumption. Unless you have a correct understanding of how the world and human beings are made and what the latter are here to do, you cannot know what is right and what is wrong. It is too facile to say that if something were not meant to be, it wouldn't be. Human beings have free will. Certainly we learn through exercising that, but I believe that now is a pivotal point in the evolution of human beings on this planet and some kind of sorting out of the sheep from the goats is taking place. I don't mean this in a judgemental way but there are choices to be made at the present time. If that is the case there are necessarily going to be various options available, some better than others. They are not all right or in line with the true nature of things. I am not talking about fire and brimstone here but it is quite likely that our future evolutionary path will be determined by choices we make now. That is all the more reason to listen to the voice within, the one that is normally drowned out by our educational/cultural conditioning and innate desire not to appear too different from our peers. We all have access to this voice if we wish to hear it. Unfortunately we often prefer to listen to something else.

I think the second part of this talk is largely self-explanatory and does not need much commentary from me. Sometimes the Masters would say little, leaving me to work out the implications of what they were saying on my own. At others they would develop their theme a bit more and this was one of those occasions. Their words made a strong impression, strong enough for me to remember what was said afterwards pretty much in its entirety. Perhaps I should just say a brief word on their description of people as more and less evolved. This might sound a little controversial nowadays but it was customary then to speak of relative degrees of spiritual unfoldment in those terms. The Masters used language with which I was familiar and terms that made sense to me, and perhaps it is only over-sensitivity that sees in such words any slight. The word 'evolve' comes from the Latin and means literally 'to roll out of' which is not a bad way of describing the budding and opening up of the soul. Spiritually speaking, we are all at different stages of development and if you want a pictorial representation of that you won't do much better than to think of the opening of a lotus blossom, a commonly used image to depict the unfolding chakras which themselves are indications of an individual's spiritual evolution.

Chapter 27

Thoughts on Relationships

The return from India did mark or, at any rate, coincide with one change in our lives. It had taken a while but Michael and I at last began to establish the kind of relationship the Masters wished us to have. It had not always been plain sailing and I can still remember moments of acute frustration when I wondered if I had done the right thing in coming to Bath. I don't know if Michael ever felt the same way but I would be surprised if he had not. We were of different ages and quite different characters but we were united in our love for the Masters and that bond helped us to overcome any outer conflicts, most of which were caused by temperamental oppositions. However these had their advantages too and, as the Masters had predicted, we each began to learn from the other which also brought us closer together. Without doubt there was still progress to be made before we could truly say we were travelling on parallel lines but we were now heading in that direction. I think of this time as the end of my probationary period.

It might be wondered how there could possibly be any friction between us given that we had the inestimable benefit of being instructed by the Masters. Surely that should have been enough for us to surmount any personality differences? Perhaps it should have been, and it undoubtedly helped, but I spoke to the Masters for about 15 minutes every 2 or 3 days at best, and Michael and I were together practically all waking hours, working together in the antiques market and living together in the same small flat. This gave us plenty of opportunities for disagreement. The Masters had said that the training was intended to be an intensive process, and sometimes it did feel like a baptism of fire. Rather curiously, with them one had the strange feeling that there was all the time in the world but equally there was no time to be wasted. They lived in eternity so could never be described as impatient but that is not to say that they did not value time.

I don't want to exaggerate the differences between Michael and myself, for we had much that united us and most of the time our relationship was fine. The point I wish to make is that just because you decide to tread the spiritual path that does not mean that you are put with your perfect partner who will then support you in every way. If that were the case then progress would be minimal. You might live in sublime happiness but you would have no incentive to develop. This is not a recommendation to seek out someone with whom you have nothing in common for that would obviously be a recipe for disaster but, if there is to be learning, there must be differences. Some people are tested to the limits by extremely difficult relationships but that's not what I'm talking about here. I am saying that the most fruitful situations for spiritual growth are the ones in which there is some challenge, in which balance and harmony are not automatically present from the beginning but have to be established. You might say that this doesn't just apply in spiritual life but in all life and I would absolutely agree but that is because, in reality, all life is spiritual life. The situations we encounter, the relationships we have, are all opportunities for growth as growth is the reason we (all of us, whether we believe in a spiritual purpose to existence or not) are here.

This point prompts the interesting question of how long, from the perspective of spiritual understanding and life viewed as having as its purpose the growth of the soul, we should stay in a relationship if we feel it has broken down. Inevitably there is no simple answer to that. It must surely depend on a number of factors. Most relationships, of course, are not like the one between Michael and me. In a normal marriage or relationship between two people of the opposite sex, the first thing to consider, if there are such, is children. I would say that, unless there are very strong reasons that make continuation impossible (for instance, violence), this takes precedence over all else; at least until the children reach the age of puberty. After that other things may come into consideration but before that stage in a child's life it surely is obvious that adults have an obligation to put their children's welfare above their own feelings. That may not always be possible but it should be the general aim.

The traditional religious position is that marriage partners should stay together for life. The modern attitude is that if people don't get along they should split up. An over-simplification, I realise, but, roughly speaking, correct. Neither approach really takes into account the totality of the situation where relationships between human beings are concerned or, for that matter, the complexity. Religion recognises a spiritual purpose to marriage but can be inflexible and unwilling to adjust to development and change. The modern attitude, which limits human beings to their outer form, sees no purpose other than the mutual requirements of each partner with sometimes a nod to the wider duty of maintaining the cohesion of society.

It would hardly be an exaggeration to say that our relationships have the potential to provide us with the best opportunity for growth that we can have in this life. More than anything else we experience they give us the chance to learn about ourselves and explore our psychology. They can bring out our shortcomings as well as qualities, and give us responsibilities we might not otherwise have had, not to mention occasions for self-sacrifice. This might seem a rather cold-blooded way of looking at relationships but it doesn't preclude love and affection which should always be the basic glue of any relationship. It simply means that, from the higher standpoint, our earthly relationships come about not to satisfy the desires of the incarnate self but the needs of the soul. The one does not necessarily deny the other but it is by some margin the pre-eminent factor. This has far-reaching implications when it comes to the breaking up of relationships. Should we bail out of a marriage before we have fulfilled its purpose and learned its lessons? The fact that the romantic element may have died is irrelevant. The brutal truth is that that was not the reason the relationship was formed in the first place. Not the inner reason anyway. It was formed because of what both parties could learn from it and the spiritual progress they could make from it. If you flee your lesson, you will almost certainly find it reappearing further down the line, possibly in a more intense form that makes it harder to evade.

We have to recognise that our relationships do not arise through chance but are determined by a number of things, the chief of which, as I have said, is the requirement to bring about growth between the parties involved. Thus we will form a partnership with someone who can help to bring that about for us, and whom we also can help. The process is always mutual. That person may not be our ideal partner but he or she will be the right partner for where we are at that moment. Karma is always involved in significant relationships. Sceptics may dismiss that notion but lovers, particularly those who have fallen in love at first sight, should look at it more sympathetically. There may be links from previous lives that are being carried forward and developed or there may be karmic debts to be paid. This could well mean that the potential for problems to arise is inherent in the relationship from the beginning. This doesn't matter. What we do about it does. Do we make sincere efforts to resolve them when they arise or do we take them to mean that the relationship is at an end? Do we just blame the other person for their failings or do we ask ourselves if we too need to change in some way? Of course, a relationship involves two people and if one partner seeks some kind of rapprochement while the other is uninterested in compromise that will only exacerbate any problems and may lead to an impossible situation on which the plug has to be pulled. But if we can bring a reasonable level of maturity to the situation then it is more than possible that karmic debts can be cleared and psychological wounds healed. Then my feeling is that, if it is still wished for, a separation is spiritually permissible, maybe even spiritually beneficial for both parties who can continue their development along new lines. The question then arises how can we truly know if karmic requirements have been met? The answer to that is that we can never know for sure but we can look for an intuitive response within, making quite certain, as always, that it really is the intuition we are looking to and not personal preference masquerading as such. The intuition never misleads but neither is it is ever based on anything personal, and its voice will not be heard if the ego drowns it out with its own noisy demands.

The fact that we may feel disappointed or unfulfilled by a marriage is no indication that it is over or even that it is not fulfilling its purpose. Despite the ideals of romanticism and the occult doctrine of twin souls, we must never look to another person to complete us and never feel let down when we discover (and it is always when not if) that that is not going to be the case. True and lasting wholeness can only be found within. It can never be supplied by anything external, certainly not another human being and not even God as conceived of in an external form. That is not to say that the partners in a relationship cannot achieve some kind of union but if there is to be such, and if it is to be more than the romantic but ephemeral kind, it always needs time and work to bring about. All the more reason then not to abandon ship just because it has sprung a few leaks. Try to repair them and see if you can make port.

Marriage or the like is not the only relationship we have in our lives but it is usually the most significant one if for no other reason than we actually live with the other person on a basis of equality. In the past, when monasticism was in vogue, many people attracted to the spiritual life tended to avoid marital relationships in order to concentrate on inner development, but now it seems that the wheel has turned a little and spirituality is to be expressed in the world, so it is far more common for serious spiritual seekers to enter into marriage, hopefully, though not always inevitably, with a reasonably sympathetic partner. In this, as in most other things, it is karma that will determine. This can be wholly to the advantage of both partners if their attitude is correct. And even if the relationship runs into trouble then there are valuable lessons to be learned if one is open to them.

In conclusion what I would say is this. Everyone hopes that their relationships in life will bring them joy and happiness. Unfortunately this is not always going to be the case. The purpose of all important relationships is twofold, to satisfy karmic requirements and to further personal and/or spiritual growth. So, difficult relationships are just as important and sometimes even more so as easy ones. This means that the fact that a relationship is difficult is not a reason to bring it to an end. Our personality may be telling us one thing but the soul has its own agenda, and we would do well to try to ascertain its wishes before terminating an arrangement which may be to our long term benefit. This is certainly not to say that everyone should carry on in all circumstances. If there is violence involved or fear, coercion, manipulation or any number of situations in which one partner is dominating the other to an unnatural degree then I think we can assume that the relationship is unhealthy and should be terminated. Moreover in any situation in which two people are involved, there is always the chance that one of them might be willing to make sincere attempts to change while the other has no such intention. That too does not bode well for any kind of spiritual progress and could lead to a legitimate break up. But if things have not come to such a pass then maybe we should think long and hard before walking away from a relationship merely because it is not living up to our original hopes and expectations. It is a spiritual law that what we leave unfinished we will eventually have to complete.

In heaven there is no marrying, said Jesus, thereby hinting at the transcending of all dualities. But there is on Earth and it is an estate ordained by God as the Christian prayer book says. We would do well to look on it in that light and recognise that it exists not only for our comfort in what can sometimes truly be a vale of tears as well as to provide a safe and secure environment in which to bring up children, but also to offer an arena in which we can learn and grow. It may well be that not all marriages are destined to last a lifetime but those who recognise a higher purpose to life know that there is a higher purpose to marriage too.

This chapter has taken off in ways I did not expect when I began it but I think there is a purpose behind that. It looks at a subject that did not particularly concern me at the time this story took place and which was not discussed by the Masters then as they always restricted themselves to what was of immediate relevance. However that subject, human (and, more especially, marital) relationships, concerns a lot of people now since, as previously mentioned, the present day spiritual aspirant is not necessarily required to give up the world to pursue the path. Indeed, very often he or she is specifically required to stay in it. A person might even leave the world for a period of a few or many years and then re-enter it later on to express what they have learnt and explore a different aspect of life. This has actually become increasingly common in the modern era, as it seems that the pace of human spiritual evolution is being speeded up with several lives' experience sometimes being packed into one. The two stories below illustrate the points made here in different ways.

Cyril Scott has a story in his book *The Initiate in the New World* about a revered Indian yogi who, after death, was reborn in the West in a female body and whose destiny it was in that life to marry and have children. What a come-down, someone remarks. Not at all, they are told. Even though that yogi was nearing Masterhood he still had something left to learn and this was the best way he could do it. The story is presented as a true one which it may or may not be but that is beside the point. It illustrates a truth which can be summed up in a general sense by saying that for the spiritual to be fully spiritual it must be fully expressible in the material.

The episodes in that story were spread out over two separate lives. My next story is similar but more recent and here the two parts are compressed into a single life. It concerns a young man who adopted a contemplative, near monastic, existence from an early age. He soon made good spiritual progress, finding great peace and detachment from all worldly concerns. But suddenly in midlife everything changed. He met someone, fell in love and his apparently settled world was turned on its head, precipitating a crisis for him as he tried to work out what he should do. He eventually came to the conclusion that he should follow the direction that life was showing him so he gave up his monastic life, married and had children. Does this imply that his earlier spiritual realisation had been based on an illusion? Not at all, but it does indicate that it was incomplete and that future progress depended on him leaving a world in which he had become perhaps too comfortable and seeking to manifest his inner realisation outwardly in a new and unfamiliar environment, which was in many ways more challenging. Don't take this as a pattern for all to follow. Each individual has his or her own path. Nevertheless one might speculate that it could be a way followed by an increasing number of people as we begin to realign Earth with Heaven.

Chapter 28

Tests and Trials

A few of the Masters' talks will be of limited interest to a wider audience since they specifically concerned me and my particular needs of the time. Also, there is little in them that, from the point of view of spiritual instruction, could be regarded as in any way out of the ordinary. I feel that the next two may belong to that category but, in the interests of completeness, I have left them in. I am not saying that they do not contain valuable advice for anyone at any stage of the path but they might be regarded as treading familiar ground. Having said that, though, the last sentence in the first talk is pertinent.

October 28th 1979
The Master told me that I must become more mature and balanced. At present, when things were going my way, confidence turned to arrogance. I needed to learn to be unswayed by success or failure and become completely impersonal in my outlook. "If you wish to acquire true wisdom, you must be humble." he said, adding, "I can assure you that never has a soul attained who has not done this." He then told me that I was not yet aware of the importance of my mission and reminded me of my many responsibilities. His message was "Be mature, be humble" and he said that when I really did become more mature many things would be given to me including the power of deep meditation. He concluded by telling me to think deeply on his words and not just assume I knew them because they were simple and obvious.

I have already tried to define what the Masters meant when they talked of maturity. It wasn't just an instruction to a callow youth to grow up. It encompassed a lot more than that. It required a disciplined and emotionally balanced attitude that did not waste time with petty self-concern but got on with the job in hand with total seriousness and without thought of recompense. It demanded an approach to life that combined impersonality and detachment with humility and love. And it entailed a mental attitude that was not swayed by opinion or prejudice or belief, whether one's own or that of society, but at all times sought the truth in its purity and wholeness. By those criteria how many of us are really mature? How many of us are not driven by ego, desire or fear? How many of us are intellectually unconditioned and free of prejudice of any kind? How many of us seek nothing for ourselves, whether material or spiritual, but only wish to serve God or however we define the reality that, at one and the same time, both is and transcends the world and everything in it? This is maturity.

I've left the reference to **the importance of my mission** in only because of my reluctance to edit the Masters' words in any way. That's a decision I took when I started to write for the sake of a total authenticity that I regarded as essential if I was to present this picture of the Masters honestly. Having left it in, I must point out that the importance referred to only relates to my responsibilities to any souls the Masters might send in my direction. It has no personal implication at all and certainly does not imply that any mission I have been given (and we all have missions in life) has any large scale relevance. The mother struggling in poverty to raise her children the best she can has an important mission, as has anybody to whom it is given to help spread the good news that at the heart of the universe there lies intelligence, purpose and love and not just a blind, unfeeling, mechanical nothing. As the Masters spoke to me, it is my duty to share their words with others who may find an inner response to them. That is my task or mission. If you think it is important to pass on what you have been given, then, yes, my mission is important but in that case its importance has precisely nothing to do with me and lies entirely with the words of the

Masters. I am not "protesting too much" here. That is the plain truth.

The next talk concerned a specific incident that had occured during the day when something Michael had said or done (I don't recall what at this distance in time but I imagine it was fairly innocent) had caused me to react with annoyance. Despite being told many times not to respond in this manner, I was still unable to control my emotions. Sometimes, as on this occasion, I couldn't even hold myself back from reacting outwardly. No doubt it is better to express something and get it out and over with than let it fester inside, but far better still is not to react at all. I knew that I should let irritation wash over me and not allow myself to be swept away by it but I was still too caught up in my own feelings to put that into practice. How long it can sometimes take to do what we know we must! How hard it can be to disentangle oneself from one's own ego!

On this occasion I see that I wrote down my reactions to the Master's visit as well as what he said. Presumably I did so because I realised I had succumbed to something that I had been told about often enough and really should have gone beyond. When I say that the Master was stern I don't mean that he was cross or angry or that his love was any the less. At all times the Masters were the embodiment of love but there was nothing sentimental about them and their love did not preclude firmness or even, when necessary, severity.

October 31st 1979

When the Master came his manner was stern and I felt ashamed as I knew I had failed a test which I could not pretend I had not been warned about. He told me that the minute I let annoyance or arrogance into my aura I would suffer for it. I had allowed myself to become angry with Michael and spoken to him in a commanding way, trying to force my view of things on to him and I had done this for my own satisfaction not to help him. I may have been right but that was completely without importance. My annoyed reaction to Michael's mistakes would merely have the effect of magnifying those mistakes and cause them to become more pronounced. I had not acted out of love but from selfish motives and so the fruits of my action would be sour. I should never try to impose my will on Michael. My job was to suggest and leave it at that, not worrying about whether my suggestion was received or not. He said "Be responsible in exercising your gifts. If you try to force your way there will be an inevitable backlash. If your brother does something that you consider wrong then point it out quietly and with love. If you feel annoyed, you must ignore it. Do not be in such a hurry to press home on him his mistake. Your tests will become subtler but if you are always honest, never seeking to justify yourself, and act always with love then you need have no concerns. But if you are not watchful then the chinks in your armour will be exposed and you will stumble." When he had finished he blessed me in the usual way and told me to have no fear but to be strong. The Masters loved me and were always with me and, if my task sometimes seemed hard, I should know that I had requested this as I wished to overcome what held me back from becoming free.

During this period tests seemed to be coming my way on a regular basis. At times hardly a day passed when there was not something that brought to the surface and exposed my weaknesses but, uncomfortable as this relentless probing was, it did at least make me aware of my faults and force me to face up to them. There was no chance of evasion. Sometimes I would be lulled into a false sense of security in that Michael and I would seem to have found a point of equilibrium but then something would occur that would disturb that and, before I knew it, I would be reacting in the same old way with annoyance and irritation. But gradually I began to master these unfortunate tendencies and, as I did, found that what the Masters had always said was true. When I conquered my faults those things that annoyed me in Michael appeared much less frequently.

The incident that prompted the talk above occurred at a time when Michael and I had been getting on well together and I thought I had finally got the better of my irritability with what I perceived to be his worldly manner – see the beginning of the last chapter. In fact it was more a case that he was making fewer of the kind of remarks I deemed to be foolish so he had changed but I had not. So I relaxed and let down my guard. The time you are most vulnerable is when you think you have learnt your lesson. Even if you really have gone some way towards learning it that just means that your next test will be, as the Master said, subtler and probe a little more deeply. You can only really be said to have fully learnt your lesson when you don't even notice that a test has taken place.

If you think that this all sounds rather absurd and that surely anyone would be aware if their character was being tested, especially if warned in advance, and just not react to the test when it came then you fail to appreciate either the weakness of human nature or the downright cleverness of the powers that be. First of all, you are only tested where you are deficient. The arrow is always aimed at your Achilles heel and it is aimed unerringly. Secondly, a test in the spiritual sense is not like the ones we come across in everyday life. It reaches right down to the core of your being, or that aspect of it that is self-identified which is fairly fundamental as far as most of us are concerned. It does not test what you know but what you are, and it really does come in ways you least expect. Moreover the purpose of a test is not served if you are able to disregard it because you know what it is and can psychologically remove yourself from its impact. It's only properly effective if the situation it involves seems to you to be real. Which is not to say that you can't detach yourself from that situation but you need to experience it fully as well.

Tests and trials come to everybody but for those who have set their feet on the spiritual path they come more frequently and probe more deeply. They come through situations one encounters in life, through people one meets, through success, through failure, through hardship and also through ease. They come through having money and they come through not having money. They come in countless different ways and if you master them in one aspect they will come in another. This process is relentless and does not stop until you have become perfect, if by perfect we understand freedom from the stains of egotism. At the same time, it is largely through this same process that we do become perfected.

We are not given any tests that we are incapable of surmounting, not necessarily straightaway but, given time, eventually. In some cases a test might even span an entire lifetime, arising under numerous different guises and posing problems that we are called upon to resolve on different levels. But by this means we are cured of whatever faulty patterns of behaviour we had that initiated the need for the test in the first instance.

These faulty patterns of behaviour are frequently deep rooted so they are not going to be eradicated easily. Often they will have been built up over several lifetimes and become almost second nature in which case we cannot escape the fact that the process of getting rid of them is likely to be long and hard. That's just how it is and there is no point in pretending otherwise so those who think that the mere acceptance of the reality of the spiritual path puts one near its conclusion are in for a shock. However it is true that the sincere desire to get rid of a fault, although just a preliminary, is still an essential step as it means that we have begun to acquire a degree of self-knowledge without which there is no progress at all. Indeed, it is only through complete self-knowledge that we can liberate ourselves from the clutches of the ego, identification with which is the source of all our faults, and eventually find a measure of self-transcendence.

This may all sound quite exhausting, and in truth it often is, but for those who are serious about the spiritual path, there can be no looking back. What is more, there is joy in knowing that you are engaged in a truly transformative process and thereby serving both God and humanity. However much you are tested and tried, however dark and lonely the way may appear, you can be sure that the benevolent gaze of the spiritual guides of the world is always upon you. The path can sometimes seem very lonely but a degree of aloneness is necessary as each individual who attains must do so on his own. Each soul must be tested to the limit if it is to gain the prize, and naturally those who wish to gain the greatest prize must be prepared to make the greatest sacrifice. They must accept whatever trials and tests come in the sure and certain knowledge that by means of these ordeals they will be made worthy to enter into the light. No one can ever gain access to the Kingdom of Heaven who has one spot of darkness in his soul. If this seems an impossible task, remember the words of Jesus that nothing is impossible for God. It is God's grace that we must seek. That is always being poured forth and our only task is to accept it which we do by letting go of self. That's not something we can do merely by wanting to do it which is where the tests and trails of the spiritual path come in.

I trust I've not painted too dark a picture here. That is not my intention at all. My hope is to encourage not discourage. To comfort those who suffer by assuring them that there is a purpose to their suffering. They are being proved. They will have their reward. But I also wish to sound a little warning to those who might think that progress can be made without sacrifice. Perhaps it can if you wish to remain in the foothills of spirituality but, if you want to climb to the peaks, you have to cast off all that would hold you back and weigh you down. You have to travel light and, if you would reach the summit, you must do so quite naked and without any baggage whatsoever. It is the tests we endure that strip away our worldly coverings.

Chapter 29

A Further Look at Contemporary Spirituality

We had an acquaintance in the antiques market who was fascinated by the UFO phenomenon and regarded it as a portent of an impending spiritual upliftment of humanity. He was almost packed and ready to go. There were certain books around at the time that theorised (on, it must be said, pretty flimsy evidence) that human civilisations had been 'seeded' by aliens and that beings from other planets had been visiting this one for thousands of years. There were also quite well documented contemporary accounts of some sort of contact, though the form in which that contact took place (was it physical, was it mental?) was much less clear. Michael had absolutely no interest in any of this. I've spoken before of a sort of holy innocence he possessed that infallibly guided him to the truth. If he felt that something was not correct or not for him, he didn't worry about it or try to understand it. He just didn't bother with it. I was different. I always wanted to understand anything I found puzzling and I found the UFO phenomena puzzling. I thought there must be something real going on behind them but what that might be was another matter. One thing I was sure of, though, and that was that they had no spiritual relevance whatsoever. My conviction was intuitive but it was also based on a quite reasonable belief that spirituality operated vertically not horizontally by which I mean that the idea of men in spaceships, bringing enlightenment, was fundamentally misconceived as it materialised spirituality. Spirituality has nothing to do with technology, however advanced that technology might be. Technology is always an external thing. It relates to the world of doing rather than that of being and is always materialistic. That's not a criticism of it but it does mean that it has no connection with spirituality which is always internal.

The Masters do not use spaceships. When I write that it seems almost comical, so preposterous is the thought that they might, but there are channelled teachings purporting to come from enlightened beings that claim they do. They have nothing to do with UFOs. Any being, however intellectually capable, who needs an external vessel for transport has not transcended the material universe which the Masters have done. In fact, it is almost the definition of what a Master is. Spiritual teachings that link the idea of enlightenment with alien civilisations or other star systems or mysterious entities from far off galaxies can be disregarded. I am not saying that such beings may not exist but I am saying that they are not the spiritual teachers of humanity. Whether such teachings spring from illusion and error or deliberate deception is of secondary importance. In all cases it is safe to assume that they do not come from a source that has realised the truth. The Kingdom of Heaven is within. That is the fundamental and simple truth we need to remind ourselves of when faced with claims whose exotic nature can sometimes make them seem almost plausible, especially to a generation brought up on science fiction.

The spiritual world as it is presented in the material world can be a very confusing place nowadays. There is so much that clamours for the neophyte's attention, so many claims that are made for the veracity or superiority of this or that teaching. We live in a transitional period when old forms are breaking down and authentic new ones have yet to be built up. Into that space pours a vast amount of material of greater or lesser value, and because many people are unaware that all that is not of the physical world is not necessarily of the spiritual world, there is a lot of scope for bewilderment and misunderstanding. In this chapter I would like to address that issue. I have alluded to the problems in passing before now but here I want to focus more particularly on what they are and how best to deal with them.

The fundamental problem is that there exists between the

physical and spiritual worlds or planes what we can call the psychic plane. This is non-physical but still material in that it is a plane of form and multiplicity. It has no permanent reality but is formed of the wishes, desires and thoughts of human beings built up over many thousands of years. It is the world to which belong the emotions, the imaginative impulses and what we describe nowadays as the subconscious drives of humanity. Broadly speaking, though simplifying somewhat, the psychic world, which like all levels of manifestation is both a plane and a state of consciousness, is a reflection of the thinking and feelings part of humanity and, as such, it is, from the point of view of genuine knowledge, illusion. At best any truth to be found there is no more than relative.

The denizens of this world are numerous, comprising human beings out of incarnation as well as beings of a non-human order known by different names in different traditions, for example devas, jinn, certain members of the angelic hierarchies and so on. It has many different levels but one thing that distinguishes all its inhabitants is that they have not transcended duality. Thus it should be quite clear that this is not the field wherein the Masters work. However there are beings there who may give the impression that they have found the light and are in possession of the highest truth. They may genuinely believe this of themselves and they may also have a reasonably advanced knowledge of the inner planes but this does not mean that they have attained liberation from the worlds of becoming and freedom from self. There are also beings who may imitate Masters, or the like, adorning themselves with this name or that title, and, given that this is a plane where subjective thoughts can take objective form, there are thought-forms of the Masters (as there are of the major figures of all religions), created and fed by the concentrated devotion of aspiring devotees and capable of repeating all that such devotees may already know so giving the impression of a certain spiritual attainment but having no true connection with the Masters themselves.

Those familiar with the Tibetan concept of a *tulpa* might know to what I am referring here. In Tibetan Buddhism a *tulpa* is a form created by the concentrated thought of a lama or magician that materialises and can actually, under certain circumstances, acquire a semi-independent reality of its own. A thought-form is similar. It too can appear real and, if contacted by an unwary medium, channeller or psychic, give the impression of deriving from a genuine spiritual source. It is said that most supposed contacts with Masters are, in fact, of this type. This is why inner discernment is so essential. Common sense and humility are invaluable in such circumstances but *buddhi* or spiritual intuition is the only real means of telling true from false. As a basic guide I would say that any contact that gives the name of a Master that is already known should be treated with suspicion[18]. Names denote personalities and distract from the core of the spiritual message because they bring unwanted attention to the outer and the impermanent. The Masters are concerned only with the inner which is not to say that they do not cherish their disciples as individuals but their work has to do with the soul not the personality and they will do nothing, absolutely nothing, to give any focus to the personality.

Once I asked the Masters about all the many false and misleading spiritual forms and was briefly told. **These are distractions. You must learn to ignore them.** But in my younger days I would be quite disturbed by the corruptions to which I believed true spirituality was subjected. That was partly because I could never be completely sure what was true and what was not and that unsettled me. But also I was looking for perfection in this world and that is an obvious impossibility in a world of "change and decay". When I thought about the matter, I realised it was my ego that wanted reality to conform to the way I wanted it to be. I sought emotional security. I had to learn to combine discernment of the real with acceptance of the way things were in this world. I mean by that not being affected by them rather than giving validity to them. Michael had a much more mature attitude. He simply focussed on what he thought was right and disregarded the rest. What is true is true, what is not, is not, that's all there is to it, he would say. He knew that truth prevails and that time would sift out the false. Meanwhile he believed, correctly, that human beings have free will and should be allowed to make their own mistakes. These will have their inevitable consequences and that is how we learn.

None of that means that one should not attempt to clear the path and point out falsehood. Does not the ancient Vedic prayer say "Lead me from the unreal to the real"? It is legitimate to expose the unreal. There are powers that seek to lure the inexperienced spiritual traveller down byways that end in confusion and illusion, and, while it may be true that no one can be led away from the real if there is not something in them that corresponds to the unreal, it is still the duty of those who may already have made these mistakes to point them out so that others have the chance to avoid making similar errors and wasting time. Then it is up to each individual to do what he or she thinks best.

I am not saying that there cannot be useful instruction to be gained from beings existing in the psychic plane (which term I am using here to include what is known in occultism as the astral and mental planes). The higher levels of these worlds contain spirits of much knowledge and understanding who may not have reached the stage of enlightenment but are still more than capable of giving helpful teachings. Do not expect infallibility though. Remember the previously quoted words of the Buddha who told us not to believe something that does not ring true to you no matter who says it.

Complications arise from the fact that in channelled or mediumistically received material, as with teaching given in this world, truth and falsehood can often be mixed up together. This is for two reasons. The first of these can be spilt into two further ones concerning the source and the medium through which that source comes into this world. If the spiritual source of any teaching or message has less than full realisation, which will be the case in the great majority of instances, then however sophisticated or elevated what is communicated might seem to people in the physical world, it is still subjective and can have no more than limited value. Secondly, in ninety nine cases out of a hundred the medium will affect the message. Unless they have reached a very high stage themselves, they will condition anything that comes through them by their personal thoughts, prejudices and beliefs. Think of a light being shone through a glass. The condition of the glass will always affect the quality of the light transmitted. So, test all teachings in your heart. The mind in the head is subject to the limitations of the personality. The mind in the heart is supra-personal and infallible.

There are even teachings that I believe do originally emanate from the Masters that still need sifting because of how they have come through[19]. This may be intentional so that people have to work to discern the real from the unreal and must exercise discrimination rather than just passively absorb, but it may also be because at this present time of not especially high spiritual attainment the Masters must work with what is available. That does not mean that anyone can serve as a medium for the Masters. A basic requirement would be to be able to raise consciousness to the spiritual level where the Masters are to be found, and that would involve, at least to a certain extent, being able to still the mind and transcend the personal. But there is nothing perfect in this world and even genuine messengers will not be entirely free of conditioning, erroneous belief and prejudice. Moreover it must be understood that any contact with the Masters would not be in the form of words. The receiving channel is sensitive to an impulse or impression from the spiritual plane but translates this, which comes from the world of ideas so is not expressed in language, into his own words and so, as described above, the spiritual light is modified by the refracting and sometimes distorting prism of his personal consciousness, and given concrete expression in this world in a form that is more or less affected by the background and prevailing beliefs of the messenger. The only exception to this would be what comes through in the way that teachings from the Boy and Michael did, in which the medium is entirely absent. But these are very rare.

I spoke of two reasons for truth and falsehood being mixed up together in channelled material. The first is due to the limitations of source and medium and might be responsible for error but is still relatively innocent. The second, however, is deliberate. There are disembodied spirits who seek energy from incarnate human beings and to get their attention must include at least some truth in their communications because if they did not they would attract no-one. These communications, however, will be heavily contaminated and should be avoided. There is no benefit to be had from them but there is potential harm. Here again spiritual discernment and a refusal to fall for what may flatter the ego are required to sift out the false from the true. And finally it must also be said that there are indeed dark powers that seek to subvert the truth by leading people astray and muddying the spiritual waters. Their aim is to distort reality and this they do by mixing falsehood in with truth. The corruption of the best is the worst runs the saying, and it's very true. As always clear-sightedness and humility will be unerring guides in separating the pure springs that refresh from the polluted wells.

Lest it be thought that I am warning people off any channelled material or teachings supposedly originating from the higher planes or higher beings on the grounds that they might be misleading, let me say here that I am not. Given my personal history that would be eccentric, to say the least. I am certainly advising that one should exercise discrimination. ("Beloved, believe not every spirit, but try the spirits whether they are of God"[20].) I would also suggest that it might be wise, in order to avoid confusion arising from information overload and/or excessive focus on the theoretical side of things, not to run after every teaching that exists. The watchword is balance. With that proviso by all means investigate what is available. You will surely be directed to wherever it is you should go whether that be for spiritual sustenance, instruction that will enable you to take the next step or even (and this is possible) to something that is false, but whose very falseness will serve to bring out any latent faults or imbalances you might have within you.

Not only is there more channelled and psychically received material readily available today than ever before but the scriptures of practically all religions, dead or living, are published and online, occult and mystical literature abounds and spiritual guides representing almost any tradition you can think of or none at all are more numerous than at any time since Moses brought the tablets down from Mount Sinai. No one could deny that this profusion of spiritual information is a great compensation for those living during the current dark age of materialism even if, inevitably, it also has a downside. It is wonderful that so many valuable teachings from the past are easily accessible now though there does sometimes seem to be a law of diminishing returns operating here. And if, in certain areas, quantity often appears to exceed quality, that does not mean that quality is not to be found.

The widespread dissemination of traditional esoteric teachings might be regarded as a universal benefit for the spiritual seeker at the present time. On the other hand the drawbacks of all that might loosely be grouped together under the banner of the New Age are all too apparent. In a nutshell, the New Age mistakes the psychic for the spiritual and is fascinated by the spurious glamours of the occult and the marvellous. Rather than having a genuine metaphysical basis, it is rooted in the phenomenal which explains its absorption in the external trappings of spirituality rather than spirituality itself. Ancient civilisations, earth energies, auras, chakras, channelling, workshops to discover your past lives or contact your guardian angel and so on are all very well but they are not what true spirituality is about. They all exist in the outer worlds of becoming and manifestation. They are to do with creation not the Creator. A further serious criticism that could justifiably be levelled at New Age spirituality is that it focuses on God Immanent to the neglect of God Transcendent, with the unfortunate consequence that it tends to deify the human self, a potentially disastrous spiritual error. It may pay lip service to transcending ego but all too often it is actually more about inflating the personal self to divine proportions.

As far as spiritual guides are concerned there is no point in pretending, in the name of some kind of misplaced tolerance, that many who claim to be such are not the wolves in sheep's clothing we have been warned about. Some may be charlatans, some may be self-deluded and some may be sincere but under-qualified[21] but even if the first category is the most to be avoided, the other two are just as likely to do more harm than good. Which is not to say that a person must be fully realised to serve as a spiritual teacher (as I have said before, if that were the case we would not have many spiritual teachers) but, if he is not, then he must not give the impression that he is. Actually, even if he is, he should not give the impression that he is. Let us be clear, the quest for enlightenment is for the spiritually immature and any teacher who panders to this desire should be regarded with suspicion. The true teacher has as the core of his teaching love of God, service to others and forgetfulness of self, and the true student focuses only on these.

The spiritually naïve may be taken in by a charismatic personality or the possessor of psychic powers assuming that these denote a spiritually accomplished person when, in point of fact, the very opposite might be a better assumption. Certainly, to exhibit such things is usually the sign of someone who has not understood, or is deliberately transgressing, the real. Then there are those who claim to be modern representatives of defunct traditions to which they might be linked by previous incarnation or inner plane contact. I would say such claimants should be treated with caution. Even if they are making their claims sincerely that does not mean that their contacts are true. Long before they passed away most of these traditions had become degenerate and lost their spiritual fire – that's why they passed away. In the majority of cases it is merely the astral carcass, the decaying psychic form, which is being contacted. If, of course, anything is. If you ever come across an Atlantean or ancient Egyptian high priest it's worth asking yourself why such beings are still so identified with their old persona. Those who are now Masters may once have been such in their incarnated forms. They are not now.

The revival of paganism and associated cults is an interesting development of the mid to late 20th century but we should be careful before regarding any of these as on the same level, spiritually speaking, as the great mystical philosophies and revealed religions. Paganism, in the sense I am using that word here, originally had to do with the energies of the land. Nowadays it may acknowledge a supreme spirit and the oneness of all life but its main focus is still on the gods and goddesses of the subtle levels and so its attention is more on expressions of spirit than spirit itself. Paganism is a type of Nature worship (hence its emphasis on the Goddess) and, as such, does not reach further than the world of creation which, may I remind the reader, is not just the physical world but is always the world of change and becoming. As for neo-paganism, that is an attempt to revive what belongs to the past and it is artificial because not natural for modern men and women who live a totally different life to men and women of the past and can never be those people. It is understandable to want to seek out a belief system with links to the Earth in our deracinated times. And who, in whom a particle of imagination is present, is not moved by the great stoneworks at Avebury, Stonehenge and elsewhere? I have lived in Dorset and Wiltshire and visited many of the ancient sites in those two counties. Like many people, I have felt their pull. I am aware of the power, the magic even, dormant but not dead, to be found there. But we are 21st century people and cannot pretend to be otherwise. That's not to say we should embrace our epoch wholeheartedly. It is all too evident that it is totally out of step with spiritual reality so we need to maintain a critical detachment towards it. But we are what we are and cannot revert to an earlier epoch, however much we might like to. Westerners cannot pretend to be Easterners and nor can modern people pretend to belong to the 10th century B.C. Or, at least, they can so pretend but pretence is what it will be and their experience will ultimately be artificial because it will always be at one remove from what they really are.

While we are on the subject of ancient humanity and prehistoric sites, it is worth drawing attention to the error that equates the psychological state of prehistoric man or even of relatively modern tribal man with a spiritual state. To be sure, early man lived in a condition of oneness with nature, a condition in which time was perceived to be cyclic rather than linear and in which the analytical mind had not assumed the dominance it has today. Thus he was not fully separate. But that does not mean that he had transcended self. It was more that in him self had not yet fully crystallised. His consciousness was still more tribal than individual so he would have to be seen as unconsciously one with life rather than consciously so. His oneness was that of a passive onlooker not that of a participating co-creator with God who had become godlike himself in love, wisdom and creative power. In effect, he may have been one with nature but he was not one with God whose essential being would have been even further beyond his comprehension than it is beyond ours.

Deep within all of us is a nostalgia for a lost Golden Age, and I have no doubt that, in the childhood of humanity, such an age existed. Before the Fall, in an Edenic paradise, we may well have led an existence without pain or sorrow. But paradise is not enlightenment and although the Fall is normally regarded as the result of error or disobedience, it can be looked at in another way. It might be that, by falling, we eventually have the chance to rise higher. After labouring like the prodigal son in the hard and dusty fields of earthly existence, we can return to our Maker with a greater degree of realisation than would have been possible if we had never left. I am not saying that the Fall was not the result of error on the part of humanity, but might it not be the case that it was used by God so that out of evil might come good? I am definitely not one of those who believes that evil was part of the divine plan but I see no reason not to suppose that, given the fact of its arising, it could not be co-opted to bring about a greater good. Be that as it may, the main point I wish to make is that the bliss of our spiritual childhood, the pre-lapsarian

Adamic state, is not the same as the attainment of Christhood, becoming a fully conscious son or daughter of God.

From the foregoing remarks about paganism and the psychological state of early humanity, it should be appreciated that although the trance of the shaman is sometimes equated with the enlightened state of a Buddha, it is by no means the same thing. The traditional shaman operated in the psychic levels of existence. He served his tribe as a healer, a teacher and a link with the gods of the inner worlds of creation. His work and his realisation were more magical than spiritual which I do not say to belittle him for I believe that the shaman performed an essential function in traditional tribal societies. But, once again, I would say that it is a mistake for modern people brought up in the technological West to imitate something that belonged to other cultures and other times. No doubt it is possible to acquire psychic and magical power by following the path of the shaman if that is what you want. However, if you wish to discover the essential truth of what you are, you have to go beyond the quest for higher states of consciousness and the allurements of magic. The ecstasy of the shaman was not the enlightenment of the sage. He still lived in the world of experience and subject/object duality. He may have been a voyager in the unknown from the perspective of physical consciousness but he had not transcended identification with form and self, and shamanic techniques will not help you to do that. That is not what they were designed for. I know that some might disagree with me on this but the spiritual state of a Christ or Buddha is to the shaman as the sun is to the moon.

The purpose of this brief trawl through the contemporary spiritual landscape is not, as it might seem, to criticise or condemn but to try to bring some clarity to what can be a confusing jumble of competing ideologies and claims. Organised religions certainly have their faults, all well known today, but they do at least strive to maintain a degree of order in an area which can be very disordered especially as it is not subject to the same checks and balances that the scientific method brings to the world of material knowledge. In a time when genuine spiritual authority is lacking, the field is wide open for all kinds of unsubstantiated assertions. We need to try and sort out the true from the partially true but incomplete and that from the downright false and misleading. In this we have two guides. The first is the religious teaching of the ages as it comes down to us from the mystics, saints and realised sages of the past. This may differ in its inessential external aspects which vary according to time and place but is fundamentally identical. The second is our own intuition though we must make sure that we do **not confuse it with wishful or conditioned thinking** or identify the pristine intuition with the cultural, fashionable or personal clothing that gets put on it as it travels down from spiritual to mental levels.

As we are living during a period when a large number of men and women are becoming interested in the mystical path and, in varying degrees, having experiences of the soul, which coincides with one in which the religions of the past (which, make no mistake about it, all served humanity very well in their time) are much diminished in spiritual power, there is increased potential for understanding if these experiences are rightly reacted to and illusion if they are not. One of the aims of this book is to put spiritual experiences in some kind of context and help those who have them to make sense of them and know what are and what are not the next steps to take. For there are always next steps to take and there is always a right and a wrong path on which to take them. The awakening to the realities of the spiritual world shines a bright light into the human psyche, but where the light is strongest there the shadows can be darkest too and it is a fact that the devil is far from defeated when people start to have spiritual experiences. On the contrary, it is then that we can be at our most vulnerable as we are setting out on a journey which is still relatively uncharted. We need good maps that show the safe routes, the treacherous bogs and the ways that may seem to pass through pleasant country but in the end go nowhere.

Chapter 30

"Awaken!"

The last entry in my notebook is for November 11th. That is simply because I had reached the end of that particular book and has no other significance. The Masters kept on talking to me as before and I started a new book. However, although I still kept notes of their talks, these were not as meticulous a record as they had been. Instead I just jotted down the salient points as I understood them. With hindsight I rather wish I had kept a fuller account but at the time it did not seem so necessary and, from my personal point of view, it wasn't. The basic message of the Masters did not change. My task was as it always had been, my lessons were unaltered. As I hope to have made clear the spiritual path is not easy but it is simple and can be boiled down to relatively few instructions.

This talk was slightly unusual in that, for the first time, when the Master came through Michael during meditation, he seemed to be talking to him as much as me. He said that he spoke through Michael's body so as to impress him more strongly and also because he wished me to hear his words to Michael. Generally Michael had no recollection of what had been said through him, and I have no idea as to how the actual mechanics on this occasion differed from normal in order to enable him to be aware of what was going on. But he confirmed afterwards that he was aware of the Master's words though not of them coming through him. He had been taken out of his body and was with the Masters' helpers who, as always, were on hand to assist with the operation. The trance was as deep as usual and the voice was not Michael's as was also always the case. This is what was said.

November 11th 1979

Do not resist him. He has much knowledge. You have experience in this life. He has difficulty in communicating his knowledge but it is deep. Do not resist him. Both of you have great power. Do not squander it. Use it well to benefit others. Call on us during meditation and we will rend the veil that separates you from us. Do not lie down and go to sleep. Awaken!

Once again you might think that there is not much here for the general reader but I include it as it points to the quite unusual relationship that existed between these two people that the Masters had put together to learn from each other. A rather extrovert man with wide experience of the world, and a wordly manner to boot, who nevertheless had great love and a strong pull to the spiritual life, and somebody, thirty six years his junior, who was decidedly introverted and for whom the inner world was more real than the outer, but who still had much to learn before he could use that awareness constructively rather than be overwhelmed by it. We both needed each other for balance and support. For the Masters it must have been a delicate operation to get us to stay together and develop a relationship that would overcome our differences particularly as the relationship was not one recognised by the world. Without them we would never have done it but with their encouragement and guidance we knew that the difficulties were only there to be conquered, and that any problems on the level of the personality could be surmounted by going beyond the personality. In a sense the problems were good because it forced us to do just that.

I also include this brief message because I truly believe there is power in every utterance of the Masters and that that power can transmit itself even through the printed page. By reading and pondering their words one can be brought into contact with them, even if it is only a matter of attuning oneself to a certain vibration. That very attunement will have an uplifting effect and help kindle one's intuitive powers. A picture of a saint or saviour can have this effect too, as can the reading of sacred scriptures, though we need to remember that in every case we will only get out of the experience what we bring to it. It is by no means a mechanical affair that acts independently of the participant and has the same effect for all. That means it can't be proved scientifically but it can experientially.

This passage makes it quite clear that spirituality can never exist in a vacuum. We pursue the path not for ourselves but to increase our capacity for service. **You have great power. Do not squander it. Use it well to benefit others.** It is sometimes asked why God does not manifest Himself on Earth. I would suggest that He does, through each and every person who lets Him come through them. Might it not be that human beings are the means whereby God experiences the world from inside creation, and that what we are is God in the form of Him doing this? All we have to do is realise that fact. This does not mean that we, individually, are God but when we have transcended our individual selves then we find that our being and God's being are one and the same. Then God manifests Himself in the world through us. So we are one another and all of us are part of God. This being the case how could anyone pursue the path only for themselves? It is a complete contradiction in terms, albeit inevitable at its earlier stages when motive is at best mixed. But the more progress we make, the more apparent it becomes that we do not exist in isolation and, if we are to receive, then we must give because the receiving and the giving really are the two inseparable sides of the one coin.

The fact that the aspirant has to realise his identity with God and his oneness with his fellow men and women does not mean that he will not feel alone at many times during his quest. Oneness exists at a spiritual level but most people are totally ignorant of that, so identified are they with the form their soul has taken, and this cannot help but cause a distance, a gulf even, between one who is detaching himself from identification with the world and the great majority who are still completely caught up in the grand illusion. Their interests, their concerns, their goals, their whole outlook on life will be completely different. It can be hard to find a point of contact and that unfortunately can make it rather too easy to feel a touch of superiority over others labouring away in the vale of illusion. But guard against pride if you have seen through the veil of *maya* while others have not. Don't allow that fact to engender a sense of exclusiveness. This is one of the classic traps for the unwary. What you have seen, you have been shown. By looking down on others who have not yet seen through this illusion you are falling right back into the always open arms of that which causes it, namely the ego. Don't let the fact of your advancement result in its own loss.

Loneliness comes to all on the path. It is at once a sign of progress and a test. You are pulling yourself free of the entanglements of the world. At the current stage in the history of humanity that puts you in a minority. What is more, the further you go the more alone you will be. The climb to the summit narrows as it ascends. But, at any stage of the way, to pursue the spiritual path in a serious sense puts you at odds with other people. You might be called selfish, egotistical, lazy, misguided, unbalanced or even mad. You just have to put up with these epithets without reacting to them in kind. In the light of wordly understanding you could be any or all of these. In the light of truth you are doing what needs to be done both as concerns you as an individual and as concerns humanity as a whole. It is the task, the only task, of a human being to realise his or her spiritual source so have no fear or doubt about whether you are doing the right thing. You are following your true destiny. At the same time, do not disdain those who might criticise you. Separating yourself from the mainstream upsets those still swimming in that current. By your action you are implying that their life is incomplete which they naturally don't appreciate. You are attacking the foundations of their self-made belief systems, rejecting their world, and that inevitably creates a certain insecurity in them which leads to criticism. Of course, it can't be denied that a sizeable proportion of those claiming to pursue the spiritual path actually are either unbalanced or egotistical but, assuming that is not the case (and, if it is, that is the fault of the individuals concerned and their reaction to the path not the path itself), then you must simply stand firm in your convictions and not allow the criticisms of others to deflect you from what you know to be right. It can be hard to be criticised without returning the criticism, even internally, but that is what you must learn to do. Do not attempt to justify yourself and do not water down your endeavours in order to placate others. At all times, be true to yourself. Do your spiritual duty, remembering that an important part of that duty is to serve as an example of spiritual truth whether others acknowledge it or not, and an important part of serving as a spiritual example is always to turn the other cheek, whatever the provocation. You might be insulted, you might be condemned but to these you must respond with perfect equanimity, accepting the rebuke if it be merited, ignoring it without the desire to retaliate if it is without foundation.

Loneliness is not just a result of detaching oneself from the norm. It is also a test because each person who passes through the gateway of initiation must do so on their own. Each person must prove themselves worthy on their own merits. We have to transcend our individuality but we can only do that as individuals hence the necessity of learning to stand alone without external or internal support. We have to climb the steep path, dropping all wordly attachments and letting go of whatever still binds us to the three worlds of form because, before we can be filled with God, we must become quite empty of everything else. And all of that we must necessarily do alone. To an extent aloneness is the lot of the aspirant at every stage of the path but it becomes near total towards the end as depicted so harrowingly in the story of Christ when he prayed in agony in the garden of Gethsemane and later, even more intensely, when he suffered on the cross. Then everything must be given up and for that one is thrown back entirely on oneself. But, real as it may seem, this aloneness is ultimately an illusion. God is always there but one must be purified in the fires of isolation before one can become worthy to join the assembled ranks of saints and sages of humanity.

Do not lie down and go to sleep. I have met people who imagine that once someone attains enlightenment there is nothing more to do but rest in permanent bliss. Having not attained that state myself, I can't say with any certitude but my impression from the Masters is that their life was not like that at all. I am sure that their inner state was one of peace and spiritual completeness but they were by no means inactive. It is their job to bring salvation to the world and for that they work unceasingly. No doubt for them this is not work as we would understand it but it is certainly not idleness. For us too, spirituality means work though, again, not as it would normally be conceived. It means vigilance, awareness, endeavour and alertness for opportunities for service even if that is just acting as a channel for light which, incidentally, is probably the best form of service any disciple can render.

Awaken! That is our task expressed in one word. We are all asleep. Whatever our intellectual capacity, whatever our creative ability, whatever our achievements in whatever field, be it material or what the world calls spiritual, until we become aware of the reality of the universe we are asleep and will continue to wander in the dreamlike worlds of form and becoming. Awaken means open your spiritual eyes. Look up from the Earth. Be aware and act on that awareness. This is the Masters' clarion call to slumbering humanity. This has been their call throughout the ages but as yet relatively few of us have heeded it to any great extent. It is a sad but true fact that many people who think of themselves as spiritual have simply developed a spiritual ego. But time, I believe, presses. There are natural cycles to human development and there is a gathering feeling that matters are presently coming to a head. Some talk of the advent of the Aquarian Age, some of the impending end of a cycle as enigmatically described in the book of Revelation and some seem to think that the year 2012 marks a critical moment. All these varying interpretations of what might lie in the future are attempts to give form to an intuition which a number of people have today that an old world is passing away and a new one preparing to be born. That intuition can take decidedly strange forms and sceptics might say that there have always been cults that predicted the end of the world which is true enough. Psychically sensitive people, who may not be that spiritually developed, can pick up impressions and over-react to them. Weak, easily influenced individuals can follow charismatic leaders who promise salvation, playing on fear and the very human desire to be part of the chosen few. But misconceptions and misinterpretations of something real do not mean that it has no reality. Human beings may bend and twist reality to suit their desires and prejudices but reality remains. There are so many voices raised nowadays proclaiming that these are the "latter times" that I think we would do well to consider that there might be some substance behind them without allowing ourselves to be swept away by certain of the wilder prognostications or even committing ourselves to any interpretation of what may lie ahead. Many may sense that something does but nobody can be sure of the form it will take despite claims to the contrary.

The Masters commented to me on more than one occasion that we live in a time of greater separation from the source than ever before. They did not appear to anticipate any sudden improvement. This is in line with the predictions of many religions and, though not willed by the powers that be, anticipated by them as humanity develops its intellectual capacity without developing sufficient spiritual wisdom to counterbalance the excesses of that. It is permitted because of free will and also, perhaps, because all potentialities of a cycle must eventually be expressed within that cycle before it comes to an end. There is also the fact that as matter becomes denser towards the conclusion of a particular cycle so it becomes harder to be aware of the reality that lies beyond it. Despite that, this period of spiritual neglect can also be a time of opportunity since much that was previously hidden has been revealed for anyone to avail themselves of if they so desire though that brings its own responsibilities as what we do use, we must use correctly.

What should we do in these "latter times"? Quite simply we should do what we have always been called upon to do which is "watch and pray". That is, stay aware, stay awake and centre ourselves in God. The year 2012 is widely predicted as a time of upheaval, a turning point if you like. Without denying that such a time may be approaching I think we should be sceptical of anyone who seeks to pin a date on it. There are those who deem it necessary to prepare for impending doom by taking all kinds of outer precautions. Again, while not disputing the need for prudence and preparation, I submit that the best thing we can do is prepare inwardly. Build an inner ark, an ark of purity and spiritual dedication. Concentrate on what you *can* take with you. For those who worry about survival in times to come, let me echo the famous words of Oliver Cromwell who, combining pragmatism with faith, told his men before battle to "Trust in God and keep your powder dry". The survival of the physical body is of small importance and, if in line with your destiny, will happen regardless. Whatever takes place, you will be where you are meant to be when it does.

I know that statement is one a lot of people will find difficult to accept. To some its implications might even seem offensive. Nevertheless the fact is that the conditions we experience in life, the circumstances we encounter, the people we meet, are largely those it is our destiny and purpose so to do. We are where we are meant to be. I realise that a remark of this nature will be rejected by anyone schooled in the contemporary worldview but it is not intended to advocate a passive acceptance of all that happens to us. We have free will and learn by exercising it. Nor should it be taken to mean that we cannot stray from our allotted path, if we so choose, but that will be a conscious decision on our part, a rejection of an opportunity or a refusal to accept conditions which our outer self finds constricting in some way but which may be spiritually beneficial. What it does mean is that what happens in life, certainly as far as the major events are concerned, is what is meant to happen. Let me stress once again that this does not imply that everything that occurs in the world is the result of God's will. Mankind has free will and has exercised that for good and ill for millennia. Much in the world is not as it should be or as its Creator would will it but nevertheless, on the level of an individual life, there is a pre-existing structure laid down before birth which may not be rigidly set in stone but which exists as a sort of blueprint. This is not a matter of an inflexible destiny but it does tell us that circumstances over which we seemingly have no control are not to be feared. It confirms that there is a plan and a purpose to life even if we do not necessarily recognise that, and it makes clear that the success or lack of it of a person's passage through this world cannot be judged by outer appearance.

Because this is such an important point from the aspect of understanding the patterns of our life, and because the tension between free will and destiny has existed in human minds for so many centuries, let me try and be as clear as possible. Life is not random. Destiny does exist. We do have a path. However we are faced with choices throughout life and there is always a better choice to make which is where free will comes in. Thus although we do have a path the way we react to it is not pre-determined

What about the Holocaust, it might be asked? What about those born with severe disabilities? How can this be part of anybody's life plan? The doctrine of karma has often been crudely interpreted in the past with the result that in certain quarters it has been taken to mean that if you suffer now it is, on some level, your own fault. We instinctively react against that as it seems to add insult to injury. Here's a better way of looking at it. If you suffer now it may very well be the karmic consequence of a previous lifetime's behaviour. That is quite true. But it may also be a learning experience that you have agreed to before taking birth in order to overcome something in you that blocks further progress. In certain cases, it may even be a voluntary sacrifice that you have accepted in order to help others, even perhaps to help humanity as a whole. I would speculate that among victims of major tragedies there are some who, in their higher selves, have offered themselves as innocent victims precisely so that the sleeping conscience of humanity might be awakened. I know many will reject this and I certainly don't claim to have the last word on this far from simple subject but two things I have learned from the Masters and these are that, one, every soul has a path but also free will, and, two, the universe is nothing other than the manifestation of love.

Awaken! This was not the last word the Masters spoke to me as they came on many occasions over the next twenty years. However it was the last word in my first notebook and that is the only one that remains to me, subsequent notes having, for the most part, been lost over the course of various moves, and it is a very suitable word on which to conclude the main part of this book. It sums up the Masters' message as well as any single word ever could. The essential part of that message is contained in the talks they gave over the period of the single year that the first set of notes covers, and it remains as valid for any seeker today as it was for me then. Spiritual truths are unchanging. The task of the disciple remains the same as it always has been, namely to extricate him or herself from the swamp of ego. The teachings contained in this book, which are those of the Masters not mine, will help one in that task and I feel sure that anyone who sincerely puts these teachings into practice will come to the Masters' notice.

Afterword

In the introduction to this book I said that although it is written in the form of an autobiography it is not actually about me at all and that is true. The bulk of it concerns a period in my life of less than a year and has to do with the spiritual path as it was expressed in my case but as it could be expressed in anybody's case. But, more than that, the book is about the Masters. It is intended as a testimony to their existence and, at the same time, an attempt to show them as they are, correcting the sometimes misleading impression put forward by certain individuals and organisations that present themselves as representatives of the Masters but end up either vulgarising or sentimentalising the latter in the eyes of most intelligent people. I do this in order to preserve their integrity as it exists in our world. Not for their sake evidently (they are far above such concerns) but so that aspiring disciples might not be put off the idea of spiritually realised beings who are the embodiment of love and wisdom, and who are there to be contacted when one has raised one's consciousness sufficiently. By contacted I do not mean in the direct manner that was used with me, which either shows my good fortune or spiritual denseness or both, but inwardly at the level of the soul, that being the plane on which they exist. The Masters are far greater than I have shown them to be but equally you who are reading this are greater than you imagine yourself to be. Follow the path in humility and love and you will discover what you truly are.

My story continued and took a new turn which, for those who might be interested, I will set down here, at least those aspects of it that relate to my spiritual journey and so have a broader relevance than just the personal one. Shortly after Christmas of 1979 Michael and I decided that we should return to India and not just for a holiday this time but to live there. Predictably, as they later confirmed, this was an idea that the Masters had put into our heads and was in accordance with their intentions for us. Now that we had

ironed out the preliminary bumps in our relationship and got used
to each other they wished us to continue with our life together in a
country whose vibrations were more sympathetic to spirituality than
the modern West. I am not saying that contemporary India is any
more spiritual than the Western world but there is still an influence
which lingers there that comes from thousands of years of mystical
practice. India remains a sacred land, albeit one in which the sacred
is more frequently talked about than lived. The Masters also told us
that it would be easier for them to come to us there though why this
was so, whether it was a matter of a lesser degree of psychic
pollution or an association they had with that country, I do not know.

We decided to go to the south of the country even though it was
not a part Michael was familiar with or one whose language he
spoke. The south has long been a more stable area of India on which
foreign influences have made less of an impression. Traditions have
remained largely unchanged there for centuries so it retains a greater
degree of ancient India than elsewhere in the sub-continent though
that is relatively speaking of course. The few arrangements we had
to make fell quickly into place. The flat sold almost straightaway and
we booked our flight to Bombay (now Mumbai) for April with the
aim of settling somewhere in the region of Mysore. Our intention
was to make ends meet by running a small guest house.

Before we departed we went on a brief visit to Ireland. Michael's
stepfather had been Irish and he knew and loved the country from
many visits in his youth. I had had an Irish grandmother but had not
been there and he considered that to be a gap in my education.

We took the boat to Cork and then went on to Killarney which
Michael assured me was a magical place with one foot in the other
world. As he was not normally given to flights of fancy I was
intrigued but, actually, having one foot in the other world could be
said about much of the western part of the British Isles, especially
those parts that are thought of as Celtic. The veil between the worlds
often does seem thinner there and there is something about the
Celtic temperament, perhaps imbibed from the land, which

resonates particularly strongly to myth and poetry. And what are the sources of myth and poetry if not an instinctive awareness that this world is but the outer garment of something much grander?

The lakes of Killarney were certainly most beautiful and I could see what Michael had meant. Rowing out on their smooth waters it seemed by no means impossible that the approaches to paradise could be just around the corner. That glowing light that spread over the lakes at sunset must surely be spilling over from a source beyond this mortal plane. Those misty hills in the distance, did they not once form part of the lost continent of Atlantis? There are certain places in this world where the gates of the next one can seem just about to swing open and I agreed with Michael that here was one of them.

I have a serious point to make behind this rhapsodising. That there are special localities on Earth where the material crust is thin was accepted by all traditional societies. Visiting such places for spiritual renewal was one of the original purposes of pilgrimage. Nowadays we may have replaced the idea of pilgrimage with that of holidays but people are still instinctively drawn to places of holiness and power. Sometimes the guru is the land itself and going to holy sites in a spirit of openness is a valuable means of attuning oneself to the inner currents of existence. If human beings have centres of force within their bodies so too does the planet and making pilgrimage to such spots can stimulate the corresponding centres within ourselves.

Michael and I spent five years in India. When people hear that they often assume I was there to follow some guru or other but I only saw a couple of individuals who might be regarded in that light whilst there, though I did have contact with the followers of several more and also met a number of sannyasis and swamis. My spiritual mentors continued to be the Masters but I had an outer teacher of sorts and that was India herself. Her ancient history, her traditional culture, her deep mystical roots nurtured me on a spiritual level as they have so many others. From the windswept peaks of the

Himalayas to the hot dense jungles of the south India is a land loved by the gods and, even in our sad and distracted times, it continues to be so.

Most of the time we lived up in a hill station called Yercaud in the state of Tamil Nadu where we did indeed run a small guesthouse as had originally been our plan. Yercaud had been developed in the 19th century by coffee planters and there were still many coffee estates scattered around the town. It was situated 5,000 feet above sea level in the Shevaroy hills and offered a pleasant escape from the heat of the southern plains in summer. We let out rooms on a bed and breakfast basis charging the equivalent of about £1 a night which was the local going rate. To supplement that we had a large vegetable patch, some bananas, oranges and guavas and a couple of bee hives. But fundamentally our lives revolved around meditation. I walked a lot in the surrounding hills, Michael rather less so. It was a quiet life and I consider it to have been a spiritually fruitful one but eventually it was time to move on. In effect, it was a five year retreat but if it had gone on for much longer than that it might have lost its creative aspect and descended into stagnation. I gained much from it but knew when the time came to go back to a more active phase of existence. There are cycles for everything.

The Masters spoke to me frequently during those days but very little written record remains of what they said. To begin with I did make notes as before but eventually gave that up as it seemed redundant to carry on copying down everything they said when so much was in a similar vein to the talks of earlier days. There was instruction, encouragement and regular pointing out of my weaknesses. The Masters are stern but loving taskmasters. When they spoke to me they went straight to the point. They had no interest in anything to do with the personality and it would have seemed almost blasphemous to have asked them anything on that subject. I don't mean that I would have been afraid to do so. Fear was impossible with them but my love and respect for them prevented me from saying anything which I knew to be foolish. However there was one occasion when I did ask them something non-spiritual and, because it had an interesting outcome, I will mention it here. I had been suffering from a bad back for a few weeks which a visit to the local doctor had done nothing to help. One night when the Master came I mentioned my back and asked if he knew of anything that might ease the pain. He told me of a simple exercise that involved lying on my back, raising my outstretched feet a few inches above the ground and then pushing the heels forwards. He told me to do this a few times every day and the pain would go. I did and it worked. Some years later I met a back specialist and, without saying where I got it from, told him of this exercise. He said it was exactly what he would have recommended.

The first place we had stayed in after our arrival was Bangalore which we intended to use as a base from which we could look around to find somewhere more permanent. We explored Mysore as a possibility but that didn't work out and, as the process of finding somewhere was taking longer than anticipated, we moved out of the hotel we had been staying in to a guesthouse which was a colonial era bungalow run by a friendly old gentleman called Mr Gupta. I was never sure if Mr Gupta was a true devotee of Sai Baba or just sensed a good business opportunity. At any rate, he had pictures of Sai Baba up all round the guesthouse and there was a constant stream of Western devotees of that guru staying there. Sai Baba had an ashram at Whitefield, a small town a few miles out of Bangalore, and when he was *in situ* devotees flocked there to receive a sight of him. We met many in the guesthouse and they were always trying to persuade us to come along for a view of their holy man but neither of us were attracted to him. To me, his pictures gave off a decidedly unspiritual vibration and Michael, in typical no nonsense fashion, just thought he was ridiculous, an example of someone who might have had genuine magical powers but whose ego had become as overblown as his hairstyle (his words). No genuine spiritual master would make the claims he made or descend to vulgar exhibitionism of his powers in the way he did. That extraordinary things happened around him could not be denied but the lesson to all seekers was to look beneath the surface and not to be taken in by marvels and wonders.

Because we were friendly with some of the devotees, who were for the most part good and sincere people, but also out of curiosity, we eventually agreed to go out to the ashram for morning *darshan*. This was the moment that Sai Baba displayed himself to receive the adoration of his devotees. After he had walked around in a lordly manner, accepting the homage and petitions of his acolytes, he sat down in a chair cum throne to listen to the singing of devotional songs. Then he went back inside and it was time to go. We were asked for our opinion but what do you say to someone who believes that the person you have just seen is God Incarnate when you view him as tending more to the other end of the spiritual spectrum? I think we fell back on the line that it had been an interesting experience and left it at that.

It is instructive to speculate on what sort of person becomes a follower of a self-proclaimed messiah. To say it is just the gullible does them an injustice, I think. Many, no doubt, do fall into that category but there are genuine seekers too. However in my experience they usually lack one or both of two things which are spiritual discernment and the resolve to take full responsibility for themselves. The messiah figure makes the claim that belief in him personally is all that is necessary for salvation but anyone who seriously makes such a claim is not a true teacher whatever powers he might appear to possess. Unusual powers may impress and could lead one to suspend judgment but I believe that what really attracts many seekers to those who claim messiahship is the hope that someone else will do the work for them. All they have to do is hand over personal responsibility and their salvation is assured. But the spiritual path is not like that. God created us as individuals and, while we certainly have to transcend the sense of a separate self, we must work out our own salvation. God wants us to be fully individual but not restricted to that. **Be individual but not individ-**

376

ualistic. Yes, you must surrender the ego but you are responsible for your own soul and no-one else can save that for you but you yourself.

I don't know if Sai Baba genuinely believed he was a divine incarnation, possibly because of an erroneous interpretation of Hindu mythology, or else just used his powers and charisma to advance his personal goals. I do know that he was in no sense a realised human being and that was clearly illustrated in his behaviour and even written on his face.

Someone who was the opposite of Sai Baba in almost every respect was Krishnamurti. Occasionally Michael and I left our hill top retreat to go travelling and in early 1981 we were in Madras when we heard that Krishnamurti was also there giving his regular winter talks. As he was one of the few contemporary spiritual teachers who I thought spoke from the source I wanted to go and hear him speak. Michael was not so interested in his teachings, which were too abstract for his tastes, but recognised his authenticity; a thoroughbred in a field of many donkeys was his verdict.

One evening as dusk fell we went and sat in the compound of the bungalow where Krishnamurti gave his talks to a few hundred people. I don't remember the subject of the talk but well recall the atmosphere of peacefulness created by this rather frail old man in his eighties who still retained a certain youthfulness as he unobtrusively walked to his position on a slightly raised platform to begin his talk. There was no announcement or introduction. He just began talking and did so for about an hour during which time he held the audience's attention completely. Then, again without ostentation, he got up and walked back to the house where he was staying, in the garden of which the talk had taken place. To get there he had to walk around the edge of the crowd and a few of the Indian members of the audience prostrated themselves before him which called forth no visible response. But then suddenly Michael got up from his seat, positioned himself directly in Krishnamurti's path, and, folding his hands together in the traditional Indian form of salutation, said

"Thank you for the talk, Swamiji". I was getting ready to deny all knowledge of him. For one thing, I thought he was insensitively forcing himself on Krishnamurti who had finished his talk and now probably just wanted to get back to the house to rest. For another, Krishnamurti was not a swami and explicitly disassociated himself from all that sort of thing. But, far from carrying on past Michael at a slightly faster speed as I fully expected him to do, Krishnamurti stopped and looked at him intently. He then put both his hands around Michael's and, still looking him fully in the face, held them close. He remained like that for at least a minute without saying anything before finally letting go and moving on, all the while with a solemn expression which was somehow more impressive than if he had smiled.

Now I don't know why Krishnamurti stopped and held Michael's hands in that way but I am convinced that, although he may outwardly have discouraged belief in (of the sort that led to dependence on) the Masters, he knew perfectly well that they existed, and he was without a doubt one of their representatives in this world. What he was against, in my view, was not the idea of Masters but the vulgarisation of that idea, that reality, which to him was sacred. And so to preserve the purity, the holiness of it, he denied it or, as I'm not sure if he did actually deny it, he spoke of it as if it were irrelevant. In the final analysis the Masters are part of duality (not them, of course, but the idea of them and us as separate) and Krishnamurti came to teach non-duality in a pure form. But I have no doubt that he loved the Masters and was loved by them as a cherished son. So my explanation of what happened is that Krishnamurti recognised their presence in Michael. When later I asked Michael why he had got up and spoke to Krishnamurti as he did, he said he had no idea why he had behaved in that way but had felt impelled to do so.

Krishnamurti has been accused of teaching the goal but not the path. I imagine he would say that the goal is the path, and it is perfectly true that the relative can never realise the absolute. There is an insurmountable gulf between the two that cannot be crossed, only seen never to have existed and that is a process that cannot take place in time. But it does need time to get to that point and, glad as I am that Krishnamurti took his totally uncompromising stance, since by doing so he showed up so much of the shallowness of modern day spirituality, there is some justification to this criticism. To bring the relative to the point at which it can make the non-existent leap does require some sort of path. Ego itself can never transcend ego but only one who has fully purified the ego will ever be able to transcend it. You must make it transparent before you can see through it. This is why we need spiritual practices and it is why we need spiritual teachers and, for that matter, religions. Krishnamurti is certainly not wrong in what he says but he does tend to speak as though only the absolute were real which, on the highest level, might be so but the relative is part of the absolute as it is in manifestation and cannot simply be dismissed or denied any sort of reality at all, even a relative one, especially by those of us who are still caught up in it.

Despite my reservation about some of the practical aspects of Krishnamurti's teaching (I have none about his personal attainment) I would question if there were really that much difference between his spiritual rigour and Christ's injunction to "be perfect even as your Father in heaven is perfect". (Note that Christ said that we should be perfect not that we should try to be perfect.) The Masters may have had a more nuanced understanding of the various stages of the path than Krishnamurti appeared to but they are just as uncompromising in their attitude to truth and just as demanding in what they expect of their disciples. There is no room for imper-fection of any kind if you seriously wish to join their ranks. That doesn't mean that perfection is expected of you straightaway but you should know that it is the condition of entry to the Kingdom of Heaven and that nothing can be hidden from those who guard the gates. Everything is required from you and you will be tested to the utmost in order that you may become perfect. However you should also know that if your heart is true and your motive sincere you will be given all the help you need in order to overcome the trials of the path. Everything may be asked of those who tread the path but in return they are given eternal life.

Krishnamurti was a genuine spiritual original. Since his time others have tried to assume his mantle, often, I would guess, in imitation of him, but it is not given to everyone to be a pure conduit for truth, and the great majority of those who have followed after him may have a perfectly good intellectual understanding of that of which he spoke but do not embody it as he did. Shall I tell you the difference between a spiritual original and the imitators? It is innocence. True spirituality comes from inward purity and non-responsiveness to this world. It has nothing to do with knowledge or experience which is not to say that the spiritual person does not have these things but they are not the source of his understanding.

It was during our time in Bangalore that we heard about Yercaud and, as it seemed the ideal sort of place for our purposes, we went there to see what it was like. At that time it comprised a large village with surrounding coffee estates and a couple of hotels to cater for the small number of people who came up from the plains to get away from the hot weather. There was a lake, an orchidarium and a private school run by Catholic priests and that was about it. A few shops in the bazaar sold the basics but for anything more you had to go to Salem, a town at the foot of the hills about one hour and twenty one hairpin bends' bus ride away. We found a property consisting of two old bungalows on a hillside that had been cut into a three tiered terraced garden and, although it was rather run down, it was just what we wanted. We lived in the bungalow on the top level and the second one on the next level down became the guesthouse. On the lowest level there was a well and all the water had to be carried up to the top until we eventually got an electric pump which was fine as long as the electricity was working but it frequently was not. I might have implied above that we spent all our time meditating but that was not the case. It took a good year of hard work to get the bungalows and compound into shape, and when we got the guesthouse up and running that inevitably demanded a certain amount of time and energy too. Although we did have Indian guests many of those who stayed with us were Westerners who had come up to the hills to escape the heat of the plains and the stresses and strains of the spiritual quest. Michael was particularly adept at restoring souls bruised and battered by the Indian experience and the search for enlightenment. Sometimes I wondered if that was why we were there.

Practically all my records of the Masters' talks during this period are lost but I do have a few fragmentary notes left. Here's something they said early on during our time in Yercaud.

Much of our work with you involves teaching you to break bad habits. When you feel yourself about to succumb to irritation or anger do not react thoughtlessly but simply ignore what has prompted the reaction. Rise above it. This will require an effort on your part because years of faulty behaviour have made reaction automatic but you must break that cycle and replace bad habits with good ones. Then you will move beyond your current state of spiritual frustration which is caused by a true knowledge of what lies beyond the emotions coupled with an inability to detach yourself sufficiently from them. You react to protect yourself but you must realise that there is nothing to protect.

What does it mean that we react to protect ourselves (because this applies to everyone, not just me), and what does it mean that there is nothing to protect? Two feelings are fundamental to human beings as they exist in this world and these are the desire for self-preservation and the fear of death. (Note we talk of self-preservation not bodily preservation since the latter is really only important insofar as the destruction of the body is taken to mean personal extinction). Obviously these are two aspects of the same thing so we can think of them as one. It is this that causes us to react when threatened whether that be physically or emotionally. We identify falsely with a limited aspect of ourselves instead of knowing ourselves to be the uncreated spirit. So we react to perceived attack to protect that which feels threatened, namely the separate self. But there is nothing to protect because that separate self we seek to maintain, believing it to be what we are, is but a mind created form which disappears when mind is no longer the centre of identification. It is basic to all human beings to seek to perpetuate the self because that is what we think we are and this causes us to live in a constant state of subliminal fear. But we are more than the self and when we realise this then we have nothing to protect and no need to react to any form of threat. There can be no threat because there is nothing in us that can be threatened.

On another occasion I made a complaint about no longer experiencing the spiritual upliftments I had done when I first started to meditate. This is the reply.

We pay you the compliment of assuming you no longer need to be fed sweets in order to make you behave. Do you think that the spiritual path is the path of pleasure and self-gratification? Do you follow the path for what advantages it brings you or because it is the way of truth? Let me tell you that if someone is given constant ecstasies they are unlikely to make further progress and could well slip back. They will become attached to these feelings and see no reason to go any further along the way. Many people have become stuck at a certain stage of the path thinking they have reached the end. Would you wish to join their company?

The purpose of spiritual experiences is to show us that God and the higher worlds, hitherto intuited perhaps but not truly known, are real. They can be thought of as the carrot that lures us to take our first proper steps along the path. Thus they are more often than not a mark of spiritual awakening than one of spiritual maturity. They are there to encourage us to continue along a path that will sometimes lead us into times of inner privation, such times being inevitable as we seeks to eradicate ego identification and move into higher states of being. Spiritual experiences are like a beacon, the recollection of which can guide us through times of darkness but which, if allowed to shine all the time, would not allow the purifying work of the darkness to have its proper effect.

If someone is given constant ecstasies they ... will become attached to these feelings. Jesus famously said that it is harder for a rich man to get to heaven than for a camel to go through the eye of a needle. This is not because of the rich man's wealth but his attachment to it. If the mystic becomes attached to his spiritual riches then he will find himself in exactly the same position.

The goal of the spiritual life is not to have spiritual experiences but to transcend the ego. It is not to bask in bliss (if it were, why be born at all?) but to develop virtue. It is not to receive but to give. Spiritual experiences are not necessarily a sign of spiritual growth and can even be a positive hindrance to it as they tend to focus attention on the self which may be seen as transcended in the course of the experience but afterwards can actually be stimulated as a result. This then has precisely the opposite effect to that anticipated. Like many people I had imagined that my early experiences were the dawning rays of light on the horizon that prefigured the full glory of the rising sun but that was not what happened at all. Now I realise that one should just accept such things if and when they come but not see them as anything other than gifts, and do not demand or expect repetition. I also know that spiritual experiences might actually be given to you as a test to see how you react. Will it be with pride and attachment or will it be with humility and gratitude?

Accept what comes to you whatever it is. Do not demand the good and reject the bad. Know that ultimately all is good as all serves to take you forward.

This is not a personal history so, although there are many other things I could write about our time in India, here is not the place to do it. In 1985, after realising that it was time to move on, we packed our bags and returned to England. On a purely personal level I was reluctant to leave but I knew that we had done what we had come to India to do and a new phase in our lives was beginning, one in which we had to demonstrate our ability to stay spiritually focussed while in the world. To have stayed longer would have risked turning something that had once been fresh into something stale. We took a train up to Delhi and boarded a flight to London. Once again Michael bade farewell to India and this time it was a final farewell.

The ensuing years found us living first in England and then in France and, though the Masters continued to speak to me through Michael, I have only a few records of their talks from this time. I did sometimes note down what they said but these notes have gone missing in various moves. It's possible they exist in a trunk in an attic somewhere. Perhaps one day they will turn up. However the gist of what they said was as before. Their teaching does not change though its presentation may adjust to changing circumstances. They continued to be the embodiments of love, wisdom and pure goodness they had always been, guides who demonstrated in themselves the highest truth of every spiritual teaching. I have always maintained that I learned more from their presence than their words and I learned a great deal from their words. Their presence, though, was a sacred benediction that humbled and inspired in equal measure. In them there is no trace of ego whatsoever, not even the slightest shadow or remnant. In them ego has been totally eradicated, leaving them as open windows to God insofar as God can be manifested in human form. They are men made perfect, and they point to what we can be if we follow their teachings which are not theirs but the teachings of truth.

In 1996 we returned to England. Michael felt he did not have much time left to live and thought it better for my sake that he should die in England. In the event he lived for another three years but, as related earlier, after the eclipse in August of 1999 he had a heart attack and two weeks later he was dead.

He had lived an interesting life. It spanned a period that saw

probably more change than any other period in human history, and
during that time he packed in enough experience for two or three
lifetimes. He had known film stars, writers and eminent politicians.
He had mixed in aristocratic circles and lived on his own in a bedsit.
He had led the high life in New York, Paris and London in the 1950s
and '60s, and he had been a Benedictine monk and initiated by a
swami in the Ramakrishna order as well. All that, he said, meant
nothing compared to being contacted by the Masters. He served
them devotedly, asking nothing for himself, for the last twenty odd
years of his life and, I have no doubt, is with them now.

Spiritual people can be divided into three classes. There are the
ordinary believers who see God as outside themselves. They might
be devout or they might not be but they see God as a separate being
who reigns over all. They seek salvation as their highest goal. Then
there are the aspiring mystics who practise an esoteric form of spirituality and see God as within. Their goal is liberation or enlightenment. But there is a third class who, on the face of it, might seem
to lead perfectly ordinary lives in the world. They do not practice
any particular discipline and, though they may engage in prayer or
meditation, they have no personal motive for doing so. They do so
because that is a natural part of what they are. They have no goal.
They simply live their lives in harmony with God wherever they
might find themselves. This was the state that Michael had reached
by the end of his life.

As for me, I remain what I have been since first meeting Michael,
a disciple of the Masters. I have not had outer contact with them for
over ten years but I strive to be aware of them inwardly and it is
because I was given what seemed to me a clear message to set down
a record of my experiences with them that I have written this book.

How to finish this account of my life as a pupil of the Masters?
The most important point I would like to leave the reader with is
that there is nothing special about me and that what I experienced is
open to all. No doubt I am being a little disingenuous in saying that
as all my life, even before I was consciously aware of their existence,

I loved the Masters and desired to serve them. But the fact is that anyone who feels similarly will become known to them. You may not encounter them in your outer life, as I no longer do, but you will, if you love them, assuredly meet them on the inner planes and the effects of that will filter down. However let me sound a small note of warning. To be a pupil of the Masters has nothing glamorous about it. It demands hard work and personal forgetfulness. You will not have a constant stream of light poured down upon you but you will be required to soldier on in often trying circumstances, asking nothing for the separate self. You will not be taken on for your personal benefit but so that you may be the better equipped to serve. Having said that, there really is no greater joy than such service.

Today more than ever the Masters need people willing to work with them which means people able to lift their consciousness up to the spiritual plane and happy to work for no pay. Not that they won't be rewarded but only those can be taken on who seek no reward other than to do the will of God. I believe such people exist in reasonably large numbers today but prevailing worldly forces can sometimes divert them from their proper path. Understanding what these forces are can help us to see past them.

Principally there are two, apparently opposite but really quite complementary. To begin with, there is the ever-increasing descent into materialism which is too obvious to require further discussion. However what is less apparent is how this is aided and abetted by the excessive use of the many forms of technology on which we have become so dependent. All technology separates us from reality to a degree but the highly sophisticated nature of contemporary technology means that it is doing that to a greater degree than ever before. We have to use such things in the modern world but we should remain alert to their dangers and know that all tools that liberate us in some ways enslave us in others, and the more sophisticated or further removed from nature a tool is, the more spiritually dangerous it can be; that is, the more its use divorces us from our source. Thus, to those who are serious about spiritual progress, I would suggest that the correct approach to modern technology is to use it as and when necessary but avoid being seduced by it. The internet and computer technology in general, which are seen as liberating and consciousness expanding by some, are in fact more likely to have precisely the opposite effect given that they are materialistic imitations of spiritual realities (for instance, access to all knowledge) which encourage dependence on the external and the artificial. That is not to deny their obvious benefits but look beneath the surface and a different picture emerges.

So, on the one hand, there is the denial of the transcendent dimension of life but there is also the spurious spirituality that can arise as a reaction to the inner emptiness that causes. You might think that reaction to be a good thing but if it takes place on the level of the ego then the individual is easily lured into more forms of unreality in the search for personal fulfilment. Such forms, posing as truth, exist in abundance in our day, and many of them promise much but can deliver little.

If our spirituality comes from the ego and reflects its desires and goals then it is worthless. It is common nowadays to hear people say, "I'm not religious but I am spiritual". Possibly this means I can find no contemporary religion that truly answers my inner yearnings but very often it means that my concern with the spiritual lies in what I can get from it, what it might give me. I do not wish to sacrifice, I do not wish to transcend, I do not wish to submit to a higher power, I do not wish to give up my self. I wish to remain what I am and add some spiritual possessions to the ones I already have. This is emphatically not the way to any kind of depth or holiness. The only reason to tread the path is love of God or love of the changeless reality that both transcends the universe and lies at the core of our being, if you prefer. You do it not because of any benefits it might bring you but because you must, because it is your nature to do so and you would follow it regardless of where it might lead.

How do we react to the downward spiral in which we find ourselves at the present time by which I mean how do we respond to the recognition that we are living through a time of spiritual decline even if outwardly there appears to be a continuing amelioration of conditions? All we can do is seek to live the truth as far as we understand it. Live it and demonstrate it. Then let God do the rest. Let His Will be done. We need to be in the world because that is where we are but we should not allow ourselves to become of it because that is not where we want to stay.

Partisans of New Age ideology believe that humanity is poised to make what they call a giant evolutionary leap in the relatively near future, predicting a mass expansion of consciousness and a new enlightened age of love and brotherhood. I don't reject this idea out of hand but nor do I think there is any compelling evidence for it. The advances on the horizontal plane that are sometimes cited as evidence, such as improvements on the level of human relations in the form of greater democratic freedom and equality, have little to do with spiritual understanding in any real sense which, let us remind ourselves, is always based on a full recognition of the vertical pole of existence. Other than that there are various channelled messages, which probably have as much disagreement as agreement among them, and (perhaps most significantly) hope. That's about it. It did not seem to be the Masters' view and it is flatly denied by every single religious tradition I am aware of, all of which are in complete agreement that the latter days are a time of spiritual decline. The wonders of the Aquarian Age are a recent innovation and have no support from traditional religions which are unanimous in their eschatological views predicting a falling away from truth not a sudden return to it.

Humanity may be fallen but we are also made in the image of God, and the somewhat sombre picture I have painted is relieved by more positive aspects of the current situation. I have described the essential spirit of the times, the general trend, which might apply to society collectively but certainly does not apply to all individuals within it. Here is where the Aquarian vision may have some substance for, although the world has largely descended into materialism and atheism, many people have reached a point in their evolutionary development at which they are ready to start climbing out of that and begin their journey back to the source. Even in the darkest of times truth is ever present as is access to it. The fact that it may be behind thicker veils in this age even has its compensations in that those who make sincere efforts to progress are given every possible help. That does not mean that less is asked of you but if you think of the contemporary availability of the wisdom teachings of all ages compared to what there was in the past then we are spoiled indeed. Moreover the Masters, who are God's emissaries to humanity, are always there to help us if we sincerely reach out to them. That is what I hope to have made clear in this book.

I would like to conclude with what were the last words I heard through Michael from the Masters. They were spoken sometime in 1999 when we were living in Eastbourne and, for some reason, I wrote them down on a scrap of paper and kept them in my wallet. There was no indication at the time that this would be the last occasion the Masters would speak to me in that way.

All is well. Trust your intuition. Have faith, courage and carry on.

Notes

Chapter 4

1   I have adopted from those books the useful practice of putting the Masters' words in bold.

2   According to Hindu chronology, the Kali Yuga is the current dark age of materialism and inversion of real values in which true spirituality is hard to find though the counterfeit variety abounds. It is the time in a particular cycle when matter is at its most material and spirit its least perceptible. In truth, the entire historical period is regarded as falling within the Kali Yuga but now is when it is reaching its point of greatest development.

Chapter 11

3   I discovered *'The Boy and the Brothers'* in the local library a few weeks after the Masters began talking to me. When I read it I was very struck by the similarities to my experience but as it was out of print I couldn't buy a copy which I would have liked to have done for reference's sake. But then I came across it in a second hand bookshop shortly afterwards and found the sequel soon after that. Most spiritual seekers have 'lucky coincidences' like that. Or maybe they are just more inclined to notice them.

4   One of the problems of the current materialistic worldview is that many people react to it by turning to false forms of spirituality thinking that because they are not material they must be spiritual. This is by no means necessarily the case.

Chapter 12

5   A Sanskrit word for which there is no real equivalent in English, meaning a combination of duty, purpose, role and life mission but in a spiritual sense.

Chapter 16

6   It is sometimes said that the later Christianisation of these stories distorted what are essentially Celtic and pre-Celtic fertility tales. In my view precisely the opposite is the case with the Christian element elevating them to a higher spiritual plane. The figure of Galahad, fictitious though he may be, is a greater spiritual archetype than either Arthur or Merlin despite appearing somewhat bland and less interesting in human terms due to his near perfect nature. That is not to deny Arthur the king and Merlin the magician their due as supreme exponents of 1st (Will) and 7th (Magic) ray energies or their fundamental place in the British psyche but the purely spiritual realisation of Galahad goes beyond these two.

7   Regarding this statement. The Masters would never forbid one to do anything. The law of free will is sacred in their eyes and, within reason, we have the right to do whatever we want. The corollary of that, though, is that we must accept the consequences of our actions.

Chapter 20

8   As the Psalms have it. A fine and eloquent phrase if one allows for its slightly old-fashioned nature.

9   I am not talking about simple atheism here. It is not a question of disbelieving in God but of saying no to all that God is. Most atheists, mistaken as they are, believe in God in the sense that they would not deny the good and the true.

Chapter 21

10 Kali is obviously a primitive tribal goddess of death and war who has acquired or, perhaps better put, usurped higher functions, that in her original incarnation she never had, as a deeper metaphysical understanding developed. *Pace* Ramakrishna and Tantrics everywhere, I don't think her form (and that's basically all she or any deity really is, a form symbol-

ising a divine function) is very inspiring as it only resonates with her assumed higher function in a crude even misleading way. A similar thing, by the way, happened with some of the Bon deities of Tibet who were transformed from their original demonic status after a higher Buddhist metaphysics took root in Tibet.

11 Curiously Michael, who was of pure English stock, was often asked if he had any Tibetan ancestry. He had the round face and slightly slanted eye shape typical of that ethnic group. He used to joke that it must have been because he was conceived in Simla.

12 It's not quite as straightforward as that. Michael need not have reacted to my provocation and then they would not have got into him. But he was, as you might say, programmed by the Masters to respond to me in the same way plus as I had behaved to him in order to reflect my behaviour back to me so once I had set the ball in motion the rest was inevitable.

Chapter 22

13 "As many as I love, I rebuke and chasten". Revelation 3:19. "For the Lord disciplines those he loves, and he punishes each one he accepts as his child". Hebrews 12:6. More humorously there is the famous story of St Teresa of Avila who, when riding a donkey, was thrown off into a muddy puddle, 'Lord, why this?' she asked and was answered, 'That is the way I treat my friends.' 'Then no wonder you have so few' was Theresa's quick as a flash riposte.

Chapter 23

14 In case of misunderstanding, may I say here that I am not in the least bit anti-science. I am just anti the assumption that science often makes that what it knows is all there is to be known, and that the way it acquires knowledge is the only way to do so. Of course, scientists themselves realise they have by no means

reached the frontiers of knowledge but they often seem to envisage its extension exclusively in a quantitative direction rather than a qualitative one which would encompass the spiritual dimension. So I am very much for science as the search for knowledge but I am against it as a belief system.

15   Some people do indeed deny the existence of free will saying that the choices we make are inevitably dictated by what we are which is based on our genetic inheritance and life experience but I don't think even they would renounce the idea of themselves as individuals. The point is that at any one moment we do have the power to choose and this power goes beyond any pre-determined factors though it will frequently be influenced by them. As an intellectual exercise we may deny the existence of free will but none of us live like that because in our hearts we know it is there. Faced with any given situation we are always free to make a choice.

Chapter 25

16   'My Dear Alexias. Letters from W. Tudor Pole to Rosamond Lehmann'. Neville Spearman 1979.

Chapter 26

17   'My Dear Alexias', letter of 14 2 68

Chapter 29

18   I'd like to quote the esteemed Tudor Pole again here who says in one of his letters to Rosamond Lehmann. "The 'Masters' who work quietly in our midst deprecate curiosity. They need complete anonymity. How foolish the T.S. and Bailey people are to try to personalize them, giving them this attribute and that. 'Infants in the night' are they, poor dears, spying among the Gods" (My Dear Alexias, p.13).

19   For example, the well-known Alice Bailey books which combine a wealth of occult teachings which have the unmistakeable

stamp of a Master with other material that seems rather less authentic.

20 1st epistle of John, chapter 4, verse1

21 Note that the fact that someone may have had a genuine spiritual experience does not necessarily mean that they are a spiritual person or that their interpretation of their experience is correct.

AXIS MUNDI
BOOKS

Axis Mundi Books provide the most revealing and coherent explorations and investigations of the world of hidden or forbidden knowledge. Take a fascinating journey into the realm of Esoteric Mysteries, Magic, Mysticism, Angels, Cosmology, Alchemy, Gnosticism, Theosophy, Kabbalah, Secret Societies and Religions, Symbolism, Quantum Theory, Apocalyptic Mythology, Holy Grail and Alternative Views of Mainstream Religion.